Healing The Shame
That Binds You

John Bradshaw

Health Communications, Inc.
Deerfield Beach, Florida

John Bradshaw
Houston, Texas

Library of Congress Cataloging-in-Publication Data

Bradshaw, John E., 1933-
    Healing the shame that binds you.

    1. Shame.   2. Psychotherapy.   I. Title.
RC455.4.S53B73   1988   616.85'22   88-21228
ISBN 0-932194-86-9

ISBN 0-932194-86-9

Published by: Health Communications, Inc.
            Enterprise Center
            3201 S.W. 15th Street
            Deerfield Beach, Florida 33442

Cover design by Reta Thomas

DEDICATION

To Nancy, my wonderful wife, who heals my toxic shame by loving me unconditionally.

To my long-time friends (who used to be my children) Brad, Brenda and John. Forgive me for all the times I've transferred my shame to you.

To my father, Jack. Toxic shame took your life and robbed us of our time.

ACKNOWLEDGMENTS

I want to thank Gershan Kaufman for his ground-breaking work on shame. Kaufman's book *SHAME* has been my number one resource in naming the demon I call toxic shame. My book would not be possible without his pioneering efforts.

I'm also indebted to the anonymous writer of the Hazeldon publication entitled *SHAME* for my understanding of healthy shame as that which signals our essential human limitation and, of the more than human/less than human polarity of toxic shame.

Several other people have been important to me in understanding the dynamics of shame. They are Sheldon Kopp, Marilyn Mason, Merl Fossum and Terry Kellogg.

Kip Flock, my friend and co-training therapist in Los Angeles has been extremely helpful in my developing the concepts in this book. Kip and I have spent countless hours discussing and clarifying the concept of shame.

I want to thank my colleagues at the Center for Recovering Families in Houston (especially Mary Bell) for their continued support.

I thank John Daugherty, George Pletcher, and Rev. Mike Falls, my best friends, for sharing their pain and vulnerability with me. Their non-shaming acceptance has allowed me to share my toxic shame with them. Together we've reduced the power of toxic shame in our lives.

Thanks to my publishers, Peter Vegso and Gary Seidler, for their continued commitment and total support of my work. I'm grateful to Marie Stilkind for her painstaking editing and for encouraging me to trust my own style, and to the production staff at Health Communications.

My publicist Diane Glynn and her able associate Jodee Blanco, have gone far beyond the call of duty in promoting my work.

This book would not have been possible without the incredible patience of Barbara Evans, who diligently typed and retyped my manuscript (at all hours of the day and night). Barbara's grasp of this material made her far more than a typist for me.

And lest I forget (which I too often do) my greatest gratitude goes to my Higher Power, whose Grace has saved me from my toxic shame.

CONTENTS

v

The Videotape and Audiotape series for Bradshaw's first book

BRADSHAW ON: The Family

as well as other tapes are available for purchase from

John Bradshaw
5003 Mandell
Houston, Texas 77006
(713) 529-9437

John Bradshaw gives workshops and lectures throughout the country in the areas of management, addiction, recovery and spirituality.

PREFACE

"And they were not ashamed."
Genesis

Ten years ago I had one of those life-jolting discoveries that significantly changed everything. I named the core demon in my life. I named "shame". Naming shame means that I became aware of the massive destructive power that shame had exerted in my life. I discovered that I had been *bound* by shame all my life. It ruled me like an addiction. I acted it out; I covered it up in subtle and not so subtle ways; I transferred it to my family, my clients and the people I taught.

Shame was the unconscious demon I had never acknowledged. In becoming aware of the dynamics of shame, I came to see that shame is one of the major destructive forces in all human life. In naming shame I began to have power over it.

In itself, shame is not bad. Shame is a normal human emotion. In fact, it is necessary to have the feeling of shame if one is to be truly human. Shame is the emotion which gives us permission to be human. Shame tells us of our limits. Shame keeps us in our human boundaries, letting us know we can and will make mistakes, and that we need help. Our shame tells us we are not God. Healthy shame is the psychological foundation of humility. It is the source of spirituality.

What I discovered was that *shame as a healthy human emotion can be transformed into shame as a state of being. As a state of being, shame takes over one's whole identity. To have shame as an identity is to believe that one's being is flawed, that one is defective as a human being. Once shame is transformed into an identity, it becomes toxic and dehumanizing.*

Toxic shame is unbearable and always necessitates a cover-up, a false self.

Since one feels his true self is defective and flawed, one needs a false self which is not defective and flawed. *Once one becomes a false self, one ceases to exist psychologically.* To be a false self is to cease being an authentic human being. The process of false self-formation is what Alice Miller calls "soul murder". As a false self, one tries to be more than human or less than human. Toxic shame is the greatest form of learned domestic violence there is. It destroys human life. Toxic shame is the core of most forms of emotional illness. Gershen Kaufman writes:

> "Shame is the affect which is the source of many complex and disturbing inner states: depression, alienation, self-doubt, isolating loneliness, paranoid and schizoid phenomena, compulsive disorders, splitting of the self, perfectionism, a deep sense of inferiority, inadequacy or failure, the so-called borderline conditions and disorders of narcissism."

Shame

Toxic shame so destroys the function of our authentic self that clear syndromes of shame develop out of the false self cover-ups. Each syndrome has its own characteristic pattern. Toxic shame becomes the core of neurosis, character disorders, political violence, wars and criminality. It comes the closest to defining human bondage of all the things I know.

The Bible describes shame as the core and consequence of Adam's fall. In Hebrew Adam is equivalent to mankind. Adam symbolizes all human beings. The Bible suggests that Adam was not satisfied with his own being. He wanted to be more than he was. He wanted to be more than human. He failed to accept his essential limitations. He lost his healthy shame. The Bible suggests that the origin of human bondage (original sin) is the desire to be other than who we are . . . to be more than human. In his toxic shame (pride), Adam wanted a false self. The false self led to his destruction.

After Adam alienated his true being, he went into hiding. "And the Lord God called unto Adam . . . where art thou?" And Adam said, "I heard thy voice in the garden and I hid myself" (Genesis 3:9-10). Before the fall the man and the woman were both naked and "were not ashamed" (Genesis 2:25). Once they chose to be other than what they were, they became naked and ashamed.

Nakedness symbolized their true and authentic selves. They were who they were and they were okay with it. There was nothing to hide. They could be perfectly and rigorously honest.

This symbolic and metaphorical description of Adam and Eve is a description of the human condition. The unconditional love and acceptance of self seems to be the hardest task for all humankind. Refusing to accept our "real selves", we try to create more powerful false selves or give up and become less than human. This results in a lifetime of cover-up and secrecy. This secrecy and hiding is the basic cause of suffering for all of us.

Total self-love and acceptance is the only foundation for happiness and the love of others. Without total self-love and acceptance, we are doomed to the enervative task of creating false selves. It takes tons of energy and hard work to live a false self. This may be the symbolic meaning of the Biblical statement that after the fall, the man and the woman would suffer in their natural activities: the woman in childbirth, the man in his work.

How do we heal this shame that binds us? Wherein lies our hope? This is the matter of this book. In what follows I'd like to share with you my own journey in healing shame. This journey has been the most important issue in my life. Toxic shame is everywhere. Toxic shame is cunning, powerful and baffling. Its power resides in its darkness and secretiveness.

In Part I, I shall try to bring shame out of hiding by examining its many faces and by exposing its origins and major cover-ups. I shall show how shame creates hopelessness and spiritual bankruptcy.

Part II offers every way I know for reducing toxic shame, and transforming it back into healthy shame. My most sincere hope is that every reader who is bound by the ties of toxic shame will use this book to free himself from this menacing enemy.

PART I

THE
PROBLEM

CHAPTER

1

The Many Faces
Of Shame

Because of its preverbal origins, shame is difficult to define. It is a healthy human power which can become a true sickness of the soul. There are two forms of shame: nourishing shame and toxic/life-destroying shame. As toxic shame, it is an excruciatingly internal experience of unexpected exposure. It is a deep cut felt primarily from the inside. It divides us from ourselves and from others. In toxic shame, we disown ourselves. And this disowning demands a cover-up. Toxic shame parades in many garbs and get-ups. It loves darkness and secretiveness. It is the dark secret aspect of shame which has evaded our study.

Because toxic shame stays in hiding and covers itself up, we have to track it down by learning to recognize its many faces and its many distracting behavioral cover-ups.

Shame As A Healthy Human Emotion

Recently I heard Broadway Joe Namath being interviewed. He spoke candidly of his failure to be used by the major network that had hired him as a sportscaster. His voice carried his disappointment. What struck me was his openness and honesty. He was expressing his healthy shame. He seemed totally aware that despite his many achievements, he had some real limitations.

3

Shame As Permission To Be Human*

What our healthy feeling of shame does is let us know that we are limited. It tells us that to be human is to be limited. Actually we humans are essentially limited. We are by definition limited. *Not one of us has or can ever have unlimited power.* The unlimited power that many modern gurus offer us is false hope. Their programs calling us to unlimited power have made them rich, not us. They touch our false selves and tap our toxic shame. We humans are finite. Limitation is our essential nature. Grave problems result from refusing to accept our limits.

Healthy shame is an emotion which signals us about our limits. Like all emotions, healthy shame is an energy-in-motion. Like all emotions it moves us to get our basic needs met.

One of our basic needs is structure. We insure our structure by developing a boundary system within which we safely operate. Structure gives our lives form. Boundaries and form offer us safety and allow a more efficient use of energy.

There is an old joke about the man who "got on his horse and rode off in all directions". Without boundaries we have no limits and easily get confused. We go this way and that, wasting a lot of energy. We lose our way. We become addicted because we don't know when to stop; we don't know how to say no.

Healthy shame keeps us grounded. It is a yellow light warning us that we are essentially limited. *Healthy shame is the basic metaphysical boundary for human beings.* It is the emotional energy which signals us that we are not God — that we have made and will make mistakes, that we need help. Healthy shame gives us permission to be human.

Healthy shame is part of every human's personal power. It allows us to know our limits, and thus to use our energy more effectively. We have better direction when we know our limits. We do not waste ourselves on goals we cannot reach or on things we cannot change. Healthy shame allows our energy to be integrated rather than diffused.

Shame As A Developmental Stage

According to Erik Erikson, a sense of shame is part of the second stage of psychosocial development. In the first stage a child needs to establish a sense of basic trust. This basic trust must be greater than his sense of mistrust. We can understand healthy shame best by understanding this trust stage of psychosocial development.

We needed to know from the beginning that we could trust the world. The world came to us first in the form of our primary caretakers. We needed to know that we could count on someone outside of us to be there for us in a humanly predictable manner. If we had a caretaker who was mostly predictable, and who touched us and mirrored all our behaviors, we developed a sense of basic trust. When security and trust are present, we begin to develop an interpersonal bond, which forms a bridge of mutuality. Such a bridge is crucial for the development of self-worth. The only way a child has of developing a sense of self is through a relationship with another. We are "we" before we are "I".

In this earliest stage of life, we can only know ourselves in the mirroring eyes of our primary caretakers. Each of us needed a relational bridge with our primary caretaker in order to grow.

The Interpersonal Bridge

The relationship between child and caretaker gradually evolves out of reciprocal interest along with shared experiences of trust. Actually trust is fostered by the fact that we come to expect and rely on the mutuality of response. As trust grows, an emotional bond is formed. The emotional bond allows the child to risk venturing out to explore the world. This bond becomes an interpersonal bridge between child and caretaker. The bridge is the foundation for mutual growth and understanding. The interpersonal bridge is strengthened by certain experiences we have come to accept and depend on. The other person, our primary caretaker, becomes significant in the sense that that person's love, respect and care for us really matters. We allow ourselves to be vulnerable in that we allow ourselves to need the other person.

Once basic trust has been established, the child is in a position to develop shame. The shame may be healthy or toxic.

The Development Of Healthy Shame

At about 15 months a child begins to develop musculature. He needs to establish a balance between "holding on and letting go". The earliest muscle development focuses on gaining balance when standing up and walking. This triggers the desire to roam and explore and in order to roam and explore, the child needs to separate from his primary caregivers.

In fact, Erikson says that the psychosocial task for this stage of development is to strike a balance between autonomy and shame and doubt. This stage (15 months to three years) has been called the terrible two's because children begin to explore by touching, tasting and testing. Two-year-olds are stubborn. They want to do it their way (always within eyesight of their caregiver). When two-year-olds are thwarted (like every three minutes), they have intense anger and temper tantrums. At this stage the child needs to take possession of things in order to test them by purposeful repetition. The world is brand new — sights, sounds and smells all have to be assimilated through repeated experience.

The Child's Needs

What a child needs most is a firm but understanding caretaker, who needs to be getting her own needs met through her spouse. Such a caretaker needs to have resolved the issues in her own source relationships, and needs to have a sense of self-responsibility. When this is the case, such a caretaker can be available to the child and provide what the child needs.

The child needs good modeling of healthy shame and other emotions. The child needs the caretaker's time and attention. Above all the child needs good boundaries. A child needs to have a caretaker available to set limits. Outer control must be firmly reassuring. The child needs to know that the interpersonal bridge will not be destroyed by his new urge for doing things his own way — his new urge toward autonomy. Erikson writes:

> "Firmness must protect him against the potential anarchy of his yet untrained sense of discrimination, his inability to hold on and to let go with discretion."

> *Childhood And Society*

If a child can be protected by firm but compassionate limits; if he can explore, test and have tantrums without the caregiver's withdrawal of love, i.e., withdrawal of the interpersonal bridge, then the child can develop a healthy sense of shame. It may come as a moment of embarrassment over one's normal human failures or as timidity and shyness in the presence of strangers. This sense of shame is crucial and necessary as a balance and limit for one's new found autonomy. Healthy shame signals us that we are not omnipotent.

I can remember once beginning a lecture on the 'farther reaches of human nature'. As I started to approach the podium, someone gently pointed out that my fly was unzipped. My blush and momentary embarrassment was the voice of my good shame telling me not to get carried away.

Pascal once said, "He who would be an angel must become a beast."** Thomas Aquinas said that man is a spiritual being who in order to be truly spiritual needs a body. This is similar to George Santayana's statement, "It is necessary to become a beast if one is ever to be a spirit."** We need the boundary of our finitude — ever reminding us that we are human not divine.

Shame As Embarrassment And Blushing

In an embarrassing situation one is caught off guard — one is exposed when one is not ready to be exposed. One feels unable to cope with some situation in the presence of others. It may be an unexpected physical clumsiness, an interpersonal sensitivity or a breach of etiquette.

In such situations we experience the blush that accompanies the feeling of healthy shame. Blushing manifests the exposure, the unexpectedness, the involuntary nature of shame.

Helen Lynd writes,

"One's feeling is involuntarily exposed; one is uncovered."

On Shame And The Search For Identity

Blushing is the manifestation of our human limits. The ability to blush is the metaphor of our essentially limited humanity. With blushing comes the impulse to "cover one's face", "bury one's face", "save face", or "sink into the ground". With blushing we know we've made a mistake. Why would we have such a capacity, if mistakes were not part of our essential nature. Blushing as a manifestation of the healthy feeling of shame keeps us grounded. It reminds us of our core human boundary. It is a signal for us not to get carried away with our own excellence.

Shame As Shyness

Shyness is a natural boundary which guards us from being exposed or wounded by a stranger. Many of us feel shy when we are faced with the prospect of walking up to a stranger. We feel self-conscious, we stammer in speech or speak in an awkward manner. This may trigger embarrassment. Contained in the experience of shyness is the healthy feeling of shame, of a reluctance to expose oneself.

The stranger, by definition, is one who is un-family-iar. The stranger is not of our family. The stranger poses the threat of the unknown. Our shyness is our healthy shame in the presence of a stranger. Like all emotions shyness signals us to be cautious, to take heed lest we be wounded or exposed. Shyness is a boundary which guards our inner core in the presence of the unfamiliar stranger.

Shyness *can* become a serious problem, when it is rooted in toxic shame.

Shame As The Basic Need For Community

There is an ancient proverb which states, "One man is no man." This saying underscores our basic human need for community, which underscores our need for relationships, our need for social life. No one of us could have made it without someone being there for us. We human beings need help. No one of us is so strong that he does not need love, intimacy and dialogue in community.

At birth we are symbiotically bonded to our mother. We are we before we are I. A great deal depends on that source relationship. After a year and a half of establishing the bond of mutual trust, we start to move out to test our autonomy. We need a sense of shame to remind us of our limits. We need our shame and doubt to balance our newly found autonomy.

We will need our parents for another decade before we are ready to leave home. We cannot get our needs met without depending on our primary caregivers. Our healthy feeling of shame is there to remind us that we need help. We cannot make it alone. No human beings can. Even after we have achieved some sense of mastery, even when we are undependent, we will still have needs. We will need to love and grow. We will need to care for another and we will need to be needed. Our shame functions as a healthy signal that we need help, and that we need to love and be in caring relationships with others.

Without the healthy signal of shame, we would not be in touch with our core dependency needs.

Shame As The Source Of Creativity And Learning

I once did a workshop with Richard Bandler, one of the founders of Neuro-Linguistic Programming (NLP). It was a very powerful experience. One aspect of that experience I've never forgotten. Richard asked us to think of a time in our lives when we knew we were right. After a few seconds, I remembered an incident with my wife. He asked us to go over the experience in our memory. Then he asked us to make a movie of the experience: to divide it into acts and to run it as a film. Then he asked us to run the film backwards. Then we were to run the acts out of sequence: the middle act first, the last act in the middle, etc. Then we were to run through the experience again as we had done it the first time. We were to pay exquisite attention to the details of the experience and to the feeling of rightness.

By the time I reran the experience, it no longer had the voltage it had the first time. In fact, I hardly felt anything of the initial intensity. Richard was introducing us to a form of internal remapping called submodality work. That was not what was important for me. What was important for me was a statement Richard made about creativity. For me the greatest human power is the creative power.

Richard Bandler suggested that one of the major blocks to creativity was the feeling of knowing you are right. When we think we are absolutely right, we stop seeking new information. To be right is to be certain, and to be certain stops us from being curious. Curiosity and wonder are at the heart of all learning. Plato said that all philosophy begins in wonder. So the feeling of absolute certainty and righteousness causes us to stop seeking and to stop learning.

Our healthy shame, which is a feeling of our core boundary and limitedness, never allows us to believe we know it all. Our healthy shame is nourishing in that it moves us to seek new information and to learn new things.

Shame As The Source Of Spirituality

Abraham Maslow, the pioneering Third Force Psychologist, once wrote,

> "The spiritual life is . . . part of the human essence. It is a defining characteristic of human nature . . . without which human nature is not full human nature."
>
> *The Farther Reaches Of Human Nature*

What is spirituality? I believe it has to do with our life-style. I believe that life is ever-unfolding and growing. So spirituality is about expansion and growth. It is about love, truth, goodness, beauty, giving and caring. Spirituality is about wholeness and completion. Spirituality is our ultimate human need. It pushes us to transcend ourselves, and to become grounded in the ultimate source of reality. Most call that source God.

Our healthy shame is essential as the ground of our spirituality. By signaling us of our essential limitations, our healthy shame lets us know that we are not God. Our healthy shame points us in the direction of some larger meaning. It lets us know that there is something or someone greater than ourselves. Our healthy shame is the psychological ground of our humility.

Shame As Toxic

Scott Peck describes both neuroses and character disorders as disorders of responsibility. Peck writes,

> "The neurotic assumes too much responsibility; the person with a character disorder not enough. When neurotics are in conflict with the world, they automatically assume that they are at fault. When those with character disorders are in conflict with the world, they automatically assume the world is at fault."
>
> *The Road Less Traveled*

All of us have a smattering of neurotic and character disordered personality traits. The major problem in all of our lives is to decide and clarify our responsibilities. To truly be committed to a life of honesty, love and discipline, we must be willing to commit ourselves to reality. This commitment, according to Peck, "requires the willingness and the capacity to suffer continual self-examination." Such an ability requires a good relationship with oneself. This is precisely what no shame-based person has. In fact a toxically shamed person has an adversarial relationship with himself. Toxic shame — the shame that binds us — is the basis for both neurotic and character disordered syndromes of behavior.

Neurotic Syndromes Of Shame

What is the shame that binds you? How did it get set up in your life? What happens to healthy shame in the process?

Toxic shame, the shame that binds you, is experienced as the all-pervasive sense that I am flawed and defective as a human being. Toxic shame is no longer an emotion that signals our limits, it is a state of being, a core identity. Toxic shame gives you a sense of worthlessness, a sense of failing and falling short as a human being. Toxic shame is a rupture of the self with the self.

It is like internal bleeding. Exposure to oneself lies at the heart of toxic shame. A shame-based person will guard against exposing his inner self to others, but more significantly, he will guard against exposing himself to himself.

Toxic shame is so excruciating because it is the painful exposure of the believed failure of self to the self. In toxic shame the self becomes an object of its own contempt, an object that can't be trusted. As an object that can't be trusted, one experiences oneself as untrustworthy. Toxic shame is experienced as an inner torment, a sickness of the soul. If I'm an object that can't be trusted, then I'm not in me. Toxic shame is paradoxical and self-generating.

There is shame about shame. People will readily admit guilt, hurt or fear before they will admit shame. Toxic shame is the feeling of being isolated and alone in a complete sense. A shame-based person is haunted by a sense of absence and emptiness.

Toxic shame has been studied very little. It is easily confused with guilt. Freud studied anxiety and guilt but almost completely neglected shame.

In a recent New York Times article entitled "Shame Steps Out of Hiding and into Sharper Focus", Daniel Goleman writes,

> "Psychologists, admittedly chagrined and a little embarrassed, are belatedly focusing on shame, a prevalent and powerful emotion, which somehow escaped rigorous scientific examination until now."

Shame As An Identity — Internalization Of Shame

Any human emotion can become internalized. When internalized, an emotion stops functioning in the manner of an emotion and becomes a characterological style. You probably know someone who could be labeled "an angry person" or someone you'd call a "sad sack". In both cases the emotion has become the core of the person's character, her identity. The person doesn't have anger or melancholy, she *is* angry and melancholy.

In the case of shame, internalization involves at least three processes:

1. Identification with unreliable and shame-based models
2. The trauma of abandonment, and the binding of feelings, needs and drives with shame
3. The interconnection of memory imprints which forms collages of shame

Internalization is a gradual process and happens over a period of time. Every human being has to contend with certain aspects of this process. Internalization takes place when all three processes are consistently reinforced.

IDENTIFICATION WITH SHAME-BASED MODELS

Identification is one of our normal human processes. We always have the need to identify. Identification gives one a sense of security. By belonging to something larger than ourselves, we feel the security and protection of the larger reality.

The need to identify with someone, to feel a part of something, to belong somewhere, is one of our most basic needs. With the exception of self-preservation, no other striving is as compelling as this need, which begins with our caregivers or significant others and extends to family, peer group, culture, nation and world. It is seen in lesser forms in our allegiance to a political party or our rooting for a sports team. *Our* team provides a way to experience the powerful emotions of winning or losing. In my own case, I've been a Notre Dame addict from childhood. Even though I've never been to South Bend, didn't attend that university, I'm still their avid and emotional fan. When they win, I win. When they lose, I go into a "funk".

This need to belong explains the loyal and often fanatic adherence people display to a group . . . their group.

When children have shame-based parents, they identify with them. This is the first step in the child's internalizing shame.

ABANDONMENT: THE LEGACY OF BROKEN MUTUALITY

Shame is internalized when one is abandoned. Abandonment is the precise term to describe how one loses one's authentic self and ceases to exist psychologically. Children cannot know who they are without reflective mirrors. Mirroring is done by one's primary caretakers and is crucial in the first years of life. Abandonment includes the loss of mirroring. Parents who are shut down emotionally (all shame-based parents) cannot mirror and affirm their children's emotions.

Since the earliest period of our life was preverbal, everything depended on emotional interaction. Without someone to reflect our emotions, we had no way of knowing who we were. Mirroring remains important all our lives. Think of the frustrating experience which most of us have had, of talking to someone who is not looking at us. While you are speaking, they are fidgeting around or reading something. Our identity demands a significant other whose eyes see us pretty much as we see ourselves.

In fact, Erik Erikson defines identity as interpersonal. He writes,

> "The sense of ego identity is the accrued confidence that the inner sameness and continuity . . . are matched by the sameness and continuity of one's meaning for others."
>
> *Childhood And Society*

Besides lack of mirroring, abandonment includes the following:
Neglect of developmental dependency needs
Abuse of any kind
Enmeshment into the covert or overt needs of the parents or the
    family system needs

Feeling Need And Drive Shame Binds

The shame binding of feelings, needs and natural instinctual drives, is a key factor in changing healthy shame into toxic shame. *To be shame-bound means that whenever you feel any feeling, any need or any drive, you immediately feel ashamed.* The dynamic core of your human life is grounded in your feelings, your needs and your drives. When these are bound by shame, you are shamed to the core.

THE INTERCONNECTION OF MEMORY IMPRINTS WHICH FORM COLLAGES OF SHAME

As shaming experiences accrue and are defended against, the images created by those experiences are recorded in a person's memory bank. Because the victim has no time or support to grieve the pain of the broken mutuality, his emotions are repressed and the grief is unresolved. The verbal (auditory) imprints remain in the memory as do the visual images of the shaming scenes. As each new shaming experience takes place, a new verbal imprint and visual image attach to the already existing ones forming collages of shaming memories.

Children also record their parent's actions at their worst. When Mom and Dad, stepparent or whoever the caretaker, are most out of control, they are the most threatening to the child's survival. The child's survival alarm registers these behaviors the most deeply. Any subsequent shame experience which even vaguely resembles that past trauma can easily trigger the words and scenes of said trauma. What are then recorded are the new experience and the old. Over time an accumulation of shame scenes are attached together. Each new scene potentiates the old, sort of like a snowball rolling down a hill, getting larger and larger as it picks up snow.

As the years go on, very little is needed to trigger these collages of shame memories. A word, a similar facial expression or scene, can set it off. Sometimes an external stimulus is not even necessary. Just going back to an old memory can trigger an enormously painful experience. Shame as an emotion has now become frozen and embedded into the core of the person's identity. Shame is deeply internalized.

Shame As Self-Alienation And Isolation

When one suffers from alienation, it means that one experiences parts of one's self as alien to one's self.

For example, if you were never allowed to express anger in your family, your anger becomes an alienated part of yourself. You experience toxic shame when you feel angry. This part of you must be disowned or severed. There is no way to get rid of your emotional power of anger. Anger is the self-preserving and self-protecting energy. Without this energy you become a doormat and a people-pleaser. As your feelings, needs and drives are bound by toxic shame, more and more of you is alienated.

Finally, when shame has been completely internalized, nothing about you is okay. You feel flawed and inferior; you have the sense of being a failure. There is no way you can share your inner self because you are an object of contempt to yourself. When you are contemptible to yourself, you are no longer in you. To feel shame is to feel seen in an exposed and diminished way. When you're an object to yourself, you turn your eyes inward, watching and scrutinizing every minute detail of behavior. This internal critical observation is excruciating. It generates a tormenting self-consciousness which Kaufman describes as, "creating a binding and paralyzing effect upon the self." This paralyzing internal monitoring causes withdrawal, passivity and inaction.

The severed parts of self are projected in relationships. They are often the basis of hatred and prejudice. The severed parts of the self may be experienced as a split personality or even multiple personalities. This happens often with victims who have been through physical and sexual violation.

To be severed and alienated within oneself also creates a sense of unreality. One may have an all-pervasive sense of never quite belonging, of being on the outside looking in. The condition of *inner alienation and isolation is also pervaded by a low grade chronic depression.* This has to do with the sadness of losing one's authentic self. Perhaps the deepest and most devastating aspect of neurotic shame is the rejection of the self by the self.

Shame As False Self

Because the exposure of self to self lies at the heart of neurotic shame, escape from the self is necessary. The escape from self is accomplished by creating a false self. The false self is always more or less than human. The false self may be a perfectionist or a slob, a family Hero or a family Scapegoat. As the false self is formed, the authentic self goes into hiding. Years later the layers of defense and pretense are so intense that one loses all awareness of who one really is.

It is crucial to see that the false self may be as polar opposite as a superachieving perfectionist or an addict in an alley. Both are driven to cover up their deep sense of self-rupture, the hole in their soul. They may cover up in ways that look polar opposite, but each is still driven by neurotic shame. In fact, *the most paradoxical aspect of neurotic shame is that it is the core motivator of the superachieved and the underachieved, the Star and the Scapegoat, the "Righteous" and the wretched, the powerful and the pathetic.*

Shame As Co-dependency

Much has been written about co-dependency. All agree that it is about the loss of selfhood. Co-dependency is a condition wherein one has no inner life. Happiness is on the outside. Good feelings and self-validation lie on the outside. They can never be generated from within. Pia Mellody's definition of co-dependency is "a state of dis-ease whereby the authentic self is unknown or kept hidden, so that a sense of self . . . of mattering . . . of esteem and connectedness to others is distorted, creating pain and distorted relationships." There is no significant difference in that definition and the way I have described internalized shame. It is my belief that internalized shame *is the essence of co-dependency.*

Shame As Borderline Personality

Kaufman sees many of the categories of emotional illness which are defined in DSM III as rooted in neurotic shame. It seems obvious that some of these types of disorders are related to syndromes of shame. These include dependent personality, clinical depression, schizoid phenomena and borderline personality. My own belief is that toxic shame is a unifying concept for what is often a maze of psychological definitions and distinctions. While I realize that there is clinical and psychotherapeutic value in the kinds of detailed etiological distinctions offered by accurate and precise conceptualizing, I also think some of it is counterproductive.

My own study of James Masterson's work on borderline personalities, as well as my experience with watching his working films, convinces me that there is minimal difference in the treatment of some toxically shame-based people and his treatment of the Borderline Personality. I'm convinced that Masterson's Borderline Personality is a syndrome of neurotic shame. It is described as follows.

It is a syndrome of these roughly related complaints:

1. Self-image disturbance
2. Difficulty identifying and expressing one's own individuated thoughts, wishes and feelings and autonomously regulating self-esteem
3. Difficulty with self-assertion

Borderline Adolescent to Functioning Adult: The Test of Time

Shame As The Core And Fuel Of All Addiction

Neurotic shame is the root and fuel of all compulsive/addictive behaviors. My general working definition of compulsive/addictive behavior is "a pathological relationship to any mood-altering experience that has life-damaging consequences".

The drivenness in any addiction is about the ruptured self, the belief that one is flawed as a person. The content of the addiction, whether it be an ingestive addiction or an activity addiction (like work, buying or gambling) is an attempt at an intimate relationship. The workaholic with his work, or the alcoholic with his booze, are having a love affair. Each one mood alters to avoid the feeling of loneliness and hurt in the underbelly of shame. Each addictive acting out creates life-damaging consequences which create more shame. The new shame fuels the cycle of addiction. Figure 1.1 gives you a visual picture of how internalized shame fuels the addictive process, and how addictions create more shame, which sets one up to be more shame-based. Addicts call this cycle the squirrel cage.

I used to drink to solve the problems caused by drinking. The more I drank to relieve my shame-based loneliness and hurt, the more I felt ashamed. Shame begets shame. The cycle begins with the false belief system that all addicts have, that no one could want them or love them as they are. In fact, addicts can't love themselves. They are an object of scorn to themselves. This deep internalized shame gives rise to distorted thinking. The distorted thinking can be reduced to the belief that I'll be okay if I drink, eat, have sex, get more money, work harder, etc. The shame turns one into what Kellogg has termed a "human doing", rather than a human being.

Figure 1.1. The Compulsive/Addictive Cycle Fueled by and Regenerating Shame

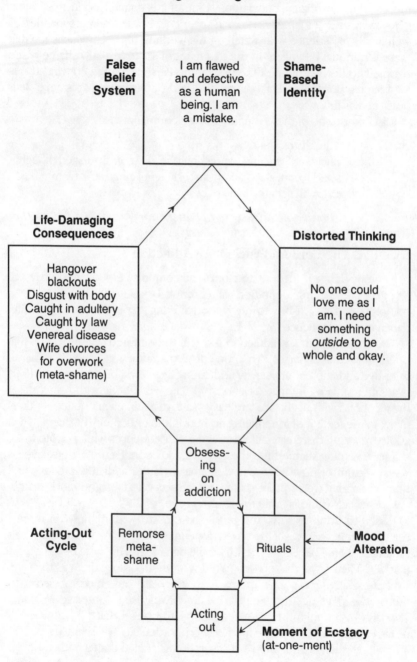

Worth is measured on the outside, never on the inside. The mental obsession about the specific addictive relationship is the first mood alteration, since thinking takes us out of our emotions. After obsessing for a while, the second mood alteration occurs. This is the "acting out" or ritual stage of the addiction. The ritual may involve drinking with the boys, secretly eating in one's favorite hiding place or cruising for sex. The ritual ends in drunkenness, satiation, orgasm, spending all the money or whatever.

What follows is the feeling of shame over one's behavior, and the life-damaging consequences — the hangover, the infidelity, the demeaning sex, the empty pocketbook. The meta-shame is a displacement of affect, a transforming of the shame about self into the shame about "acting out" and experiencing life-damaging consequences. This meta-shame intensifies the shame-based identity.

"I'm no good; there's something wrong with me," plays like a broken record. The more it plays, the more one solidifies one's false belief system. The toxic shame fuels the addiction and regenerates itself.

Shame And Guilt

Toxic shame needs to be sharply distinguished from guilt (guilt can be healthy or toxic). Healthy guilt is the emotional core of our conscience. It is emotion which results from behaving in a manner contrary to our beliefs and values. Guilt presupposes internalized rules and develops later than shame. According to Erikson, the third stage of psychosocial development is the polar balance between initiative and guilt. This stage begins after age three. Guilt is developmentally more mature than shame. Guilt does not reflect directly upon one's identity or diminish one's sense of personal worth. It flows from an integrated set of values. Fossum and Mason write,

> "A person with guilt might say, 'I feel awful seeing that I did something which violated my values.' Or the guilty person might say, 'I feel sorry about the consequences of my behaviors.' In so doing *the person's values are reaffirmed. The possibility of repair exists and learning and growth are promoted.* While guilt is a painful feeling of regret and responsibility for one's actions, shame is a painful feeling about oneself as a person. *The possibility for repair seems foreclosed to the shameful person* because shame is a matter of identity . . . not of behavioral infraction. There is nothing to be learned from it and no growth is opened by the experience because it only confirms one's negative feelings about oneself." (Italics mine)
>
> *Facing Shame*

Figure 1.2 offers a composite contrast between toxic shame, healthy shame, toxic guilt and healthy guilt. The main point of focus is that toxic

Figure 1.2. Shame - Guilt Contrast

	Toxic Guilt	Healthy Guilt	Toxic Shame	Healthy Shame
Origins and Description	Abortive development due to superego distortion; results from perfectionism, family enmeshment	Develops later than shame (age 3-6); Erikson's 3rd psychosocial stage; initiative versus guilt; conscience former	Abortive development a. shame-based models b. abandonment trauma c. shame images interconnected	Develops early, 15 months - 3 years; Erikson's 2nd psychosocial stage
Responsibility* and Power	Grandiose responsibility; way to be powerful in a powerless system	Adequate responsibility; accountability; exercise of power choice	No responsibility; lack of power; failure of choice; incapacity	Limited power and responsibility; power comes by knowing limits; I need help
Felt Sense	Somber-serious; no place for mistakes; I can't make a mistake — it would be terrible	I made a mistake; transgressed my values; I feel bad — sense of wickedness	I'm a mistake; it's hopeless; I'm no good; I'm worthless	I can and will make mistakes; it's normal and mistakes can be remedied
Fault *	Fault of role rigidity; fault of thought distortion (belief you are responsible for *other's* life)	Fault of action; about doing; remedial	Fault of Being; about being defective and flawed as person — irremedial	Limits of being; fault of natural finitude
Morality Goodness	I can be good if I'm perfect; if I follow all rules (legalistic) and do my duty (my role)	What I did was not good; I'm adequate to repair the damage	I'm bad; I'm no good; I'm inadequate, pre-moral	I'm good but limited — permission to be human.
Boundary	No right to a boundary, except through my rigid role or performance	Transgressed moral boundaries (values)	No boundary; nothing about me is okay	Core boundary
Sports Analogy *	Violation of a simple rule — like being off-side, with excessive penalty, like expulsion from game	Violation of a restraining boundary like running out of bounds on a football field	Violation of the game itself; failure to attain goal — like never reaching the end zone	Violation of the rules; simple infraction; too much time — 5 yds

* The ideas about responsibility and fault aspects of healthy guilt and toxic shame, as well as the idea about sports analogy are adapted from **SHAME**, Hazelden, 1981.

shame is about being flawed as a human being. Repair seems foreclosed since no change is really possible. In its ultimate essence, toxic shame has the sense of hopelessness.

Character Disorder Syndromes Of Shame

NARCISSISTIC PERSONALITY DISORDER

According to James Masterson, the main clinical characteristics of the narcissistic personality disorder are:

> "Grandiosity, extreme self-involvement and lack of interest and empathy for others, in spite of the pursuit of others to obtain admiration and approval."
>
> *The Narcissistic And Borderline Disorders*

The Narcissist is endlessly motivated to seek perfection in everything he does. Such a personality is driven to the acquisition of wealth, power and beauty, and to find others who will mirror and admire his grandiosity. Underneath this external facade there is an emptiness filled with envy and rage. The core of this emptiness is internalized shame.

PARANOID PERSONALITY

The paranoid defense is a posture developed to cope with excessive shame. The paranoid person becomes hypervigilant expecting and waiting for the betrayal and humiliation he knows is coming. The paranoid person interprets innocent events as personally threatening and lives constantly on guard.

Harry Stack Sullivan described the self of the paranoid as "feeling hopelessly defective". The sources of the paranoid's own sense of deficiency are blamed elsewhere. It's as if the inner eyes of shaming, contempt and disdain are projected outward. Wrongdoings, mistakes and other instances of personal failure cannot be owned by the paranoid-type personality. They are disowned and transferred from the inner self to others.

OFFENDER BEHAVIOR

Criminality In General

Alice Miller has shown convincingly that much criminal behavior is "acting out" behavior. "Acting out" is also called reenactment. What this means is that a criminal offender was once victimized in much the same way as he criminalizes. Children from violently abusing families, children from families where high voltage abandonment takes place, suffer terrible victimization. They generally either take on a victim role and reenact it over and over again, or they identify with their offender and reenact the offense on helpless victims (as they once were). This reenactment is called "repetition compulsion" — the urge to repeat.

In Alice Miller's book, *For Your Own Good,* she outlines in detail the reenactments of a teenage drug addict and a child murderer. While no one can or has proven that every criminal is acting out his own abandoning shame, I believe there is enough data to support the hypothesis that this is most often the case. Surely no one has offered any other solution to the everlasting problem of crime and criminality. Without any doubt, criminals feel like social outcasts and bear enormous toxic shame.

Physical Abuse

The physical offender was once a victim who was powerless and who was humiliated. Parents who physically humiliate and abuse their own children were typically abused when they were young. They have never resolved the internalized shame in their own lives. Their own childhood traumas are embedded in a series of inter-related memories. These original scenes become reactivated by their own children and compel reenactment like a Pavlovian trigger. The NLP people refer to these scenes as "anchors" (see Chapter 6 of Part II). Kaufman suggests,

> "Parents who are about to abuse their own children are simultaneously reliving scenes in which they were also beaten, but they relive the scene from the perspective of their own parent as well. They now play their parents' role."

Why would parents, who were once abused and beaten children, want to play their parents' role? This answer lies in the dynamic of identification. Offender identification was clearly defined by Bettelheim with the phrase "identification with the aggressor". When children are physically hurt and in psychological pain, they want out of it as quickly as possible. So they cease identifying with themselves, and identify with their shaming oppressor in an attempt to possess that person's power and strength. In forming the identification with the parent, one becomes at once the weak bad child *and* the strong transgressor parent. The internal image of the abusive parent triggers the old scene and mediates the process. Physical abuse can trigger compulsive reenactment of the abuse either toward oneself, one's spouse or one's children. Internalized shame maintains the process. It compels the reenactment.

The victims of physical violence may also remain victims. Martin Seligman has done extensive studies on what is called "learned helplessness". In essence, arbitrary, random and unpredictable beatings create a state of passivity in which the victim no longer feels that there is anything that she can do. A negative belief system is adhered to. The person no longer believes she has a choice.

A simpler explanation for the bonding to violence is the fact that as one is beaten more and more, one is shamed more and more. The more internalized shame, the greater is the belief in oneself as defective and flawed. The more one believes one is defective and flawed, the more one's choices diminish. Internalized shame destroys one's boundaries. Without boundaries one has no protection.

Sexual Abuse

Sexual abusers are most often sex addicts. Sometimes they are reenacting their own sexual or physical violation. Sexual abuse generates intense and crippling shame, which more often than not, results in a splitting of the self. Incest and sexual abuse offenders are fueled by internalized shame. Kaufman writes,

> "The perpetrator of the assault or violation also is shame-based. Such acts are acts of power and revenge, born of impotence and fueled by shame . . . that scene of forcible violation is a reenactment, a transformation of a scene of equal powerlessness and humiliation experienced by the perpetrator at the hands of a different tormentor . . . The victim, the target of revenge, is confused with the source of the perpetrator's shame. By defeating and humiliating the victim, the perpetrator is momentarily freed of shame."

The victimization could be incest, molestation, rape, voyeurism, exhibitionism, indecent liberties or phone calls. In every case there is an acting out of shame and a victimization of the innocent.

GRANDIOSITY — THE DISABLED WILL

Toxic shame also wears the face of grandiosity. Grandiosity is a disorder of the will. It can appear as narcissistic self-enlargement or wormlike helplessness. Each extreme refuses to be human. Each exaggerates: one is more than human; the other is less than human. It's important to see that the less than human, the hopeless one, is also grandiose. Hopelessness says that nothing and no one could help me. I'm the sickest of the sick . . . I'm the "best/worst" there ever was.

Grandiosity results from the human will becoming disabled. *The will is disabled primarily through the shaming of the emotions.* The shamed and blocked emotions stop the full integration of intellectual meaning. When an emotional event happens, emotions must be discharged in order for the intellect, reason and judgment to make sense out of it. Emotions bias thinking. As emotions get bound by shame, their energy is frozen, which blocks the full interaction between the mind and the will.

The human will is intensity of desire raised to the level of action. The will is an appetite. It is dependent on the mind (reasoning and judgment) for its eyes. Without the mind, the will is blind and has no content. Without content the will starts willing itself. This state of disablement causes severe problems. Some of which are:

- The will wills what can't be willed.
- The will tries to control everything.
- The will experiences itself as omnipotent or when it has failed as "wormlike".
- The will wills for the sake of willing (impulsiveness).
- The will wills in absolute extremes — all or nothing.

Toxic Shame As Spiritual Bankruptcy

The problem of toxic shame is ultimately a spiritual problem. I call it "spiritual bankruptcy". I suggested earlier that spirituality is the essence of human existence. We are not material beings on a spiritual journey; we are spiritual beings who need an earthly journey to become fully spiritual.

Spirituality is life-style — that which enhances and expands life. Therefore, spirituality is about growth and expansion, newness and creativity. Spirituality is about being. Being is that victorious thrust whereby we triumph over nothingness. Being is about why there is something, rather than nothing. Being is the ground of all the beings that are.

OTHERATION AND DEHUMANIZATION

Toxic shame, which is an alienation of the self from the self, causes one to become 'other-ated'.

Otheration is the term used by the Spanish philosopher Ortega Y. Gasset to describe dehumanization. He says that man is the only being who lives from within. To be truly human is to have an inner self and a life from within. Animals live in constant hypervigilance, always on guard, looking outside themselves for sustenance and guarding against danger. When humans no longer have an inner life, they become otherated and dehumanized.

Toxic shame with its more than human, less than human polarity is dehumanizing. The demand for a false self to cover and hide the authentic self necessitates a life dominated by doing and achievement. Everything depends on performance and achievement rather than on being. Being requires no measurement; it is its own justification. Being is grounded in an inner life which grows in richness.

'The kingdom of heaven is within,' says the scripture. Toxic shame looks to the outside for happiness and for validation, since the inside is flawed and defective. Toxic shame is spiritual bankruptcy.

SHAME AS HOPELESSNESS — THE SQUIRREL CAGE

Toxic shame has the quality of being irremedial. If I am flawed, defective and a mistake, then there is nothing that can be done about me. Such a belief leads to impotence. How can I change who I am? Toxic shame also has the quality of circularity. Shame begets shame. You saw in Figure 1.1 how addicts act out internalized shame and then feel shame about their shameful behavior.

FUNCTIONAL AUTONOMY

Once internalized, toxic shame is functionally autonomous, which means that it can be triggered internally without any attending stimulus. One can imagine a situation and feel deep shame. One can be alone and trigger a shaming spiral through internal self-talk. The more one experiences shame, the more one is ashamed and the beat goes on.

It is this dead-end quality of shame that makes it so hopeless. The possibility for repair seems foreclosed if one is essentially flawed as a human being. Add to that the self-generating quality of shame, and one can see the devastating, soul-murdering power of neurotic shame.

The reader can begin to see how dramatic it was for me to discover the dynamics of shame. By being aware of the dynamics of shame, by naming it, we gain some power over it.

---

* See **SHAME**, Hazeldon, 1981.
** I'm indebted to the Hazeldon publication on **SHAME** for the quotations of Pascal and Santayana.

2

The Sources Of
Toxic Shame

The Family System

Introduction

Toxic shame is primarily fostered in *significant* relationships. If you do
not value someone, it's hard to imagine being shamed by what he says or
does. The possibility of toxic shame begins with our source relationships. If
our primary caregivers are shame-based, they will act shameless and pass
their toxic shame onto us. There is no way to teach self-value if one does not
value oneself.

Toxic shame is multigenerational. It is passed from one generation to the
next. Shame-based people find other shame-based people and get married.
As a couple each carries the shame from his or her own family system. Their
marriage will be grounded in their shame-core. The major outcome of this
will be a lack of intimacy. It's difficult to let someone get close to you if you
feel defective and flawed as a human being. Shame-based couples maintain
non-intimacy through poor communication, nonproductive circular
fighting, games, manipulation, vying for control, withdrawal, blaming and
confluence. Confluence is the agreement never to disagree. Confluence
creates pseudo-intimacy.

When a child is born to these shame-based parents, the deck is stacked
from the beginning. The job of parents is to model. Modeling includes how
to be a man or woman; how to relate intimately to another person; how to

acknowledge and express emotions; how to fight fairly; how to have physical, emotional and intellectual boundaries; how to communicate; how to cope and survive life's unending problems; how to be self-disciplined; how to love oneself and another. Shame-based parents cannot do any of these. They simply don't know how.

Children need their parents' time and attention. Giving one's time is part of the work of love. It means being there for the child, attending to the child's needs rather than the parent's needs.

For example, I used to spend lots of time with my son. Often it consisted of my watching a football game, while my son played in the room. If he made too much noise, I scolded him. We spent time together but it was quantitative rather than qualitative.

Part of the work of love is listening. Children are clear about what they need and will tell us in no uncertain terms. We need to listen to them. This requires a fair amount of emotional maturity. To listen well, one must have one's own needs met. If one is needy, it's hard to listen. Our neediness is like a toothache. When we are shame-based, we can only focus on our own ache.

Needy, shame-based parents cannot possibly take care of their children's needs. The child is shamed whenever he or she is needy because the child's needs clash with the parents' needs. The child grows up and becomes an adult. But underneath the mask of adult behavior there is a child who was neglected. This needy child is insatiable. What that means is that when the child becomes an adult, there is a "hole in his soul". He can never get enough as an adult. Adults make what they get be enough and work harder to get more the next time. An adult child can't get enough because it's really a child's needs that are in question.

For example, in my beginning relationships I always went too far and wanted too much. If I met a girl and we hit it off, I immediately began talking about her in terms of marriage, *even after one date!* Once she was in love with me, I expected her to take care of me like a mother. Needy children need parents. So adult children turn lovers into parents, someone to take care of their needs.

The bottom line is that shame-based needy marriages create shame-based needy families. The children grow up in the soil of shame rather than the nurturing arms of love.

Shame-based families operate according to the laws of social systems. When a social system is dysfunctional, it is rigid and closed. All the individuals in that family are enmeshed into a kind of trancelike frozenness. They take care of the system's need for balance.

Children then go to school, to church or synagogue and grow up to live in society. Each of these social systems adds its own unique contribution to the toxic shame induction process.

Max's Story*

Max was perhaps the most tragic figure I encountered over a 20-year period of counseling. He came to me at age 44. I liked him instantly. Everyone seemed to like him. His problem was one I had never heard of before. Max ran away. He had done it nine times. At certain points in his life, most often when he was doing very well and the pressures of success were mounting, he would just pack up his car with a few necessities and start driving. He would leave everything — clothes, furnishings, family and job. Max was a Sales Engineer.

On the ninth runaway, he left his five children, all under 17. They had come to live with Max after he divorced his third wife. Three children were from his first marriage, the fourth from his second, the fifth from his third. As I talked to Max, the deep hurt and pain of his life was apparent. His shame was more apparent. In fact, Max's life was a metaphor of internalized shame.

He embodied many of the faces of shame and was the product of the major sources of shame. He also acted out many of the major cover-ups of shame.

He broke eye contact continually when he talked. He frequently blushed. He was painfully self-conscious and hypervigilant. Sometimes he would defiantly look me in the eyes and make matter of fact statements about the things he had done, severely condemning himself. And then he would follow this with long delusional descriptions of how he had been responsible and successful. When I gently confronted his denials, he would become energetically reactive and defensive and sometimes go into a rage. What became clear to me was his despair, his desperate loneliness and his shame-based hopelessness. Although he was gifted intellectually and evidently a skilled salesman and engineer, he would subject himself to the most demeaning jobs during his runaways. He had been a janitor, a dishwasher, a garbageman's helper, a lumberjack, a stagehand, a short-order cook and on his last "trip", as he referred to it, he collected and sold aluminum cans.

Max, although quite attractive to women, always stayed alone and celibate on his trips. He was tall, 6'3" and handsome. By the time he saw me, he was impotent with women. This was partly due to years of isolation, marijuana smoking and sexualizing.

Max was what Pat Carnes, in his book *Out Of The Shadows*, calls a Level I and II sex addict.

---

*Max is a composite symbol — a sort of Everyman of Toxic Shame. I have taken bits and pieces from the tragic lives of actual shame-based people. One of them is now dead — a tragic victim of toxic shame.

Level I sexual addiction involves the following:
Multiple affairs or sex partners
Compulsive masturbation with or without pornography
Chronic cruising of either a homosexual or heterosexual nature
Fetish behavior, bestiality and prostitution

Level II involves voyeurism, exhibitionism, indecent liberties and lewd phone calls.

Carnes also speaks of **Level III** sexual addiction which includes incest, rape and molestation. The levels refer to the level of victimization and legal punishment accompaning the sexual act. Levels II and III always have a victim and are punishable by law.

In Max's case he had multiple affairs during his three marriages. During the early part of his second marriage he had engaged in voyeurism. He described the voyeurism with a great feeling of degradation and shame. On one occasion he hid in the branches of a tree for three hours to get a two-minute glimpse of a young woman in her bra and panties.

Max also cruised shopping malls, engaging in subtle forms of indecent liberties. By the time Max came to me for counseling, he had completely given up any relationship with women. He was isolated, and without any real relationships of any kind. He had resigned himself to a menial job as a bookkeeper in a hardware store.

Max's children were all addicts. His oldest was already in her second marriage at 26 years of age. She was a severe caretaker co-dependent who confused love with pity. She found men who were down and out and nourished them back to health. Her second husband was an ex-European drug dealer who had served time for drug dealing in France. Max's two sons and the daughter from his second marriage were all serious drug addicts and had major problems with sex and relationships. The youngest, a male child from his third marriage, had been arrested and jailed four times for violent alcohol and drug-related behavior by age 13.

I saw Max off and on for almost seven years. Just when I thought we were making progress, Max would quit (run away from me). I became more involved with Max than any counselor should. Max hooked my own shame and co-dependency. I wanted to help Max so much that I was overly invested in the outcome of our work. In September of 1974, Max died at the age of 52. This was the exact age his own father had died.

Max had a grandiose melodramatic quality to his personality. At the same time, there was true generosity and nobleness about him. His compassion for the suffering of others was boundless. He died of emphysema in the back ward of a public county hospital. At his funeral, I wept in a way I could not have imagined.

Max represented all of us shame-based people. I said he died of emphysema. What he really died of was toxic shame. His internalized shame was the source of his co-dependency, chemical and sex addictions. Max was the Everyman of Toxic Shame. His life, from beginning to end, illustrated the sources and the demonic power of toxic shame.

I shall use the elements of Max's life to outline these sources of toxic shame: his dysfunctional family of origin, his shame-based parental models, his multigenerational family history, his abandonment issues, his schooling, his religious background and the shaming culture which we all share with him.

Dysfunctional Families

Toxic shame originates interpersonally, primarily in significant relationships. Our most significant relationships are our source relationships. They occur in our original families.

As Judith Bardwick says so well,

> "Marriage and thus family are where we live out our most intimate and powerful human experiences. The family is the unit in which we belong, from which we can expect protection from uncontrollable fate, in which we create infinity through our children and in which we find a haven. The stuff that family is made of is bloodier and more passionate than the stuff of friendship, and the costs are greater, too."
>
> *In Transition*

Our families are where we first learn about ourselves. Our core identity comes first from the mirroring eyes of our primary caretakers. Our destiny depended to a large extent on the health of our caretakers.

In Max's case, his father, Jerome, was a full-fledged alcoholic and womanizing sex addict. Jerome was shame-based. He had been abandoned by his own father and raised by an emotionally incesting alcoholic mother. Max's description of his grandmother was frightening.

By the time Max was eight, his mother Felicia had divorced his father Jerome. From eight years on, Max was neglected emotionally and financially. His older brother Ralph took over the role of being Max's father. His older sister Maxine also took on a parenting role. They were his Little Parents.

Max's mom and dad married at ages 17 and 18. They married because they were pregnant with Max's older sister Maxine. Felicia came from a staunchly religious Christian family. The family demanded that Jerome marry Felicia. Felicia was extremely prudish and shut down emotionally. She carried her mother's repressed sexuality. Her mother had been sexually violated by her own father (also an alcoholic) and two of her nine brothers.

Felicia's mother had never dealt with her incest issues and carried them as her shame secret. Felicia, while ostensibly proper and prudish, had "acted out" the sexual shame of her mother by getting pregnant at 17. Felicia had also been sexually violated by her maternal grandfather.

Felicia was her father's emotional spouse. She became his little woman and confidante after her mother withdrew with hypochondria.

Jerome was also the emotional caretaker of *his* mother. He was her little man and became her Surrogate Spouse. Both of Max's parents were Surrogate Spouses. This means they both were emotional incest victims. Both were severely shame-based, co-dependent and addicted. Max's mother was dutiful but cold and nonsensual. Max was born five years after Jerome and Felicia were married. He was not planned and not really wanted. He was an accidental pregnancy. Max was what is called the Lost Child in family systems theory (Sharon Wegscheider-Cruse).

Families As Social Systems

You noticed that I've capitalized the words Lost Child, Surrogate Spouse, Little Parents. I capitalize these words to show that they are rigid roles necessitated by the needs of the family system. In my book, *Bradshaw On: The Family*, and my PBS TV series by the same name, I outlined a newly emerging understanding of families as social systems.

Families are social systems which follow organismic laws. The first law of social organisms is that the whole is greater than the sum of its parts. A family is defined by the interaction and inter-relationships of its parts, rather than the sum of its parts.

A way to illustrate this holistic principle is to think of the human body. Our body is a whole organic system composed of many subsystems. There are the nervous system, the circulatory system, the endocrine system, etc. The human body as an organism is not the sum of its parts, but rather the inter-relationship of the parts. My body is not my body if it is cut into parts. For example, if you cut my legs from my body, you'd hardly look at them and think of me. In a system every part is related to every other part. Each part is wholly a part and partly a whole . . .

In a family, the whole family as an organism is greater than any individual in the family. The family is defined by the relationship between the parts, rather than the sum of the parts. As social systems families have components, rules, roles and needs that define the system.

The chief component in the family as a system is the marriage. If the marriage is healthy and functional, the family will be healthy and functional. If the marriage is dysfunctional, then the family is dysfunctional.

In Max's case, his parents' marriage was extremely dysfunctional. When the chief component of a system is dysfunctional, the whole system is thrown out of balance. When the system is out of balance, another law comes into play, the law of dynamic homeostasis. This is the law of balance.

Dynamic homeostasis means that whenever a part of the system is out of balance, the rest of the members of the system will try to bring it back into balance.

I used a mobile on my TV series to illustrate this. If you touch one part of the mobile, the rest of it is affected. If one part moves, all the parts move. The mobile will always return to a state of rest. In a healthy functional family, the mobile will be in gentle motion. In a dysfunctional family, the mobile will tend to become frozen and static.

The children in a dysfunctional family take on rigid roles necessitated by the family's need for balance. For example, if a child is not wanted, he or she will try to balance the family by not being any trouble, by being helpful, perfect, super-responsible or invisible. This is the Lost Child role. I capitalize it to show that it is a dysfunctional role.

Both Max and his older sister Maxine were Lost Children. Max's brother, Ralph, was a family Star or Hero, i.e., he superachieved to give his shame-based alcoholic family a sense of dignity. Max's older brother and sister became Max's Little Parents.

As Jerome became more and more alcoholic, he abandoned all his children. Since the family system had no father, Ralph took on that role and became Max's Little Father. Since the family had no Marriage (chief component), Ralph took on the role and became Felicia's Surrogate Spouse. The system had no money earner, so Ralph and Maxine became Super-responsible Caretakers.

As a child, Max was sheltered from his father's drinking by being taken to the homes of relatives. He was The Protected One. He experienced this as abandonment. It's crucial to see that all these roles are cover-ups for shame.

Ralph covered up his shame by playing his Star Hero role. He also acted shameless towards Max by demanding that Max be perfect. He tried to over-discipline Max, continually measuring him with shoulds and oughts. Ralph was a constant source of shame for Max. Max loved and admired his older brother. He willingly accepted his brother's interpersonal transfer of shame. Ralph was also extremely religious. He studied to be a Christian minister. He used religious righteousness as a cover-up for his shame and dumped it on Max by moralizing and making judgments of him.

When the fear, hurt and loneliness of the shame in a dysfunctional family reaches high levels of intensity, one person, often the most sensitive, becomes the family Scapegoat. The function of this role is to lessen the pain all the members are in. At first Maxine took on this role for Felicia. She became Mom's Scapegoat. Later Ralph became the Scapegoat due to his active alcoholism in his teenage years. Ralph repented and went into the ministry. This left the job for Max. Max started his drinking and running away at age 15. His first major disappearance was for four days, winding up on a beach in New Orleans. As his bizarre runaways continued, the family focused more and more on him. By discussing and obsessing on Max, everyone in the family system could avoid his own pain.

Max became like the sacrificial goat in the Jewish Atonement Ritual. In that Ritual the goat is smeared with blood and is sent into the desert. In this way the scapegoat atones for the people's sins. Max became the sacrificial goat. He literally went to his death carrying the shame of several generations of his family.

All of the roles in Max's family system were played as a way to control the distress of Jerome's alcohol addiction and Felicia's co-dependent addiction. In functional families the roles are chosen and are flexible. The members have the choice of giving up the roles. In dysfunctional families the roles are RIGID. Figure 2.1 outlines the various roles in Max's family of origin. I've added a few from my notes on Max. Notice that all the roles cover up the shame-based inner core. As each member of the system plays his rigid role, the system stays frozen and unchanging. Dysfunctional families are frozen in a trancelike state. The shame-core keeps the system frozen. Everyone is in hiding. The roles cover up each person's true and authentic self.

SHAME-BASED FAMILIES AND MULTIGENERATIONAL ILLNESS

One of the devastating aspects of toxic shame is that it is multigenerational. The secret and hidden aspects of toxic shame are the wellsprings of its multigenerational life. Since it is kept hidden, it cannot be worked out. *Families are as sick as their secrets.* The secrets are what they are ashamed of. Family secrets can go back for generations. They can be about suicides, homicides, incest, abortions, addictions, public loss of face, financial disaster, etc. All the secrets get acted out. This is the power of toxic shame.

The pain and suffering of shame generate automatic and unconscious defenses. Freud called these defenses by various names — denial, idealization of parents, repression of emotions and dissociation from emotions. What is important to note is that we can't know what we don't know. Denial, idealization, repression, dissociation once formed are unconscious survival mechanisms. Because they are unconscious, we lose touch with the shame, hurt and pain they cover up. *We cannot heal what we cannot feel.* So without recovery, our toxic shame gets carried for generations.

I've already suggested that Max's mother and father had both come from shame-based families. Figure 2.2 gives you a visual picture of Felicia's

Figure 2.1. Max's Dysfunctional Family of Origin

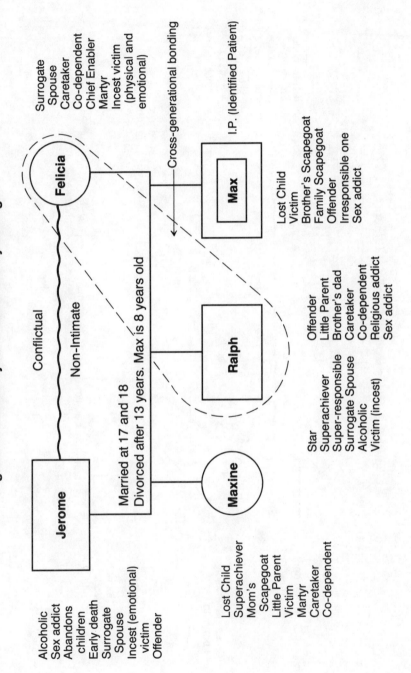

Figure 2.2. Max's Mother's (Felicia) Genogram

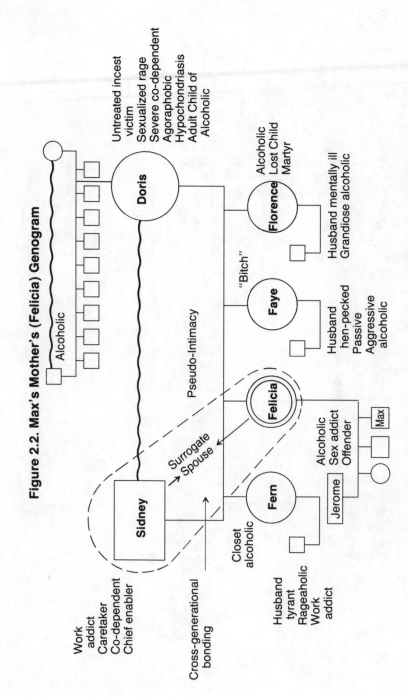

Work addict
Caretaker
Co-dependent
Chief enabler

Cross-generational bonding

Alcoholic

Untreated incest victim
Sexualized rage
Severe co-dependent
Agoraphobic
Hypochondriasis
Adult Child of Alcoholic

Doris

Pseudo-Intimacy

Surrogate Spouse

Sidney

Closet alcoholic

Felicia

Fern

Faye

"Bitch"

Florence

Alcoholic
Lost Child
Martyr

Husband mentally ill
Grandiose alcoholic

Husband hen-pecked
Passive
Aggressive alcoholic

Jerome

Alcoholic
Sex addict
Offender

Max

Husband tyrant
Rageaholic
Work addict

Daughters all prove that mother was right — "men are no damned good" genogram. Her mother came from an alcoholic incestuous family. Felicia's mother was an untreated shame-based co-dependent in acute stages of her addiction. She was agoraphobic and a hypochondriac. Felicia's father enabled her mother's shame by allowing her to be sick. He also set Felicia up in the Surrogate Spouse role. Felicia was an untreated emotional and physical incest victim, who repressed her sexuality and carried her mother's unresolved incest issues. She unconsciously acted it out by being seductive to both Ralph and Max. Ralph, as oldest son, became Felicia's Surrogate, repeating the incest. Felicia idealized her dad and enabled his severe co-dependency and work addiction. Felicia's three sisters all married dysfunctional men. Each daughter carried her mother's unresolved sexualized rage.

Felcia's mother continuously bad-mouthed men from her sick bed. Max reported that as a boy he remembered that one of her favorite sayings was, "Men only want one thing. They think with their penis." This statement, said in the presence of a young male, is sexually abusive. Ralph and Max were both victimized by Felicia's unconscious sexual rage and contempt for men.

When Felicia got pregnant with Jerome, she was "acting out" her mother's unresolved sexual shame. Max reenacted Felicia's acting out by getting his first wife Bridget pregnant when he was 17. Ralph also married pregnant.

In Figure 2.3 I've outlined the major parts of Jerome's genogram. Jerome's mother saw her own mother burn to death when she was seven years old. She was abandoned by her father. He sent her to live with her two man-hating aunts. She rebelled against this situation by continually getting into trouble.

She acted out sexually at an early age. I always suspected that her promiscuity was an acting out of some form of sexual abuse. Max had no data on her side of the family. So I was never able to verify this. Max greatly disliked his grandmother and had never even seen his grandfather. Jerome's mother married at age 16. Her husband died a tragic death before age 30. He was electrocuted while working at a power plant. Jerome's mother received a large amount of money as the surviving widow. She boozed and partied for the next few years. She seemed to have been genetically alcoholic.

She married Jerome's father pregnant, and after a stormy seven years, he divorced her. Jerome was eight years old. He only saw his father twice from that point on. Once he hitchhiked 300 miles to see him, only to be disappointed by being put on a bus and sent home. The other time was a chance run in. Jerome read of his father's death in a newspaper. He went to the funeral and was asked to leave, being told that it was too awkward for him to be there. His father had remarried, and had three children by his second marriage.

So Jerome grew up with no father, and was enmeshed with his alcoholic

Figure 2.3. Max's Father's (Jerome) Genogram

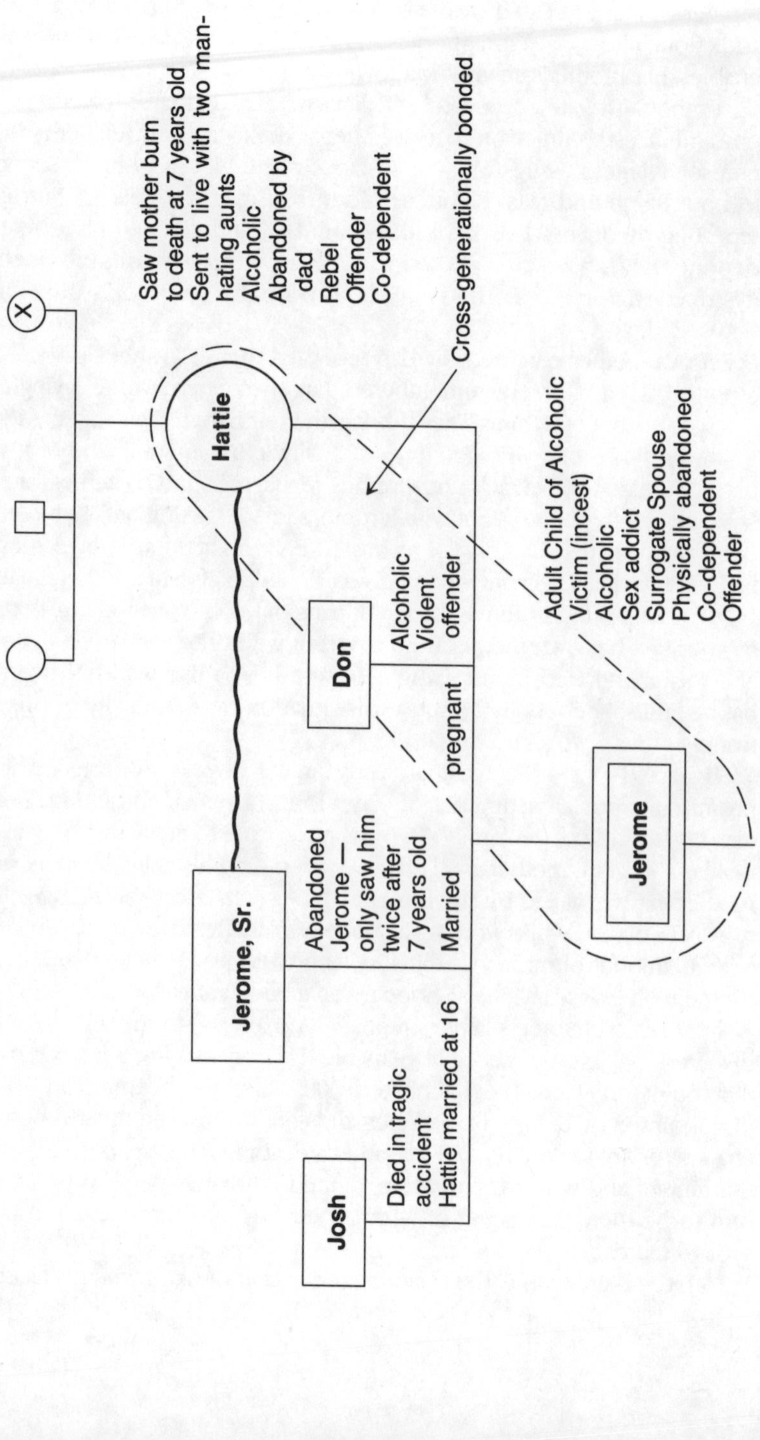

Josh
Died in tragic accident
Hattie married at 16

Jerome, Sr.
Abandoned Jerome — only saw him twice after 7 years old
Married

Don
Alcoholic
Violent offender

pregnant

Hattie
Saw mother burn to death at 7 years old
Sent to live with two man-hating aunts
Alcoholic
Abandoned by dad
Rebel
Offender
Co-dependent

Cross-generationally bonded

Jerome
Adult Child of Alcoholic
Victim (incest)
Alcoholic
Sex addict
Surrogate Spouse
Physically abandoned
Co-dependent
Offender

sex addict mother. He was her emotional incest victim. Max would *"act out" these multigenerational abandonment patterns in his runaways.* Both his parents, Jerome and Felicia, had been abandoned by their parents of the same sex. Both were used for their parents' needs, rather than their parents being there for them.

Max met his first wife, Bridget, in college. She was an Adult Child of an Alcoholic (ACoA) and the apple of her dad's eye. An only child, she was beautiful and smart. She was the family Star and was cross-generationally bonded with both her parents.

Max was the third child in the birth order position. Third children often carry the dynamics of their parent's marriage. Max literally reenacted his parents' pregnancy and early marriage. He later abandoned his children as his father had abandoned him. Max felt the loneliness and isolation his parents experienced in their marriage.

Bridget was the Caretaker in her family. She literally took care of her father's sadness, deep-seated isolation and depression. She did this by always being up and cheerful. She was a high school cheerleader. This role became so chronic, she lost any contact with her authentic self.

On one occasion Max asked me to see her because of their oldest daughter. I had suggested to Max that Bridget seemed to be in an enabling relationship with their daughter. She had bailed her out of jams on numerous occasions and was always giving her money she couldn't afford. When Bridget spoke to me, I had the uneasy feeling of not knowing who I was talking to. She had a parrotlike vocabulary and was "acting". The role was so sealed, she had no idea she was in an act. Figure 2.4 gives you a visual picture of Max's own family system. The oldest child was clearly a Lost Child who gave her all to take care of everybody. Each of the other children was acting out the family system's shame. The middle sons were severely alcoholic. The fourth child was also alcoholic and hooked on pills. The youngest son was acting out Max's internalized rage in offender behavior.

In summary, I hope the reader can feel the power of the multigenerational patterns in Max's background. I hope you can see how Max reenacted those patterns and passed them on to his children. In Max's five generation genogram there are five generations of alcoholism, physical and emotional abandonment and co-dependency. There are four generations of sexual abuse and sexual addiction. There are early pregnancies, multiple marriages and divorces. Max was abandoned by his father Jerome at exactly the same age Jerome was abandoned by his father. Max died at exactly the same age his father died. Max's five-generation family map is not atypical of shame-based families.

Figure 2.4. Max's Genogram (Immediate Family)

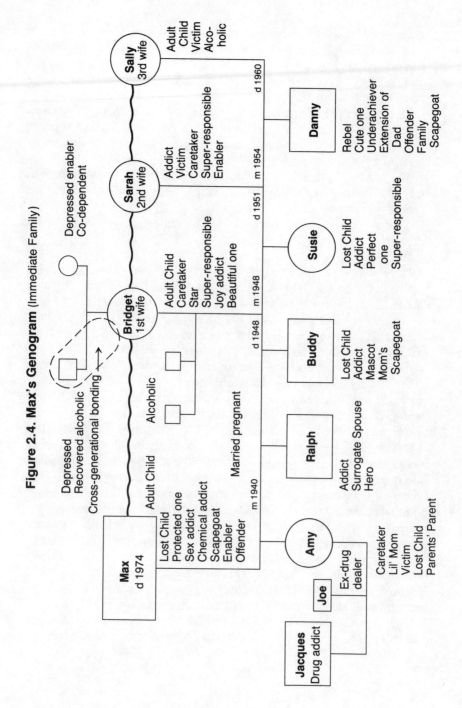

SHAME-BASED MARRIAGE AND PARENTAL MODELS

From what you have seen so far it should be obvious that a major source of toxic shame is the family system and its multigenerational patterns of unresolved secrets.

More specifically these families are created by the shame-based people who find and marry each other. Each looks to and expects the other to take care of and parent the child within him or her. Each is incomplete and insatiable. The insatiability is rooted in each person's unmet childhood needs. When two adult children meet and fall in love, the child in each looks to the other to fill his or her needs. Since "in-love" is a natural state of fusion, the incomplete children fuse together as they had done in the symbiotic stage of infancy. Each feels a sense of oneness and completeness. Since "in-love" is always erotic, each feels "oceanic" in the sexual embrace. "Oceanic" love is without boundaries. Being in love is as powerful as any narcotic. One feels whole and ecstatic.

Unfortunately this state cannot last. The ecstatic consciousness is highly selective. Lovers focus on sameness and are intrigued by the newness of each other. Soon, however, real differences in socialization begin to emerge. The two families of origin rear their shame-based heads. Now the battle begins! Who will take care of whom? Whose family rules will win out? The more shame-based each person is, the more each other's differences will be intolerable. "If you loved me, you'd do it my way," each cajoles the other. The Hatfields and the McCoys go at it again.

SHAME-BASED FAMILY RULES

Each family system has several categories of rules. There are rules about celebrating and socializing; rules about touching and sexuality; rules about sickness and proper health care; rules about vacations and vocations; rules about household maintenance and the spending of money. Perhaps the most important rules are about feelings, interpersonal communication and parenting.

Toxic shame is consciously transferred by means of shaming rules. In shame-based families, the rules consciously shame all the members. Generally however, the children receive the major brunt of the shame. Power is a cover-up for shame. Power is frequently hierarchical. Dad can yell at anyone. Mom can yell at anyone but Dad. The oldest can yell at anyone but Mom and Dad, etc. The youngest tortures the cat.

The Dysfunctional Family Rules

1. **Control** — One must be in control of all interactions, feelings and personal behavior at all times . . . control is the major defense strategy for shame.

2. **Perfectionism** — Always be right in everything you do. The perfectionist rule always involves a measurement that is being imposed. The fear and avoidance of the negative is the organizing principle of life. The members live according to an externalized image. No one ever measures up.

3. **Blame** — Whenever things don't turn out as planned, blame yourself or others. Blame is another defensive cover-up for shame . . . Blame maintains the balance in a dysfunctional system when control has broken down.

4. **Denial Of The Five Freedoms** — The five freedoms, first enunciated by Virginia Satir, describe full personal functionality. Each freedom has to do with a basic human power . . . the power to perceive; to think and interpret; to feel; to want and choose; and the power to imagine. In shame-based families, the perfectionist rule prohibits the full expression of these powers. It says you shouldn't perceive, think, feel, desire or imagine the way you do. You should do these the way the perfectionistic ideal demands.

5. **The No-Talk Rule** — This rule prohibits the full expression of any feeling, need or want. In shame-based families, the members want to hide their true feelings, needs or wants. Therefore, no one speaks of his loneliness and sense of self-rupture.

6. **Don't Make Mistakes** — Mistakes reveal the flawed vulnerable self. To acknowledge a mistake is to open oneself to scrutiny. Cover up your own mistakes and if someone else makes a mistake, shame him.

7. **Unreliability** — Don't expect reliability in relationships. Don't trust anyone and you will never be disappointed. The parents didn't get their developmental dependency needs met and will not be there for their children to depend on. The distrust cycle goes on.

These rules are not written on the refrigerator door. However, they are the operative principles that govern shame-based families in their interpersonal relationships. They continue the cycle of shame for generations.

The parenting rules used in most western world families create massive shame. Add alcoholism, incest, physical abuse to these systems, and you get major dysfunctionality. Alice Miller has summed up these rules under the title **Poisonous Pedagogy**. These rules state:

1. Adults are the masters of the dependent child.
2. They determine in godlike fashion what is right and what is wrong.
3. The child is held responsible for the parents' anger.
4. The parents must always be shielded.
5. The child's life-affirming feelings pose a threat to the autocratic adult.
6. The child's will must be "broken" as soon as possible.

7. All this must happen at a very early age so that the child "won't notice" and will therefore not be able to expose the adult.

For Your Own Good

Such beliefs about the parents' absolute power stem from the time of monarchs and kings. They are pre-democratic and pre-Einsteinian. They presuppose a world of eternal laws, a *Deus Ex Machina* view of the world. This was the world of Newton and Descartes. Such a worldview has been refuted many times over.

The poisonous pedagogy justifies highly abusive methods for suppressing children's vital spontaneity: physical beatings, lying, duplicity, manipulation, scare tactics, withdrawal of love, isolation and coercion to the point of torture. All of these methods are toxically shaming.

SHAME AS A STATE OF BEING

When healthy shame is transformed into toxic shame, it is called the 'internalization process'. The healthy feeling of shame is lost, and a frozen state of being emerges, whereby a person believes himself to be flawed and defective as a human being. This transformation involves three dynamics: first, the identification with shame-based models; second, the trauma of abandonment and the shame binding all one's feelings, needs and drives; and third, the interconnection and magnification of visual memories or scenes; and the retaining of shaming auditory and kinesthetic imprints.

The Abandonment Trauma

The word abandonment, as used here, goes far beyond the ordinary understanding of that word. I include the notion of physical desertion, which is the most common usage of the word. In naming our demons, we have to stretch the old meanings of our words.

I want to expand the meaning of the word abandonment to include various forms of emotional abandonment: stroke deprivation, narcissistic deprivation, fantasy bonding, the neglect of developmental dependency needs and family system enmeshment. My definition of abandonment also includes all forms of abuse.

Alice Miller, in her powerful book, *The Drama Of The Gifted Child*, has described the paradoxical *fact that many good, kind, devoted parents abandon their children*. She also outlines the equally paradoxical fact that many highly gifted superachieving and successful people are driven by a deep-seated chronic depression, resulting from their true and authentic selves being shamed through abandonment in childhood. I referred to this earlier as the "hole in your soul" phenomena. Alice Miller's work has expanded my understanding of the abandonment trauma. She does not use shame as a major organizing principle of her work. However, it is easy to see that the loss of authentic selfhood with its accompanying depression is another way to describe toxic shame.

When one is abandoned, one is left alone. This can happen through physical absence as well as physical presence. In fact to be abandoned by someone who is physically present is much more crazymaking.

ACTUAL PHYSICAL ABSENCE

Max began his life with two strikes against him. He was not planned or really wanted. He was an accidental pregnancy in an ever intensifying dysfunctional marriage. Jerome's drinking had escalated so that Felicia had attempted separation on several occasions in an attempt to control his drinking. Four separations occurred during Max's first eight years of life.

Max was also separated from his brother and sister during three of these separations. He and Felicia lived with two of her sisters while Ralph and Maxine lived with Felicia's mother. A child needs structure and predictability. He needs to be able to count on someone.

I remember when my son was about three years old, he would ask me to read him a story at night. His favorites were *The Little Engine That Could* and *Peter Rabbit.* After a few readings, these stories became rather boring to me. I used to try and turn two pages simultaneously (the old two-pages-at-a-time trick). I was rarely able to do this without getting caught. To my son's young mind if a piece of that story were missing, it was disastrous. It would put his world out of order. In a more dramatic way, for a child to be continuously moved from his family causes severe upset.

A child needs the presence of both parents. For a boy child to break his mother bonding, he needs a father to bond with. Bonding involves spending time together, sharing feelings, warmth, touching and displaying desire to be with one another.

Max's dad was hardly ever around. When he was not working, he was drinking. He gave Max very little of his time. A very young child cannot understand that his dad is a sick alcoholic. Children are limited in logical ability. Their earliest way of thinking is through feelings (felt thought). Children are also egocentric. This doesn't mean they are selfish in the usual meaning of that word. They are not morally selfish. They are not even capable of moral thinking until about seven or eight (the so-called age of reason). Even at that age their thinking still has definite egocentric elements in it. Children are not capable of pure altruistic behavior until about age 16.

Egocentric thinking means that a child will take everything personally. Even if a parent dies, a child can personalize it. A child might say something like — "If Mommie had really loved me, she would not have gone to God's house; she would have stayed with me."

We give time to those things that we love.

The impact of not having one's parents' time creates the feeling of being worthless. The child is worth less than his parents' time, attention or direction. The young child's egocentricity always interprets events egocentrically. If Mom and Dad are not present, it's because of me. There must be something wrong with me or they would want to be with me.

Children are egocentric because they have not had time to develop ego boundaries. An ego boundary is an internal strength by which a person guards her inner space. Without boundaries a person has no protection. A strong boundary is like a door with the doorknob on the inside. A weak ego boundary is like a door with the doorknob on the outside. A child's ego is like a house without any doors.

Children are egocentric by nature (not by choice). Their egocentricity is like a temporary door and doorknob, in use until strong boundaries can be built. Strong boundaries result from the identification with parents who themselves have strong boundaries and who teach their children by modeling. Children have no experience; they need their parents' experience. By identifying with their parent, they have someone whom they can depend on outside themselves. As they internalize their parent, they form a dependable guide inside themselves. If their parent is not dependable, they will not develop this inner resource.

EMOTIONAL ABANDONMENT AND DEPRIVED NARCISSISM

Children need mirroring and echoing. These come from their primary caretaker's eyes. Mirroring means that someone is there for them and reflects who they really are at any given moment of time. In the first three years of our life each of us needed to be admired and taken seriously. We needed to be accepted for the very one we are. Getting these mirroring needs is what Alice Miller calls our basic Narcissistic Supplies.

These supplies result from good mirroring by a parent with good boundaries. When this is the case, the following dynamics take place:

1. The child's aggressive impulses can be neutralized because they do not threaten the parent.
2. The child's striving for autonomy is not experienced as a threat to the parent.
3. The child is allowed to experience and express ordinary impulses, such as jealousy, rage, sexuality, defiance, because the parents have not disowned these feelings in themselves.

4. The child does not have to please the parent and can develop his own needs at his own developmental pace.
5. The child can depend on and use his parents because they are separate from him.
6. The parent's independence and good boundaries allow the child to separate self and object representation.
7. Because the child is allowed to display ambivalent feelings, he can learn to regard himself and the caregiver as "both good and bad", rather than splitting off certain parts as good and splitting them from the bad.
8. The beginning of true object love is possible because the parent's love the child as a separate object.

Drama Of The Gifted Child

What happens if the parents are shame-based and needy? What happens is they are unable to take over the mirroring narcissistic function for the child. Furthermore, the fact that the parents are shame-based is a clear signal that *they never got their own narcissistic supplies*. Such parents are adult children who are still in search of a parent or an object who will be totally available to them. For such parents, the most appropriate objects of narcissistic gratification are their *own children*. Again Alice Miller writes,

> "A newborn baby is completely dependent on his parents and since their caring is essential for his existence, he does all he can to avoid losing them. From the very first day onward, he will muster all his resources to this end, like a small plant that turns toward the sun in order to survive."

Drama Of The Gifted Child

What the shame-based mother was unable to find in her own mother she finds in her own children. The child is someone who is always at her disposal. A child cannot run away as her own mother did. A child can be used as an echo; is completely centered on her; will never desert her; can be totally controlled and offers full admiration and absorbed attention.

Children have an amazing ability to perceive this need in the parent(s). A child seems to know it unconsciously. By taking on the role of supplying his shame-based parents narcissistic gratification, the child secures love and a sense of being needed and not abandoned. *This process is a reversal of the order of nature. Now the child is taking care of the parents' needs, rather than the parents taking care of the child's needs.* This caretaker role is strangely paradoxical. In an attempt to secure parental love and avoid being abandoned, the child is in fact being abandoned. Since the child is there for the parent, there is no one there to mirror the child's feelings and drives and to nurture the child's needs. Any child growing up in such an environment has been mortally wounded by this narcissistic deprivation. This phenomenon can happen in the best of families.

Alice Miller writes,

> "There are large numbers of people who suffer from narcissistic disorders, who often had sensitive and caring parents from whom they received much encouragement; yet these people are suffering from severe depressions. They enter analysis in the belief, with which they grew up, that their childhood was happy and protected."
>
> *Drama Of The Gifted Child*

More often than not, these narcissistically deprived are talented, gifted, highly successful superachievers who have been praised and admired for their talents and achievements. Anyone looking at them on the outside would believe that these people have it made. They are strong and stable and full of self-assurance. The exact opposite is the case. Narcissistically deprived people do well in every undertaking and are admired for their gifts and talents but to no avail.

"Behind all this," writes Alice Miller, "there lurks depression, the feeling of emptiness and self-alienation, and a sense that life has no meaning."

Once the drug of grandiosity is taken away, as soon as they are no longer the stars and superachievers, they are plagued by deep feelings of shame and guilt.

I have worked with many individuals of this type. I am one myself. It is so difficult for anyone looking at our success to know how shame-based we really are. As children we were loved for our achievements and our performance, rather than for ourselves. Our true and authentic selves were abandoned.

In my own case it has taken me years to be able to connect with my own true feelings — my anger, jealousy, loneliness or sadness. This disconnection with feelings is a result of the abandonment. No one was there to affirm our feelings through mirroring. A child can only experience his feelings when there is someone there who accepts them fully, names them and supports them.

Another consequence of this emotional abandonment is the loss of a sense of self. When used as another's narcissistic supplies, a person develops in such a way as to reveal only what is expected of him and ultimately fuses with his own act or performance. He becomes a "human doing" without any real sense of his authentic self. According to Winnicotti, his true self remains in a "state of noncommunication". I described this earlier as no longer being in me. Such a person feels emptiness, homelessness and futility.

Perhaps the most devastating consequence of emotional abandonment is what Robert Firestone calls the Fantasy Bond and what Alice Miller calls "Bond Permanence". A child who has been denied the experience of connecting with his own emotions is first consciously and then unconsciously (through the internal identification with the parent) dependent on his parents. Alice Miller writes,

> "He cannot rely on his own emotions, has not come to experience them through trial and error, has no sense of his own real needs and is alienated from himself to the highest degree."
>
> *Drama Of The Gifted Child*

Such a person cannot separate from his parents. He is fantasy bonded with them. He has an illusion (fantasy) of connection, i.e., he really thinks there is a love relationship between himself and his parents. Actually he is fused and enmeshed. This is an entrapment rather than a relationship. Later on this fantasy bond will be transferred to other relationships.

This fantasy-bonded person is still dependent on affirmation from his partner, his children, his groups. He is especially dependent on his children. A fantasy-bonded person never has a real connection or a real relationship with anyone. There is no real authentic self there to relate to. The real parents, who only accepted the child when he pleased them, remain as introjected voices. The true self hides from these introjected voices just as the real child did. The 'loneliness of the parental home' is replaced by 'isolation within the self'.

Grandiosity is often the result of all this. The grandiose person is admired everywhere and cannot live without admiration. If his talents fail him, it is catastrophic. He must be perfect, otherwise depression is near. Often the most gifted among us are driven in precisely this manner. Many of the most gifted people suffer from severe depression. It cannot be otherwise because depression is about the lost and abandoned child within.

"One is free from depression," writes Alice Miller, "when self-esteem is based on the authenticity of one's own feelings and not on the possession of certain qualities" *(Drama Of The Gifted Child)*.

Emotional abandonment is multigenerational. The child of the narcissistically deprived parent becomes an adult with a narcissistically deprived child and will use his children as he was used for his narcissistic supplies. That child then becomes an adult child and the cycle is repeated.

Max's parents were narcissistically deprived. Jerome used fantasy bonds with alcohol and sex for his narcissistic supplies. Felicia used Ralph as her main narcissistic gratification. He became the family Star, the moralistic superachieving righteous minister. Maxine and Max were both Lost Children. Felicia, although dutiful, was never really there to mirror and affirm their emotions. Max reenacted this same pattern on his children, using them for his narcissistic supplies. He would immediately run to them for nurturing and solace after his runaways. His daughters especially were a source of nurturing. Never once did I see any of his children express anger, hurt or resentment to Max. They had never connected with their own feelings.

Max would become enraged when I spoke of his reenactment of his abandonment on his own children. His children also thought they had a good childhood. This is the delusional nature of deprived narcissism.

When emotionally abandoned people describe their childhood, it is always without feeling. Alice Miller writes,

> "They recount their earliest memories without any sympathy for the child they once were. Very often they show disdain and irony, even derision and cynicism. In general there is a complete absence of real emotional understanding or serious appreciation of their own childhood vicissitudes and no conception of their true need — beyond the need for achievement. The internalization of the original drama has been so complete that the illusion of a good childhood can be maintained."
>
> *Drama Of The Gifted Child*

Max's children idolized and idealized him. They continued the delusion of their happy childhood. Max himself showed no real anger toward his parents. Only when he was drunk would the rage toward his father come out. He had no overt anger toward his mother.

ABANDONMENT THROUGH ABUSE

All forms of child abuse are forms of abandonment. When parents abuse children, the abuse is about the parents' own issues not the child's. This is why it is abuse.

Abuse is abandonment because when children are abused, no one is there for them. What's happening is purportedly for the child's own good. But it isn't about the child at all, it's about the parent. Such transactions are crazymaking and induce shame. In each act of abuse the child is shamed. Young children, because of their egocentricism, make themselves responsible for the abuse.

"My caretakers couldn't be crazy or emotionally ill; it must be me," the child says to himself.

A child must maintain this idealization. Children's minds are magical, egocentric and nonlogical. They are completely dependent upon their parents for survival. The idealization ensures survival. *If my parents are sick and crazy, how could I survive? It must be me. I am crazy.* There's something wrong with me or they wouldn't treat me this way.

The child doesn't have a chance. All abuse contributes to the internalization of shame. Some kinds of abuse are more intensely shaming than others.

Sexual Abuse

Sexual abuse is the most shaming of all abuse. It takes less sexual abuse than any other form of abuse to induce shame. Sexual abuse is widespread. It is estimated that there are currently some 60 million victims of sexual violence. Our awareness of this problem has grown tremendously over the past 30 years.

In the past our understanding was limited to a kind of "horror story" incest victim. Such stories involved physical hands-on sexual abuse. Today we've greatly expanded our understanding of such abuse. In *Bradshaw On: The Family,* I presented material on sexual abuse adapted from the work of Pia Mellody at the Meadows, a treatment center in Wickenberg, Arizona.

The following is from *Bradshaw On: The Family:*

Sexual abuse involves whole families. It can be divided as follows:

1. **Physical Sexual Abuse** — This involves hands on touching in a sexual way. The range of abusive behaviors that are sexual include sexualized hugging or kissing; any kind of sexual touching or fondling; oral and anal sex; masturbation of the victim or forcing the victim to masturbate the offender; sexual intercourse.

2. **Overt Sexual Abuse** — This involves voyeurism, exhibitionism. This can be outside or inside the home. Parents often sexually abuse children through voyeurism and exhibitionism. The criteria for in-home voyeurism or exhibitionism is whether the parent is being sexually stimulated. Sometimes the parent may be so out of touch with their own sexuality that they are not aware of how sexual they are being. The child almost always has a kind of icky feeling about it.

   One client told me how her father would leer at her in her panties coming out of the bathroom. Others speak of having no privacy in the house, much less the bathroom. I've had a dozen male clients whose mothers bathed their genital parts up through eight or nine years old.

   Children can feel sexual around parents. This is not sexual abuse unless the parent originated it. It all depends upon the parents. Here I'm not talking about a parent having a passing sexual thought or feeling. It's about a parent using a child for his own conscious or unconscious sexual stimulation.

3. **Covert Sexual Abuse**
   (a) **Verbal** — This involves inappropriate sexual talking: Dad or any significant male calling women "whores" or "cunts" or

objectified sexual names; or Mom or any significant female depreciating men in a sexual way. It also involves parents or caretakers having to know about every detail of one's private sexual life, asking questions about a child's sexual physiology or questioning for minute details about dates. Covert sexual abuse involves not receiving adequate sexual information.

I've had several female clients who didn't know what was happening when they began menstruating. I've had three female clients who did not know that their vaginas had an opening in it until they were 20 years old!

An overt kind of sexual abuse occurs when Dad or Mom talk about sex in front of the children when the age level of the children is inappropriate. It also occurs when Mom or Dad make sexual remarks about the sexual parts of the children's bodies. I've worked with two male clients who were traumatized by their mother's jokes about the size of their penises, also female clients whose fathers and stepfathers teased about the size of their breasts or buttocks.

(b) Boundary Violation — This involves children witnessing parents in sexual behavior. They may walk in on it frequently because parents don't provide closed or locked doors. It also involves the children being allowed no privacy. They are walked in on in the bathroom. They are not taught to lock their doors or given permission to lock their doors. Parents need to model appropriate nudity, i.e., need to be clothed appropriately after a certain age. Children are sexually curious. Beginning at around age three or between ages three to six, children start noticing parents' bodies. They are often obsessed with nudity.

Mom and Dad need to be careful walking around nude with young children. If Mom is not being stimulated sexually, the nudity is not sexual abuse. She simply is acting in a dysfunctional way. She is not setting sexual boundaries.

The use of enemas at an early age can also be abusive in a way that leads to sexual dysfunction. The enemas can be a body boundary violation.

4. Emotional Sexual Abuse — Emotional sexual abuse results from cross-generational bonding. I've spoken of enmeshment as a way that children take on the covert needs of a family system. It is very common for one or both parents in a dysfunctional marriage to bond inappropriately with one of their children. The parents in effect use the child to meet their emotional needs. This relationship can easily become sexualized and romanticized. The daughter may become

Daddy's Little Princess, or the son may become Mom's Little Man. In both cases the child is being abandoned. The parents are getting their needs met at the expense of the child's needs. The child needs a parent not a spouse.

Pia Mellody gives the following definition of emotional sexual abuse. She says that when "one parent has a relationship with the child that is more important than the relationship they have with their spouse, there is emotional sexual abuse."

Sometimes both parents emotionally bond with a child. The child tries to take care of both parents' feelings. I once worked with a female client whose father would come and get her in the middle of the night and put her in bed with him in the guest bedroom. He would do this mainly to punish his wife for sexually refusing him. The daughter has suffered greatly with confused sexual identity.

Cross-generational bonding can occur with a parent and a child of the same sex. A most common form of this in our culture is mother and daughter. Mother often has sexualized rage, i.e., she fears and hates men. She uses her daughter for her emotional needs and also contaminates her daughter's feelings about men.

This issue is whether the parent is there for the child's needs, rather than the child being there for the parent's needs. And while children have the capacity to be sexual in a way appropriate to their developmental level, *whenever an adult is being sexual with a child, sexual abuse is going on.*

Some sexual abuse comes from older siblings. Generally sexual behavior by same-age children is not sexually abusive. The rule of thumb is that when a child is experiencing sexual "acting out" at the hands of a child three or four years older, it is sexually abusive.

Physical Abuse

Spare the rod and you spoil the child has been quoted forever as a Biblical justification or injunction for corporal punishment. Physical violence against children (and women) is part of an ancient and pervasive tradition.

Physical violence is second only to sexual violence in the toxic shame it creates. Furthermore, physical violence is highly addictive. I've already shown it to be a form of the character disordered syndrome of shame. Offenders are literally addicted to the violence and fueled by the toxic shame they feel in performing physical violence. Violent offenders are shame-based.

The profile of physically abusing parents includes the following: isolated; poor self-image; lack of sensitivity to others' feelings; usually physically abused themselves; deprived of basic mothering; unmet needs for love and comfort;

in denial of problems and the impact of the problems; feel there is no one to turn to for advice; totally unrealistic expectations of children; expect the children to meet their needs for comfort and nurturing; when children fail to meet their needs, they interpret this as rejection and respond with anger and frustration; deal with the children as if they were much older than they are.

There is no good data on the extent of physical abuse. The usual data covers those cases which are reported. It excludes those not treated by a physician, those cases treated by a physician but not identified as abuse and those cases identified as abuse but not reported. It's estimated that there are 200 unreported cases for every case reported.

The ownership of children by parents, and the belief that children are willful and need their wills broken accounts for the rationale of spanking children.

The victim of the physical violence is also bonded to the violence out of shame. In the beginning the victims bond out of sheer terror. But as the abuse continues, their self-worth is diminished. As the self-worth is diminished, the victims lose the ability to choose. They become like starving children looking for morsels and crumbs of love.

Because violence is irrational and impulsive, it is often random and unpredictable. The random quality of the violence sets up what Seligman calls "learned helplessness". Learned helplessness is a kind of mental confusion. The people can no longer think or plan. They become passively accepting of their abuse. I can't imagine a more soul-murdering destruction of human life.

Physical violence is common in family life because the tenets of the poisonous pedagogy promote and support corporal punishment. It's still endorsed as a way to teach children about life. Our common nursery rhyme about the old woman who lived in a shoe attests to the common acceptance of physical punishment.

Physical violence is the norm in many dysfunctional families. This includes actual physical spankings; having to go get your own weapons of torture (belts, switches, etc.); being punched, slapped, slapped in the face, pulled on, yanked on, choked, shook, kicked, pinched, tortured with tickling; being threatened with violence of abandonment; being threatened with being put in jail or having the police come; witnessing violence done to a parent or sibling.

This last is a major issue in homes where wives are battered. A child witnessing his mother being battered is equivalent to the child being battered. A witness to violence is a victim of violence.

EMOTIONAL ABUSE

Emotional abuse is universal. I believe that everyone has been shamed by emotional abuse. The poisonous pedagogy is quite clear about the fact that emotions are weak. We are to be rational and logical and not allow ourselves to be marred by emotions. All emotions must be controlled, but anger and sexual feelings are especially to be repressed. I can't imagine many people in modern American life who were affirmed and nurtured in expressing their sexual and/or angry feelings.

EMOTIONAL SHAME BINDS

Our emotions are part of our basic power. They serve two major functions in our psychic life. They monitor our basic needs, telling us of a need, a loss or a satiation. Without our emotional energy, we would not be aware of our most fundamental needs.

Emotions also give us the fuel or energy to act. I like to hyphenate the word "E-motion". An E-motion is an energy in motion. This energy moves us to get what we need. When our basic needs are being violated, our *anger* moves us to fight or run. Our *anger* is the energy that gives us strength. The incredible hulk becomes the huge powerful hulk when he needs the energy and power to take care of others.

Our *sadness* is an energy we discharge in order to heal. As we discharge the energy over the losses relating to our basic needs, we can integrate the shock of those losses and adapt to reality. Sadness is painful. We try to avoid it. Actually discharging sadness releases the energy involved in our emotional pain. To hold it in is to freeze the pain within us. The therapeutic slogan is that grieving is the "healing feeling".

Fear releases an energy which warns us of danger to our basic needs. Fear is an energy leading to our discernment and wisdom.

Guilt is our conscience former. It tells us we have transgressed our values. It moves us to take action and change.

Shame warns us not to try to be more or less than human. Shame signals our essential limitations.

Joy is the exhilarating energy that emerges when all our needs are being met. We want to sing, run and jump with joy. The energy of joy signals that all is well.

When our E-motions are not mirrored and named, we lose contact with one of our vital human powers. Parents who are out of touch with their own emotions cannot model those emotions for their children. They are out of touch and shut down. They are psychically numb. They are not even aware of what they are feeling. Hence they stop their children's emotions.

This is actually sanctified by our most sacred traditions of parenting rules. These rules especially shame children by denying emotions. Emotions are considered weak.

Religion endorses the poisonous pedagogy. Anger is especially considered bad. Anger is one of the Seven Deadly Sins. These sins send you to hell. In its most accurate teaching, the deadly sin is not really the E-motion of anger, but the behaviors resulting from the judgment often occasioned by anger. Behaviors often linked to anger are screaming, cursing, hitting, publically criticizing or condemning someone and physical violence. These behaviors are certainly prohibitive. They are behaviors based on judgment, rather than E-motions.

Many children are shamed for their anger. Children often see parents angry and rageful. The message is all too often that it's okay for parents to be angry, but it's not okay for children.

Shame Parfaits

As anger is shamed, two things happen. First the anger is shame-bound. Every time the person feels angry, he feels shame. Second, as anger is shamed, it is repressed. Repression is a primary ego defense. Once it is set in motion, it operates automatically and unconsciously. As the anger energy goes unconscious, it clamors to be expressed. As more and more anger is repressed, it grows more and more.

Virginia Satir once compared this to keeping hungry dogs in the basement. The hungrier they get, the more they try to get out. The more they try to escape, the more we must guard them. The repressed energy grows and grows and finally it has a life of its own. One day there is just no more room to stuff the energy. One day the anger energy erupts. The person who has been repressing it, finds herself "out of control". After the stormy outburst is over, she says, "I don't know what came over me today. Boy, I really lost it."

Repressed, unresolved shame-bound anger energy turns into rage. Rage is the outcome of shame-bound anger.

When sorrow is shamed, it builds its energy into inconsolable grief and despair. Sometimes it is the basis of suicidality. In our culture, children are shamed for crying. If not shamed, the crying discharge is stopped with bribes and rewards. Sometimes there is a magic timetable so that after crying for a designated number of minutes, one is told, "Okay, that's it, you've cried long enough." Often children are condemned and ridiculed for crying. Sometimes they are hit or spanked for crying as in, "I'll give you something to cry about!"

Likewise with fear — children are shamed for being afraid. Shamed and denied, fear splits off and grows into full-fledged terror or paranoia. The permission to have sadness and fear is often connected with gender and sex roles. Little boys are supposed to be strong and not cry or be afraid. Little girls are given more permission for sorrow and fear. However, I don't like to take this too far as I believe all feelings are shamed in our present cultural parenting forms.

Even joy is shamed. When we are happy, excited and rambunctious, we are curtailed. We are told things like, "Don't get too puffed up; pride comes before a fall." Or "Just remember — there are starving children in Latin America." This comes out later in the experience of feeling shame every time you feel really happy, or in feeling shame when you're very successful.

Sex Drive Shame Binds

Perhaps no aspect of human activity has been as dysfunctionally shamed as much as our sexuality. Sexuality is the core of human selfhood. Our sex is not something we have or do, it is who we are. It's the first thing we notice about each other. Sexuality is a basic fact in all created things. If we shut off this drive, we would annihilate the human race in 120 years. Our sexual energy (libido) is our own unique incarnation of the life force itself. To have our sex drive shamed is to be shamed to the core.

All children naturally have sexual curiosity. I can remember vividly when my next-door neighbor told me that the man's penis went into the woman's vagina. I was awestruck. It seemed unbelievable! Sexuality is somewhat awesome and confusing to a child. And children naturally explore their genitals, and at certain ages, engage in childhood sex play.

I have often outlined the following scenario to illustrate how our sexuality is shamed. One day little three-year-old Farquahr, while exploring his body, names his nose. He points to it and names it. Mom is exhilarated and calls Grandma to report Farquahr's brilliant achievement. Grandma comes over and asks Farquahr to perform his new found ability; which he does with grandiose pride. On each occasion when he names his nose, he receives great praise. Later on he finds other parts of his body, ears, eyes, elbows, navel . . . And then one day, one Sunday with all the family in the livingroom (receiving the preacher), Little Farquahr finds his penis!!! He's pretty excited. He thinks, if the nose got them, this will really get them. So he wanders into the living room and proudly displays his penis!

. . . Never has little Farquahr seen such action! Mom has him by the ear and he's moving faster than he's ever moved before. Her face is contorted. She is visibly shaken and tells him in no uncertain terms never to show himself off again. He's told that what he did was bad! Children internalize their parents at their worst. The more out of control the parent is, the more the child's security is threatened.

Variations of this scenario happen in the best of families. Parents who have had their own sexuality shamed cannot handle their children's natural sexuality. When their child explores his sexuality, the parent reacts with disapproval or worse, disgust. Global comments such as "That's bad" or "Don't ever touch yourself there", "Go get decent — put on your clothes" or "Cover your privates" link sexuality to something bad, dirty and disgusting. This part of us must be disowned. The shame becomes linked to sexuality.

A child growing up in such a family (probably most of us) comes to believe and feel that sexuality is shameful.

Generally speaking, most of our vital spontaneous instinctual life gets shamed. Children are shamed for being too rambunctious, for wanting things and for laughing too loud. Much dysfunctional shame occurs at the dinner table. Children are forced to eat when they are not hungry. Sometimes children are forced to eat what they do not find appetizing. Being exiled at the dinner table until the plate is cleaned is not unusual in modern family life. The public humiliation of sitting at the dinner table all alone, often with siblings jeering, is a painful kind of exposure.

I've had clients who have to eat standing up or on the run because of shameful scenes at the dinner table when they were children. When our instinctual life is shamed, the natural core of our life is bound up. It's like an acorn going through excruciating agony for becoming an oak, or a flower feeling ashamed for blossoming. What happens is that because our instincts are part of our natural endowment, they cannot be repressed. Once our instincts are shame-bound, they become like the hungry dogs which must be watched.

Shame — The Master Emotion

Shame has been called the master emotion because as it is internalized all the other emotions are bound by shame. Emotionally shame-bound parents cannot allow their children to have emotions because the child's emotion triggers the parents' emotions. Repressed emotions often feel too big, like they would completely overwhelm us if we expressed them. There is also the fear of the shame that would be triggered if we expressed our emotions.

The shaming and binding of emotions were core parts of Max's internalized shame. Max had never been physically abused. But he was certainly sexually abused. As the third child he carried his mother's and father's sexual issues. Both were unresolved incest victims. Jerome was a womanizer, although this was always a family secret. Max reported on several occasions that he felt his mother Felicia often acted seductively. Felicia certainly was emotionally abusing. She name-called, compared, yelled and did it with contempt and disgust. Most of all she continually made Max take care of her feelings. She criticized and scorned his feelings. According to Max she said things like, "What are you angry about?" or "There's nothing to be afraid of". "Stop that crying or I'll give you something to cry about." Max was profoundly sad. He could have cried for ages. I came to believe that his whole family system carried generations of unresolved grief. I could feel the sadness when I sat across from him.

ABANDONMENT THROUGH THE NEGLECT OF DEVELOPMENTAL DEPENDENCY NEEDS

As children, we had needs that depended on others for fulfillment. Children are dependent and needy. They need their parents for 15 years. Their dependency needs can only be satisfied by a caretaker. Figure 2.5 outlines these needs. Children need someone to hold them and touch them. They need a face to mirror and affirm their feelings, needs and drives. Children need a structure with limits; they need predictability. They need a mutually trusting relationship; they need to know there is someone they can count on. Children need to have space and be different. They need security; they need to have enough nutritional food, clothing, shelter and adequate medical care. Children need their parents' time and attention. Children need direction in the form of problem-solving techniques and strategies.

Need Shame Binds

When these needs are neglected, children are given the message that their needs are not important, and they lose a sense of their own personal value. They are not worth someone being there for them. They get the feeling that they do not matter. As their needs are chronically rejected, children stops believing that they have the right to depend on anyone. These dependency needs depend on the interpersonal bridge and the bond of mutuality for their fulfillment. It is the interpersonal bridge that is broken when one is abandoned through neglect. Since we have no one to depend on, we come to believe that we have no right to depend on anyone. We feel shame when we feel needy. Since these needs are basic needs, i.e., needs we cannot be fully human without, we have to get them met in abortive ways.

A neglected child may learn to get attention by getting into trouble or by annoying his parents. One will drink muddy water when he is dying of thirst. I know of children who get their touch and stimulation needs met by getting spanked. Much has been written about abortive adaptation. Suffice it to say, when one's basic dependency needs are not met at the proper time and in the proper sequence, the personality is arrested at those developmental stages. The child learns adaptive ways to get his needs met. Over the course of time, as one experiences need-deprivation, one loses awareness of these needs. Ultimately one does not even know what one needs.

Figure 2.5. Basic Dependency Needs

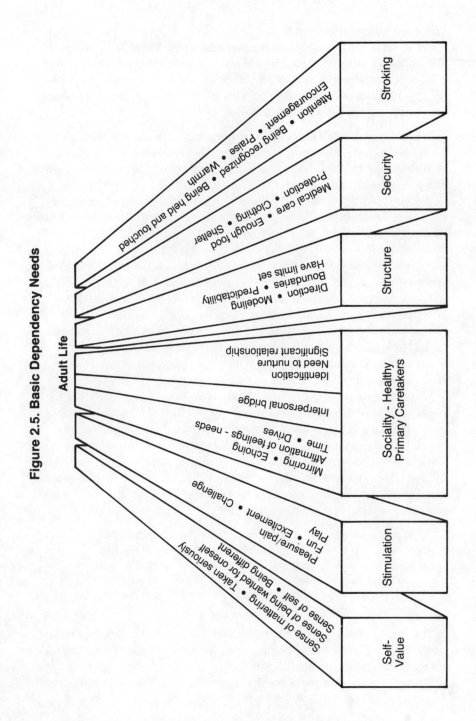

Adult Life

Stroking

Attention • Being recognized • Praise • Encouragement
Warmth • Being held and touched

Security

Medical care • Enough food • Clothing • Shelter
Protection

Structure

Direction • Modelling • Predictability
Boundaries • Have limits set

Sociality - Healthy
Primary Caretakers

Identification
Need to nurture
Significant relationship

Interpersonal bridge

Mirroring • Echoing
Affirmation of feelings - needs
Time • Drives

Stimulation

Pleasure/pain
Fun • Excitement • Challenge
Play

Self-
Value

Sense of mattering • Taken seriously
Sense of self • Being wanted for oneself
Sense of self • Being different

Being abandoned through the neglect of our developmental dependency needs is the major factor in becoming an adult child. We grow up; we look like adults. We walk and talk like adults, but beneath the surface is a little child who feels empty and needy, a child whose needs are insatiable because he has a child's needs in an adult body. This insatiable child is the core of all compulsive/addictive behavior.

In Max's case most all his needs were converted into sexual feelings. This is what accounted for his severe sexual addiction. It is also the core dynamic of all sexual addiction. Once a person is abandoned, especially through abuse, he is made into an object.

Max was used by his brother to alter his brother's shame. He was physically abandoned by his father. He was used by the family system. To be used is to be made into an object. By being objectified, Max objectified himself.

Through his internalized shame, Max became an object of his own contempt, criticism, judgment and scorn. He was his own object of rejection. To objectify self and others is to lose personhood. Since Max could no longer experience himself as a whole person, he could no longer experience anyone else as a whole person.

Max spent hours hustling women. He was obsessed by women's breasts. He had no regard for women as persons. He risked family and reputation to touch women's breasts in shopping malls or get glimpses of them through voyeuristic activities.

Another dynamic aspect of the sexual conversion of basic needs is the pleasure of sexual orgasm itself. When one is shamed through abandonment, the pain is deep and profound. One feels worth-less; one feels painfully diminished and exposed. When one experiences sexual stimulation and climax, one has available an all-encompassing and powerful pleasure. This pleasure can take the place of any other need. In a poignant passage, Kaufman sums up the process of converting all needs into sexuality. He writes,

> "A young boy who learns never to need anything emotionally from his parents . . . is faced with a dilemma whenever he feels young, needy or otherwise insecure. If masturbating has been his principle source of good feeling . . . he may resort to masturbation in order to restore good feelings about self at times when he is experiencing needs quite unrelated to sexuality."

The ego defense of conversion transforms any of the developmental needs into the need for something else. This could be food, money or excessive attention. In Max's case it was sex. Over the course of his childhood, the experience of his developmental needs became associated with his sex drive. This eventually resulted in the conversion of emotional needing into sexuality. Whenever Max felt insecure, anxious or needy, the inner event registered as sexual desire. Max turned continuously to sex to meet needs that sex cannot provide.

ABANDONMENT THROUGH ENMESHMENT IN THE OVERT AND COVERT NEEDS OF THE FAMILY SYSTEM

I have already described the family as a social system — its components, rules, roles and its law of dynamic homeostasis. You have seen how a dysfunctional family uses the members to maintain its balance. The more dysfunctional the system, the more closed and rigid are the roles it assigns. In families which are chemically, sexually or violently dysfunctional, the needs of the system are overt. The system dispenses its roles for the members to play in order to keep balance.

All the rigid roles set up by family dysfunction are forms of abandonment. To be a family Hero, I had to be strong — never showing the scared vulnerable part of me. Heroes are not supposed to be scared. The roles are like scripts given out for a play. They proscribe what feelings you can or cannot have. After playing my Hero role for years, I no longer really knew who I was. In recovery I had to learn how to give up that role. To do so I had to learn to be vulnerable. I had to learn how to be a member of a group rather than the leader, to follow rather than lead. Because the roles maintain the balance of the system, they exist for the system. The children give up their own reality to take care of the family system — to keep it whole and balanced . . .

Each form of abandonment breaks the interpersonal bridge and the mutual-intimacy bond. A child is precious and incomparable. Unless treated with value and love, this sense of preciousness and incomparability diminishes. In toxic internalized shame, it disappears completely.

Interconnection Of Imagery

The third way that internalization occurs is by internalizing images. These internal images can be of a shaming person, of a place or of an actual experience. They can also be word images, i.e., sound imprints. Hearing someone say certain words may trigger old experiences of shame. Individual shame experiences are fused together by means of language and imagery. Kaufman says, "Scenes of shame become interconnected and magnified." As the language, imagery and scenes associated with shame are fused together, the meaning of shame is transformed. "I feel shame" comes to mean "I am shameful, deficient in some vital way as a human being." Shame is no longer one feeling among many, but comes to constitute the core of oneself. Internalized shame creates a frozen state of being. Shame is no longer an emotional signal that comes and goes. It is a deep abiding, all-pervasive sense of being defective as a person. This core of defectiveness forms the foundation around which other feelings about the self will be experienced. Gradually over a period of time, this frozen feeling of belief recedes from consciousness. In this way shame becomes basic to one's sense of identity. One becomes a shame-based person.

FUNCTIONAL AUTONOMY

Once internalized, shame can be activated without any external stimuli. There is no longer any need for an interpersonal shame-inducing event. I can remember experiencing painful shame as I went to pay for a speeding ticket. As I walked up to the police station clerk, the occasion forced me to expose my mistake. The clerk was warm, pleasant and smiling. The shame feeling occurred irrespective of the clerk.

INTERNAL SHAME SPIRALS

A last consequence of internalized shame is what Kaufman terms, *the internal shame spiral*. He describes it as follows:

> "A triggering event occurs. Perhaps it is trying to get close to someone and feeling rebuffed. Or a critical remark by a friend . . . a person suddenly is enmeshed in shame, the eyes turn inward and the experience becomes totally internal, frequently with visual imagery present. The shame feelings flow in a circle, endlessly triggering each other. The precipitating event is relived internally over and over, causing the sense of shame to deepen, to absorb other neutral experiences . . . until finally the self is engulfed. In this way shame becomes paralyzing."

The spiral is one of the most devastating aspects of dysfunctional shame. Once in motion, it can cause the reliving of other shameful experiences and thereby solidifies shame further within the personality.

After shame is internalized, the fear of exposure is magnified intensely. Exposure now means having one's essential defectiveness as a human being seen. To be exposed, now means to be seen as irreparably and unspeakably bad. One must find a way to defend against such exposure. As the defenses and strategies of transference are developed, internalized shame becomes less and less conscious.

To sum up, shame internalization has four major consequences. A shame-based identity is formed; the depth of shame is magnified and frozen; autonomous shame activation or functional autonomy results; and finally internal shame spirals are made operative.

The School System

Max went to private church school through the eighth grade. He then went to a public high school. His school experience itself was fairly typical of most modern schools. Shaming has always been an integral part of the school system. Sitting in the corner with a dunce cap on is a common association with schooldays. Even though most modern forms of education no longer use dunce caps, there are powerful sources of toxic shame still operating in the school system. I taught in three high schools and four universities. I found the eductional system to be a major force in solidifying the internalization process of shame-based people.

Perfectionism

Perfectionism is a family system rule and is a core culprit in creating toxic shame. We will see it also in both the religious and cultural systems. *Perfectionism denies healthy shame. It does so by assuming we can be perfect. Such an assumption denies our human finitude because it denies the fact that we are essentially limited.* Perfectionism denies that we will make mistakes often and that it's natural to make mistakes.

Perfectionism is involved whenever we take a negative norm or standard and absolutize it. Once absolutized, the norm becomes the measure of everything else. We compare and judge according to that standard.

In school we were compared to the perfect mark of 100. As we failed to make that mark, we were graded on a descending scale, the lowest mark being an F. Think for a moment of the symbolism of the "F" as a mark. It is associated in mental imagery with the "F" word. When a child becomes a failure in school, it's not long before there is an association with being a failure as a person — a fuck-up. Children get this association very quickly in school. They also associate "bad" grades with being a bad or defective person. And most often the children who are failing, are already shame-based when they come to school. In fact, their shame base often causes their school failure. As they fail in school, their internalized shame deepens. Toxic shame begets toxic shame.

Max exemplifies another route taken by shame-based children in school. Max followed the lead of his shame-based brother and sister. He became a superachiever in school. He was a straight A student. Superachievement and perfectionism are two of the leading cover-ups for toxic shame. As paradoxical as it may seem, the straight A student and the F student may both be driven by toxic shame.

I was a straight A student. I was also the president of my class from the 7th grade on. In my senior year of high school, I was the editor of the school paper and number six academically. These were parts of my Hero role. How many high school principals would take a student who is senior class president, editor of the school paper, and number six academically, and tell him he needs help for his internalized shame problems? I was also a card-carrying alcoholic by my senior year in high school.

I had started drinking at age 14, and had had several blackouts by my senior year. High achievement is often the result of being driven by toxic shame. Feeling flawed and defective on the inside, I had to prove I was okay by being exceptional on the outside. Everything I did was based on getting authenticated on the outside. My good feelings depended upon achievement.

Toxic shame creates "human doings", people who must do to be okay. Only by accomplishment can they feel okay about themselves.

I remember a shame-based client bragging to me that he was worth one million, two hundred thousand dollars. This guy was obnoxious. He was brutally abusing his wife by flaunting affairs in front of her. His self-worth was his worth. This was the only way he had to gauge it. Since he felt flawed on the inside, he had to have verification on the outside.

The school system promotes a shame-based measure of grading people's intelligence. It would be only half bad if such a system really did measure intelligence. I believe with John Holt that the true test of intelligence is not what you know or can regurgitate from memory on an exam. It's not what you know how to do, but "what you do when you don't know what to do."

Perfectionism also spawns destructive competition. Certainly there is a nurturing form of competitiveness. Such competition moves us to do better and to expand and grow. But a perfectionistic system like the current school system encourages cheating and creates high levels of distress. Grades are often posted publicly for all eyes to see. And there is shaming exposure when one gets "bad" grades. Even the adjective "bad" lends itself to characterological shame. Each person is pitted against the next in a warfare of endeavor. The communal sense of joint venture and cooperation are lost.

Rationalism

Our schools display an enormous bias in educating the mind rather than the whole person. We place major emphasis on reasoning, logic and math, with almost no concern for emotions, intuition and creativity. Our students become memorizing mimics and dull conformists, rather than exciting and feeling creators.

Much work has emerged over the last few decades in studying the right hemisphere of the brain. This side of the brain is the source of "felt thought". Felt thought is the core of music and poetry. The right hemisphere is holistic and intuitive. It uses imagination rather than memory. Students who have a natural propensity for this side of the brain are penalized.

I know of brilliant students who were painfully shamed because of their intuitive and felt ways of knowing. Our rationalistic bias causes the shaming rejection of imagination and emotion. I remember once giving a teacher my "hunch" about a presented problem. I was told that guessing was not the mark of an educated mind. I was sent to the library to get the correct data. All in all our schools shame some of the most vibrant and creative aspects of the human psyche.

Peer Group Shaming

I remember Arnold. He was a brilliant accountant. He had been viciously shamed in high school. His presenting problem was his criticalness of women. No woman was ever good enough. As his relationship with a woman would intensify, Arnold would start finding fault. He was a nit-picker of great expertise. The outcome of all this was that he was 40 years old, fairly successful financially, but painfully alone.

Arnold had had some shaming in early childhood from an authoritarian and military-type father. But this was tempered with enough love from his mother to save him from being terribly shame-based during early and middle childhood. Later on his family moved to a small town and Arnold had to start the second semester of his sophomore year in a new high school. The town and the high school were cliquish and monied. Arnold was from a rather poor family. He rode the bus to a school where 95% of the kids had new cars. Arnold was scapegoated from the moment he set foot in the school. He was laughed at, made fun of, and ridiculed by one group of girls. Some days he was hit with waterbombs and sacks of horseshit as he waited for the bus. This treatment continued until the middle of his senior year. For two years Arnold suffered almost chronic shaming. This was an excruciating experience.

High school is the time of puberty. And puberty is a time of feeling intense exposure and vulnerability. Whatever toxic shame a person carries from childhood will be tested in high school. Often teenage groups look for a scapegoat. Someone everyone can dump and project their shame onto. This was Arnold's fate. He was viciously shamed by his female peer group. This accounted for his problem with women.

The peer group becomes like a new parent. Only this parent is much more rigid, and has several sets of eyes to look you over. Physical appearance is crucial. Acne and poor sexual development can be excruciating. Conforming to the peer group dress standards is a must if one wants to avoid being shamed. All in all, it can be disastrous if one is not physically or financially endowed.

The elementary school years can also be a source of shame. Children can be terribly cruel. Any child with deformities is especially vulnerable to ridicule. Children will shame other children the way they've been shamed. And if a child is being shamed at home, he will want to pass the hot potato by shaming others. Children like to tease. And teasing is a major source of shaming. Teasing is often done by shame-based parents, who interpersonally transfer their shame by teasing their children. Older siblings can deliver some of the cruelest teasing of all. I have been horrified listening to clients' accounts of being teased by older siblings.

School was perhaps the only place in Max's life where he was not shamed. His toxic shame motivated him to be an achiever. He put himself through graduate school by working at night. He endured tremendous hardships in order to get his degree. It was a place in his life that he felt like he accomplished something. Unfortunately, accomplishments do not reduce internalized shame. In fact, the more one achieves, the more one has to achieve. Toxic shame is about being; no amount of doing will ever change it.

The Religious System

Max's religious upbringing was rigid and authoritarian. He was taught at any early age that he was born with the stain of sin on his soul, and that he was a miserable sinner. He was also taught that God knew his innermost thoughts and was watching everything he did.

An early traumatic experience of shaming occurred when Max was nine years old. A young religious fanatic in his congregation caught Max touching himself in the church bathroom, and made an awful scene. He dragged Max into the church and asked him to prostrate himself before the altar and beg God's forgiveness.

Many religious denominations teach a concept of man as wretched and stained with original sin. Original sin as taught by some religious bodies means you are bad from the moment you are born. The teaching of original sin accounts for a lot of the child-rearing practices which are geared toward breaking a child's unruly will and natural propensity toward evil.

God As Punitive

Max often told me he hoped God would forgive him for the evils he had done. And although he had a rather brilliant intellect, he still clung to some rather childish religious beliefs. God somehow kept score, and Max could never catch up. With original sin you're beat before you start.

I often ask myself how anyone could really believe in the fires of hell. Here was Max, whose life was a continuous torment, whose inner voices never stopped their incessant shame spirals, so what more could hell possibly be? Why would a just and loving God want to burn someone like Max for all eternity? Well, Max believed it, and that's what a therapist has to work with. His shame was greatly intensified by his belief that God knew all his inner thoughts and would punish him for his sins.

DENIAL OF SECONDARY CAUSALITY

One of the most insidious and toxically shaming distortions of many religions is the denial of secondary causality. What this means is that according to some church doctrines, the human will is inept. There is *nothing* man can do that is of any value. Of himself, man is a worm. Only when God works through him does man become restored to dignity. But it's never anything that man does of himself.

The theology here is abortive of any true doctrine of Judeo/Christianity. Most mainline interpretations see man as having true secondary causality. Thomas Aquinas, in the prologue to the second part of his *Summa Theologia* writes, "After our treatise on God, we turn to man, who is God's Image, insofar as man, too, *like God, has the power over his works*" (italics mine).

This is a strong statement of human causality. Man's will is effective. In order to receive grace, man must be willing to accept the gift of faith. After acceptance, man's will plays a major role in the sanctification process.

The abortive interpretation sees man as totally flawed and defective. Of himself, he can only sin. Man is shame-based to the core.

DENIAL OF EMOTIONS

The religious system in general has not given human emotions much press. There are denominations and sects that are highly emotional. And from time to time charismatic renewal groups spontaneously arise to bring vitality and new vigor into the life of a church group. But in general, there's not a lot of permission to show emotions.

I see two basic types of religious structures — one I call the Apollonian and the other the Dionysian. Neither really permits a true and healthy expression of emotion.

The Apollonian type religion is very rigid, stoic and severe. It can also be very intellectual. In either case, outpouring of emotions are not acceptable.

The Dionysian is the charismatic or cultic type of enthusiastic worship. These types of worship seem to favor free emotional expression, but, in reality, only certain types of emotions can be shown. There are emotional outbursts, but they have no true connection with feelings. The outburst type of religiosity is often a way to get the emotions over with. They are poured out, but the subject does not experience them for long. Honest emotions, especially anger, are not permitted anywhere. The same is true of sexual feelings. Religion has added its voice to sexual shame. Some interpretations of the Protestant Reformers actually imply that Original Sin was concupiscence or sexual desire. Some religious interpretations equate desire and sexuality with the result that any kind of strong desire is prohibited.

PERFECTIONISM — THE RELIGIOUS SCRIPT

Religion has been a major source of shaming through perfectionism. Moral shoulds, oughts and musts have been sanctioned by subjective interpretations of religious revelation. The Bible has been used to justify all sorts of blaming judgment. Religious perfectionism teaches a kind of behavioral righteousness. There is a religious script, which contains the standards of holiness and righteous behavior. These standards dictate how to talk (there is a proper God voice), how to dress, walk and behave in almost every situation. Departure from this standard is deemed sinful.

What a perfectionistic system creates is a 'how to get it right' behavioral script. In such a script one is taught how to act loving and righteous. It's actually more important to *act* loving and righteous *than to be* loving and righteous. The feeling of righteousness and acting sanctimoniously are wonderful ways to mood alter toxic shame. They are often ways to interpersonally transfer one's shame to others.

RELIGIOUS ADDICTION

Mood alteration is an ingredient of compulsive/addictive behavior. Addiction has been described as "a pathological relationship to any mood-altering experience that has life-damaging consequences." Toxic shame has been suggested as the core and fuel of all addiction. Religious addiction is rooted in toxic shame, which can be readily mood-altered through various religious behaviors. One can get feelings of righteousness through any form of worship. One can fast, pray, meditate, serve others, go through sacramental rituals, speak-in-tongues, be slain by the Holy Spirit, quote the Bible, read Bible passages, say the name of Jahweh or Jesus. Any of these can be a mood-altering experience. If one is toxically shamed, such an experience can be immensely rewarding.

The disciples of any religious system can say we are good and the others, those not like us, the sinners, they are bad. This can be exhilarating to the souls of toxically shamed persons.

Righteousness is also a form of *shameless behavior*. Since healthy shame says we can and will inevitably make mistakes (the Bible says the just man will fall 70 times seven), then righteousness becomes a kind of shameless behavior.

All in all the religious system has been a major source of toxic shame for many people.

The Cultural System

T.S. Eliot wrote, "This was a decent godless people. Their only monument the asphalt road and a thousand lost golf balls." In this quote, *The Waste-Land,* and *The Love Song of J. Alfred Prufrock,* Eliot made a strong indictment on the hopelessness of modern man.

In *Bradshaw On: The Family* society itself is seen as a sick family system built on the rules of the poisonous pedagogy. These rules deny emotions. This sets us up for the psychic numbing that leads to addiction. These rules come from the time of Kings. They are non-democratic and are based on a kind of master-slave inequality. They promote obsessive orderliness and obedience. They are rigid and deny vitality. Good children are defined as meek, considerate, unselfish and perfectly law-abiding. Such rules allow no place for vitality, spontaneity, inner freedom, inner independence and critical judgment. These rules cause parents, even well-intentioned ones, to abandon their children. Such abandonment creates the toxic shame I've been describing.

Society As Compulsive And Addicted

Our society is highly addictive. We have 60 million sexual abuse victims. Possibly 75 million lives are seriously affected by alcoholism, with no telling how many more through other drugs. We have no idea of the actual impact on our economy resulting from the billions of tax free dollars that come from the illegal drug traders. Over 15 million families are violent. Some 60% of women and 50% of men have eating disorders. We have no actual data on work addiction or sexual addictions. I saw a recent quotation that cited 13 million gambling addicts. If toxic shame is the fuel of addiction — we have a massive problem of shame in our society.

Another indicator of the hopelessness that is rooted in and results from our shame is our feverish overactivism and compulsive lifestyle. Erich Fromm made an extensive diagnosis of this in his book *The Revolution Of Hope.* He saw our overactivism as a sign of the restlessness and lack of inner peace that flows from the core of our shame. We are human doings because we have no inner life. Our toxic shame won't let us go inward. It is too painful for us in there. It is too hopeless in there. As Sheldon Kopp says, "We can change what we are doing, but we can't change who we are." If I am flawed and defective as a human person, then there's something wrong with me. I am a mistake. I am hopeless.

The Success Myth

Someone once said, "Success is different at different stages of development — from not wetting your pants in infancy, to being well-liked in childhood and adolescence, to getting laid in young adulthood, to making money and having prestige in later adulthood, to getting laid in middle age, to being well-liked in old age, to not wetting your pants in senility." What's right about that description is the emphasis on making money, having prestige and being well-liked.

Perhaps the greatest modern American literary tragedy was the play, *The Death Of A Salesman* by Arthur Miller. Miller was able to create a great Aristotelian tragic hero out of an ordinary common man. Willy Loman is a symbol of the American success myth. He lives his life based on the belief that success is being well-liked and making money. Willy dies lonely and destitute, taking his own life in order to get the insurance money which would prove he was successful. In his *Poetics* Aristotle states that the power of a great tragic hero results from the combination of his nobleness coupled with some tragic flaw. Willy is noble. He is willing to die for his faith. It is his faith that is the tragic flaw. He truly believes that if a man makes money and is well-liked, he will be a success. This is what it means to make it.

The success myth also preaches a kind of rugged individuality. One is to make it on his own. One is to be self-made and to be one's own man. In this myth money and its symbols become the measure of how well you make it. A man in his 50s with a low income, has to feel the shaming pinch of this belief system. And as much as one might protest all this, money and the fame that goes with it, still have enormous power in our lives.

Rigid Sex Roles

The rigid sex roles still espoused by our society are measuring symbols of perfection. There are real men and real women. Before we were born, there was a blueprint of how to be a man and how to be a woman.

Real men are rugged individuals. They act rather than talk. They are silent and decisive. A real man never shows weakness, emotion or vulnerability. Real men win. They never give their opponent an advantage.

Real women are the helpmates of real men. They are the caretakers of the domestic scene. They are emotional, vulnerable and fragile. They are the peacemakers. In return they look for everlasting "romantic love". They look for a prince who will come and reward them for all they have given up, the reward being that they will be taken care of for the rest of their lives.

Many believe these roles are a thing of the past. But I suggest that you watch the way parents take care of little boys and little girls. Notice the way we dress the sexes and above all notice children's toys. Child's play is the precursor of the adult world of work. Children's toys are still highly sexist. Watch the way a liberated mother and father handle their girlchild, and then watch the way they handle their boychild. They won't even touch them the same way.

Our sex role scripts are rigid and divisive. They are also shaming in that they are caricatures of maleness and femaleness. They are overidentifications with parts of us, but fail to allow for completion and wholeness. Each of us is the offspring of a male and a female. Each of us has both male and female hormones. Each sex is determined by the majority hormones it possesses. And each sex needs to integrate its contrasexual opposite side in order to be complete and be whole. The rigid sex roles set standards which disallow wholeness and completion. Such standards shame our contrasexual opposite parts. A man is shamed for seeking to embrace his vulnerability. A woman is designated a bitch for becoming assertive and actualizing her maleness.

THE MYTH OF THE PERFECT "10"

Our culture presents a physical perfectionistic system which is cruelly shaming to the physically unendowed. The perfect woman or man is a "10". The movie "10" with Bo Derek gave great impetus to this mythology.

The perfect "10" has very definite attributes that enhance the sexual shaming which occurs in our society. The perfect "10" woman has perfectly round breasts, size 38D, with matching hips and buttocks. The perfect "10" man has a muscular, tanned and proportionately perfect physical body. His penis is eight inches plus.

These physical ideals have caused untold suffering and shame to an incredible number of people. I have file after file of men and women who have suffered intense shame over the size of their genitals. Small to flat chested women with histories of high school pain and isolation have peopled my counseling office over the last 20 years. Males worried about the size of their penises are commonplace in counseling annals. Sex is either secretive or banal. As banal, the bantering about genital sizes is orchestrated on the late night talk shows and in the comic routines of club comedians.

Max was obsessed with the idea that his penis was too small. He also thought himself very unattractive because of a slight harelip resulting from being hit in the mouth with a baseball. Max also had acne as an adolescent. All of this physical data added greatly to his pain and shame. And all of this was in spite of the medical data, which Max knew, that the average male genital is five to six inches erect and the absolute fact that women found

Max enormously attractive.

Comparing ourselves to the perfect "10" mythical standard is a major source of sexual shame in our society.

DENIAL OF EMOTIONS

Our culture does not handle emotions well. We like folks to be happy and fine. We learn rituals of acting happy and fine at an early age. I can remember many times telling people "I'm fine" when I felt like the world was caving in on me. I often think of Senator Muskie who cried on the campaign trail when running for president. From that moment on he was history. We don't want a president who has emotions. We would rather have one that can act! Emotions are certainly not acceptable in the workplace. True expression of any emotions that are not "positive" are met with disdain.

THE MYTH OF THE GOOD OL' BOY AND THE NICE GAL

The good ol' boy myth and the nice gal are a kind of social conformity myth. They create a real paradox when put together with the "rugged individual" part of the Success Myth. How can I be a rugged individual, be my own man and conform at the same time? Conforming means "Don't make a wave", "Don't rock the boat". Be a nice gal or a good ol' boy. This means that we have to pretend a lot.

> "We are taught to be nice and polite. We are taught that these behaviors (most often lies) are better than telling the truth. Our churches, schools, and politics are rampant with teaching dishonesty (saying things we don't mean and pretending to feel ways we don't feel). We smile when we feel sad; laugh nervously when dealing with grief; laugh at jokes we don't think are funny; tell people things to be polite that we surely don't mean."
>
> *Bradshaw On: The Family*

Playing roles and acting are forms of lying. If a person acts like they really feel and it rocks the boat, they are ostracized. We promote pretense and lying as a cultural way of life. Living this way causes an inner split. It teaches us to hide and cover up our toxic shame. This sends us deeper into isolation and loneliness.

3

The Hiding Places
Of Toxic Shame

"Where are you, Adam?"

According to the book of *Genesis*, after the fall Adam went into hiding. By trying to be more than human, Adam felt less than human. Before the fall, Adam was not ashamed; after the fall he was. Toxic shame is true agony. It is a pain felt from the inside, in the core of our being. It is excruciatingly painful.

Felt Sense Of Toxic Shame

Toxic shame results from the unexpected exposure of vulnerable aspects of a child's self. This exposure takes place before the child has any ego boundaries to protect himself. The early shaming events happen in a context where the child has no ability to choose. The felt experience of shame is the feeling of being exposed and seen when one is not ready to be seen. Toxic shame is often manifested in dreams of being naked in inappropriate places, or in not being prepared, as in suddenly having to write your final exam without having studied for it.

The unexpected quality of a shaming event creates a lack of self-trust in a child. As toxic shame develops, the child stops trusting his own eyes, judgment, feelings and desires. These faculties form our basic human

Figure 3.1. Layers of Defense Against The Agony of Internalized Shame

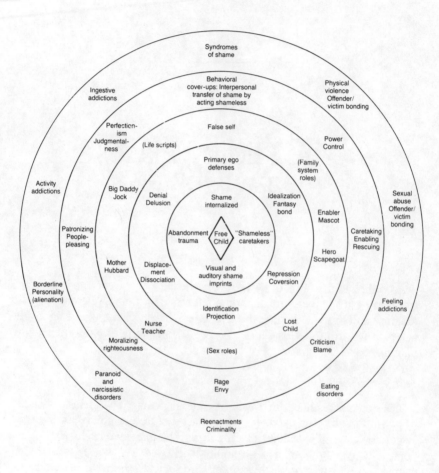

power. The distrust of our basic faculties results in the feeling of powerlessness. As vulnerable aspects of the self are shamed, they are disowned and separated from our felt sense of self. This self-separation process results in a split self. We are beside ourselves. We become an object to ourself. When I become an object, I am no longer in me. I am absent from my own experience. What I feel is emptiness and exposure. I have no boundaries and therefore no protection. I must run and hide. But there is no place to hide since I am totally exposed. They are after me and they are going to take me by surprise and catch me. I'm being hunted from moment to moment. The hunter is always approaching. There is never a moment when I can relax. I must be constantly guarded lest I'm ever unguarded. I am alone in the most complete way.

The agony of this chronic stage of being cannot be endured for long. At the deepest level toxic shame triggers our basic automatic defensive cover-ups. Freud called these automatic cover-ups our primary ego defenses. Once these defenses are in place they function automatically and unconsciously, sending our true and authentic self into hiding. We develop a false identity out of this basic core. We become master impersonators. We avoid our core agony and pain and over a period of years, we avoid our avoidance.

Figure 3.1 gives you a visual picture of the various layers of protection which we devise to create our defenses against the core agony of shame. Each layer is progressively more conscious. The deepest layers — our ego defenses, family system roles and scripts — are automatic and unconscious. All layers are compulsive and each characteristic element of our shield of secrecy seems to have a life of its own.

Primary Ego Defenses

Freud was the first to clearly define an automatic process used for self-preservation which is activated in the face of severe threat. He called this process the primary ego defense system. All of us need to use these defenses from time to time. They were intended by nature to be situational rather than chronic. Children are helpless and powerless. Their ego is undifferentiated at birth. Each child needs to develop boundaries and ego strengths. Children need their ego defenses more than adults. They need them until they can develop good boundaries. To develop strong ego boundaries children need parents with strong boundaries. No shame-based parent has these. If one is essentially flawed and defective as a human being, then everything about one is not okay. Toxic shame is without boundaries. Without any boundaries for protection, a child cannot survive. Being without boundaries is like living in a house without doors. It is like a country without borders or an army to protect its borders.

Along with their egocentricism, nature provides children with primary ego defenses to take the place of boundaries. Each ego defense allows the child to survive situations which are actually intolerable.

DENIAL AND FANTASY BONDING

Perhaps the most elementary ego defense is denial. In the face of threat, people deny what is going on, or they deny the hurt of what is going on, or the impact on their lives of what is going on.

Robert Firestone has elaborated on Freud's notion of denial. He describes the most fundamental ego defense as the 'fantasy bond'. The fantasy bond is an illusion of connectedness that the child creates in relation to the primary caregiver, who is shaming her.

Paradoxically, the more a child is violated, the more she creates the fantasy bond. Bonding to abuse is one of the most perplexing aspects of shame-inducement. Abuse is usually unpredictable, a sort of random shock. Abuse lowers one's self-value and induces shame. As one loses more and more self-respect, one's world of choices and alternatives is diminished.

Finally one feels one has no choice and often clings to one's abuser. The fantasy bond (really bondage) is the illusion that someone is there for them, someone who loves and protects them. The fantasy bond is like a mirage in the desert. Once set up, the denying fantasy bond functions automatically and unconsciously. Years later when reality is no longer life-threatening, the fantasy bond remains.

REPRESSION

Any intolerable event is signaled by strong emotions. Emotions are a form of energy-in-motion. They signal us of a loss, a threat or a satiation. Sadness is about losing something we cherish. Anger and fear signal us of actual or impending threats to our well-being. Joy signals that we are fulfilled and satisfied. Whenever a child is shamed through some form of abandonment, feelings of anger, hurt, sadness arise. Since shame-based parents are shame-bound in all their emotions, they cannot tolerate their children's emotions. Therefore, they shame their children's emotions. Repression is the way children numb out so they don't feel their emotions. It is not absolutely clear exactly how the mechanism of repression works. It certainly has to do with muscle tension, changing breathing patterns and fantasizing abandonment. Once an emotion is repressed, one feels numb. The emotional avoidance is sealed by learning to avoid the avoidance.

Erasing Subjective Experience

Kaufman posits a direct link between the emotional shame binds and the ego defense of repression. He suggests that after a period of having one's feelings shamed, one begins to enter a realm of what he calls 'experiential erasure'. This experiential erasure is equivalent to repression. Emotions are internally experienced before they are overtly expressed. Kaufman writes,

> "The very experiencing of a particular feeling can become silenced, if the binding effects of shame spread to the internal, conscious registering of the shame-bound effect. At the moment the self suddenly feels exposed, if only to itself, the awareness of the contents of consciousness (and of the triggering effect) can be erased experientially."

This erasing of experience is an ego protection. Gradually over a period of time, we learn not even to be aware of experiencing a feeling which generates shame. We learn to feel nothing. We psychically numb out.

DISSOCIATION

Dissociation is the ego defense that accompanies the most violent forms of shaming — sexual and physical violence. The trauma is so great and the fear so terrifying that one needs instant relief. Dissociation is a form of instant numbing. It involves the mechanisms of denial and regression, but includes strong elements of distracting imagination.

An incest victim simply goes away during the experience of violation — like a long daydream. The same is true of physical violence. The pain and humiliating shame are unbearable — the victim leaves her body.

This is the reason that these forms of victimization are so difficult to treat. The memories are screened while the feelings remain. The victim often feels crazy, like she is living in unreality. The victim often has a split (sometimes multiple) personality. Because the connection between the violence and the response to violence has been severed, the victim thinks the craziness and shame are about her, rather than about what has happened to her.

Dissociation is not limited to sexual and physical violation. Emotional battering, severe trauma, chronic distress are also precipitating factors in causing dissociation. Dissociation can last a lifetime.

DISPLACEMENT

Displacement is closely connected to dissociation.

A client of mine, whose alcoholic father used to come into her room and violate her shortly after the bars closed, frequently woke up about 3:00 a.m.

and saw a shadowy figure in her room. She also had a recurring nightmare of a black monster figure who poked her and punched her with his black thumb. When she came for therapy she had no idea she was an incest victim. She had a history of being sexually abused by considerably older men.

She was only 26 at the time she began her therapy. As we did her family of origin work, and while in light hypnotic age regression, she began to experience hypernesia — a flood of memories about her bedroom and her father. At first they were very general. After repeated probing for detail, she began shame-faced sobbing, describing how her father forced her to engage in fellatio. Over months of debriefing she reconstructed a two-and-a-half year trauma beginning at about age four-and-a-half. She was her dad's favorite. He threatened her with severe punishment if she told anyone. He also gave her the only warmth and attention she experienced in the family.

Once she connected the emotions with the events — her shadowy displacement and her black-thumbed monster disappeared from her dreams.

DEPERSONALIZATION

Closely related to displacement is *depersonalization.*

Depersonalization is a behavioral manifestation of being violated. It happens most often in the context of a significant other, with whom the individual no longer perceives the reality of her own subjective self. She experiences herself as an object. This results in the loss of awareness of inner experience. As violation continues, the individual no longer perceives the reality of her self or her environment.

IDENTIFICATION

When victimization takes place — the victim often identifies with the persecutor. By so doing the victim no longer feels the helplessness and the shame of humiliation of the victimization. Persecuting offenders were previously victims who identified with their offenders. In identifying they no longer have to feel the shame.

CONVERSION

I spoke of affect and need conversion when I described how Max compensated for his abusive and neglectful abandonment by converting most of his feelings and needs into sexual thoughts, feelings and behaviors. There are other ways that conversion defends us against toxic shame.

Feeling Rackets

I've already explained how in the process of internalizing shame, vital parts of our human reality are disowned. The split-off parts of our internal experience (our feelings, needs and drives) clamor for expression. They are like our hungry dogs locked in the basement. We must find some means to quiet them. One way is through feeling conversion. In feeling conversion, we convert what is forbidden or shameful into another more acceptable or tolerable feeling.

We have already seen this with the feelings of sexuality. Other feelings can be used to replace our shame-bound feelings. Anger is often blocked from conscious awareness and converted into more tolerable or family authorized feelings, such as hurt or guilt. The person feeling anger no longer feels it; he feels the acceptable feeling.

Three-year-old Herkamer is furious because his mother promised to take him to Baskin-Robbins and is now backing out. Herkamer storms and stomps, telling his mom (as three-year-olds are wont to do) that he hates her. Mom is a shame-based co-dependent. She is terrified of anger, her own and anyone else's. Herkamer's anger triggers her own anger toward her own parents. Since this anger is bound in guilt and shame, she stops herself from feeling her shame by guilting and shaming Herkamer.

She tells him how hurt she feels when he is angry at her. She begins to cry since she learned to convert her anger into sadness as a little girl. Crying when feeling angry is a common female *racket*.

A scene from Mom's childhood went as follows: Her dad was angry because she wouldn't stop playing in her room and get to sleep. When he expressed his anger, she started sobbing. Dad felt bad and picked her up and started stroking her. He gave her a glass of cold juice and rocked her to sleep. As a little girl Herkamer's mom learned that sadness is acceptable and gives her power. Anger did not work in her family. When Herkamer tells her he hates her, she cries, telling him that maybe someday she won't be home when he wants her. She may even tell him that maybe she will go away and die!

Poor Herkamer is devastated. His abandonment, terror and separation anxiety are triggered. He rushes to his mom, feeling terrible guilt. His awareness of his anger is completely lost. His anger has been converted into guilt.

Sometimes parents react with anger to their children's expression of anger, fear or sadness. When this happens the child's feelings are either bound in shame or are converted into fear or terror.

My own feeling of anger was dominated by fear much of my life. When I felt anger, it was immediately converted into fear to the point of terror. Even when I could express the anger my lips would quiver; my voice would crack; my body would tremble. Eric Berne, the founder of Transactional

Analysis (TA) called this feeling 'conversion process'. I'm describing 'Racket Formation'. *A racket is a family-authorized feeling used to replace a nonacceptable and shameful feeling.*

Somatic Conversion

A third form of conversion is the conversion of both needs and feelings into some form of bodily or somatic expression. Needs and feelings can be changed into bodily sickness.

When one is sick, one is usually cared for. When one is sick, one can feel as bad as one really feels. This conversion dynamic is especially prevalent in family systems where sickness is given attention and rewarded.

I was asthmatic as a child. Frequently when I wanted to miss a day of school, I would induce an asthma attack. I learned early on that sickness got a lot of sympathy in my family system. Getting attention with sickness is a very common phenomenon. When people want to miss work, they call in sick. Sickness works!

Conversion of feelings into sickness is the basis of psychosomatic illness. In Max's family there were several generations of hypochondriasis. His maternal great-grandmother was bedridden off and on for years. His maternal grandmother was literally bedridden for 45 years and his mom, Felicia, continually struggled with ulcers, colitis and arthritis. Max himself obsessed on illness a lot.

My own belief is that families don't convert feelings and needs to actual physical illness unless there are predisposing genetically based factors, such as a genetic history of certain disorders like asthma, arthritis and particular organ weakness. When parental modeling and high rewards for somatic illness are added to a genetic predisposition, the conversion of feelings and needs into bodily or somatic expression is all but guaranteed.

PROJECTION

Projection is one of the most primitive defense mechanisms. Its most dramatic forms of manifestion are psychotic delusions and hallucinations. Once we are shamed-based, projection is inevitable. Once we've disowned our feelings, wishes, needs and drives, they clamor for expression. They are vital parts of ourselves.

One way to handle them is to attribute them to others. If my own anger is disowned, I may project it onto you. I may ask you why you are angry.

A female client of mine hated other women. She was especially vehement about very sexy women. My client was the supervisor of a group of hard-nosed, red-neck, front-line superintendents in a chemical plant. Her father was a macho chauvinist, who shamed his wife at home and in public. As a young girl growing up, my client had been a tomboy. She had identified with her father. She was his fishing and hunting buddy. At 10 she could "shoot a gun as well as any man," her dad would brag. This woman completely rejected and disowned her femininity and her sexuality. She would project her own internal shaming onto other women, verbally disdaining them for their sexuality and femininity.

Projection is used when repression fails. It is a major source of conflict and hostility in human relationships. Projection is the basis for children considering their parents omnipotent. Children are one with the world. Christopher Morley's poem describes children as . . .

> "Born comrade of bird, beast and bee
> And unselfconscious as the tree . . .
> Elate explorer of each sense
> Without dismay, without pretense . . .
> In your untrained transparent eyes
> There is no conscience, no surprise —
> Life's queer conundrums you accept.
> Your strange Divinity still kept . . .
> There were days, O tender elf
> When you were poetry itself."

This animism and omnipotence are parts of the child's egocentricity. They easily project this onto their parents. Parents are Gods — they are omnipotent. In questioning little boys playing marbles about the origin of the rules of the game, Piaget was fascinated to realize that the children believed their fathers had made up the rules. Piaget would ask them about their grandfathers and God. The boys believed that their fathers knew the rules before their grandfathers and before God.

Such projected omnipotence is another way to understand the potential for shame in the parent/child mutual bond. Gods are perfect. If an abusing transaction takes place in the parental relationship, it can't be the parents problem (God is perfect), it must be the child's.

SECONDARY EGO DEFENSES

Freud described other secondary ego defenses. These take over when the primary process defenses seem to fail. This is especially true of repression.

For example, a shameful feeling may begin to surface. It is frightening, so the person mobilizes a secondary line of defense. Secondary defenses which are often used when primary ones fail are: Inhibition, Reactive Formation, Undoing, Isolation of Affect and Turning Against Self.

1. Inhibition

A reclusive client of mine was paralyzed and unable to move whenever he went to a club and tried to dance. During the course of our work together, he remembered an incident about dancing when he was 12 years old. His mother was a periodic alcoholic.

One night she came home partially drunk. She playfully put on some music and invited her son to dance with her, which he did. He was awkward and she was shaming to him. During one part of the dancing, my client had an erection. His mother noticed it and teased him about it. He was shamed to the core. His later inability to dance was an example of the ego defense of inhibition. By inhibiting the muscles he used to dance, he safeguarded himself against the possible experiencing of shame.

2. Reactive Formation

Reactive Formation is used to insure that a repressed disturbing feeling which would trigger shame is kept out of conscious awareness. Reactive Formation is used when repression seems to be weakening. The trait of kindness is often developed to counteract an impulse of cruelty. To be cruel would induce shame. The exact opposite of cruelty is kindness. Kindness insures that one will not be cruel and therefore can avoid feeling shame. A Reactive Formation always has some of the characteristics of the very impulse whose expression it is designed to prevent. Commenting on this, White and Gilliland write,

> "The trait of kindness . . . will have a rigid and inappropriate quality to it. It will be imposed on others under all circumstances, whether or not warranted . . . it will have a coercive and thinly sadistic quality. The person who exhibits such reactive kindness is a person who *kills with kindness.*"

> *Elements of Psychopathology*

3. Undoing

Undoing is a magical behavior aimed at canceling out a feeling, thought or behavior that one fears will cause shame or has actually caused shame.

One student I counseled spent an excessive amount of time in elaborate study rituals. He was brilliant, but was failing in college because of these rituals. He would spend hours before he started to study lining up his books, pens, pencils, note pad, etc., until he achieved a certain complicated pattern. Each item had to be positioned so as not touch any other item. This was most important in relation to his rather large collection of books.

During the time of counseling with him I noticed a general pattern of touch avoidance. He had been severely shamed as a little boy for touching and showing off his penis when the minister came to call. On a subsequent occasion he was caught masturbating by his mother and spanked abusively for it. He was subsequently told he would go blind if he ever truly masturbated (so was I, but during my adolescence I was willing to risk it).

My client's elaborate nontouching ritual was a magical way of undoing his wish to touch his penis and masturbate.

4. Isolation Of Affect

Isolation of Affect is a way to convert a shame-engendering feeling or impulse into a thought. By so doing the person can disown any responsibility for the feeling or impulse.

I once read a case of an incest victim who was obsessed with the thought of "Fucking Jesus". She was a perfectly proper Christian lady. She was also quite intelligent and realized the absurdity of the idea.

She had been incested for four years by an uncle who was the only paternal figure she had had in her life. He had come into her life when she was six years old. Her mother worked and left her with a maid who was rigidly religious and judgmental. This maid emotionally battered the child. She once expressed angry disbelief about her maid's religious teaching and was deeply shamed for it. She had also felt rage at her uncle. Yet she had deeply loved him as a child. He was the only one who showed her affection and gave her gifts. None of these conflicts had been worked out — her rage, her guilt and shame, her love for her uncle's paternal care. Since she had not worked all this out, it came together in a recurring thought of "Fucking Jesus". The thought just occurred *without any feeling.* The thought distracted her from her painful and shamefully confusing feelings.

This is a rather dramatic example of confused feelings being converted in a thought pattern. *Any mental preoccupation can distract one from one's feelings.*

5. Turning Against Self

Turning Against Self is an ego defense whereby a person deflects hostile aggression from another person and directs it onto self. This defense is extremely common with people who have been abandoned through severe abuse. Because a child so desperately needs his parents for survival, he will turn his aggressive rage about his abuse into abuse of himself. The extreme form of this is suicidality. In such cases, (the French call it self-murder), the person so identifies with the offender that he is killing the offender by killing himself.

Common but less intense examples include nail biting, head banging, accident proneness and self-mutilation. In later life people may injure themselves socially or financially. In all cases the rage at the offender is so fearful and shameful it is turned against self.

As one grows up, these primary defenses are translated into new levels of sophistication. Secondary type ego defenses include rationalization, minimization, explanation, sublimation, compensation and all the types of shameless behaviors used to interpersonally transfer shame to others.

While first in the order of self-preservation, these primary process defenses will be last in the order of healing the shame that binds you. Their power and strength lie in the fact that they are automatic and unconscious. They were the best decisions available to you at the time. And they kept you sane. They literally saved your life. The very defenses which were once life-giving, later on become the very preservers of our toxic shame.

The False Self

I spoke earlier about the rupture of the self as the deepest cut of internalized shame. Once internalized we no longer have the feeling of shame — we are it. Because we experience ourselves as flawed and defective, we cannot look at ourselves without pain. Therefore we must create a false self. The false self is the second layer of defense erected to alleviate the felt sense of toxic shame.

All major schools of therapy speak about this false self. The Jungians call it the *persona* (the mask). The T.A. people call it the *adapted child.*

Bob Subby speaks of the *public self* which he contrasts with the *private self.* He uses a fantastic drawing to illustrate the point. Figure 3.2 is an adaptation of Bob's drawing. The tiny little figure that gets smaller and smaller is the shame-based authentic self. The larger figure is the false or public self.

The Bible speaks of the Pharisee hypocrite. In Greek *hypocrite* means an *actor,* one who is pretending. Jesus didn't like false selves.

The *est* Training (The Forum now) confronts people's act: their melo-dramatic story. The act or story is the mythologized self: the phony performing self.

I divide the false self into three categories: The Cultural False Self, Life Scripts and The Family System Roles.

The Cultural False Self

In the previous section I outlined our cultural sex roles, pointing out how these roles set up a perfectionistic system of measurement. Since each of us is utterly unique and unrepeatable, there is no way to compare us or measure us. In this way our rigid sex roles are shaming.

It's important to see the dynamics of how sex roles come into being. Sociologists describe the process under the phrase "the social construction of reality". As we understand this social construction process, it is easier to see how we can readily identify with these roles and make them our false self.

Figure 3.2. Shame Internalization
Adaptation of Robert Subby's Private Self/Public Self

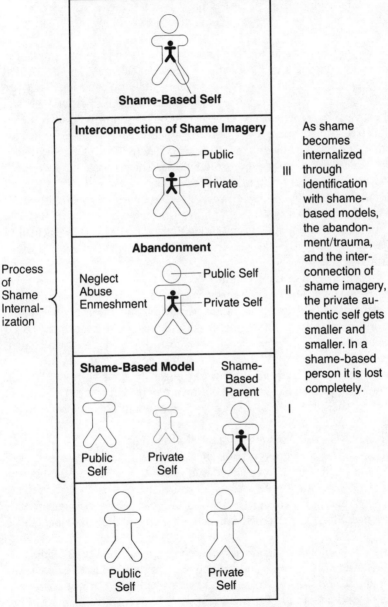

Shame-Based Self

Interconnection of Shame Imagery

— Public

III

— Private

As shame becomes internalized through identification with shame-based models, the abandonment/trauma, and the interconnection of shame imagery, the private authentic self gets smaller and smaller. In a shame-based person it is lost completely.

Abandonment

Neglect
Abuse
Enmeshment

— Public Self

II

— Private Self

Process
of
Shame
Internal-
ization

Shame-Based Model   Shame-
Based
Parent

I

Public
Self

Private
Self

Public
Self

Private
Self

Adapted from Robert Subby's *Lost in the Shuffle: The Co-dependent Reality*

THE SOCIAL CONSTRUCTION OF REALITY

Each of us is born into a social order that has already arrived at a "consensus reality". This phrase is used by sociologists to describe the product of our social construction of reality. Human beings are creatures of habit.

As we humans act in repetitious ways, necessitated by circumstances relating to survival, these repetitions become habitual. These habitual behaviors soon become socially acceptable ways of behaving. They are socially agreed upon. After a while these socially agreed upon habitual ways of behaving become what sociologists term "legitimized". After being legitimized for a while, they become unconscious. The unconscious legitimizations gradually evolve into *laws of reality*. We no longer question them. We accept them: they are predictable. They insure our security. If someone tries to change them, we get very upset.

In fact, they are not reality at all. As cultural anthropologists have continuously pointed out, other cultures do things quite differently. The laws of reality that emerged from our legitimized habituations are actually a 'consensus reality'. The 'consensus reality' is what we've all agreed on as constituting reality.

A prominent part of every culture's consensus reality is its notion of what a man is, what a woman is and what a marriage and family are. At birth it was already decided how you and I must be and behave in order to be a real man and a real woman. These stereotyped roles are perfect for shame-based identities. When I play the role of a real man, I receive generous cultural rewards. These stereotyped roles often shame the parts of our authentic self which does not correspond to the role ideal. In their current form our cultural sex roles were legitimized during the period of western expansion. Men were the hunters and warriors, and women kept the children and the wagons.

I certainly believe in some biological grounding in the sexes. But our current sex roles go far beyond biological grounding. They are caricatures of their biological ground. As I pointed out before, they also deny the obvious androgenous polarity in every man and woman. Each of us resulted from the union of male and female. Each of us embody both male and female hormones. A healthy person is a balance between so-called male and female traits.

These roles not only shame us but they become our refuge of hiding. As we pretend to be real men and women, we can hide the fact that we really don't know who we are. We can mood alter by playing our role to the hilt. In the mood alteration of being a real man or woman, we can avoid our painful shame.

Life Scripts

Eric Berne, the founder and original creator of Transactional Analysis, developed the notion of life scripts. He observed the fact that a part of the population live very tragic lives. Their lives are tragic because they seem to have no choice. They are like actors playing their roles according to a script. Berne felt that the majority of the population acted out banal or melodramatic lives. The melodramatic scripts were described by Thoreau when he said that the mass of humanity live lives of quiet desperation. Berne felt that very few people live truly authentic lives.

Scripts are like the scripts for a movie or a play. They describe a certain type of character. They proscribe what he is to feel and not feel and how he is to behave in life. Tragic scripts usually end in killing someone or oneself; or living out one's life in a form of chronic suicide; or in being considered crazy.

Claude Steiner, the T.A. therapist, speaks of three basic Tragic Scripts: the *no mind* (crazy) script, *no love* (kill someone or yourself) script, and the *no feel* (addictions) script. These tragic scripts are set up through the shaming of our basic powers: to know, to love and to feel.

The formation of scripts is complicated. The core mechanism of the process occurs by means of choices resulting from injunctions and attributions, script modeling and life experiences.

INJUNCTIONS

Injunctions come from the shame-based child in the parent. Injunctions are usually nonverbal. They take the form of messages like don't be; don't be a girl; don't be a boy; don't be important or successful. All toxic scripts have the injunction *"don't be you"*. An injunction shames the authentic self and causes self-rupture.

ATTRIBUTIONS

Attributions are more conscious and usually come from verbal emotional abuse. Messages like "How can you be so dumb or stupid?" or "What do you use for brains?" sets one up for the no mind script. Messages like "You really love your brother, don't you?" or "That's not my little boy who is acting hateful," sets one up to never know what his own feelings of love are. Messages like, "I know you're not really angry," or "There's nothing to cry about," discount one's feelings and cause confusion.

Attributes can come directly as when Mom is talking to her friend and says of your brother, "He's my well-behaved child," and of you, "She's my little hellion." Other types of parental attribution messages are, "You're always

going to have trouble with your studies, weight, anger, etc.," "You're never
going to amount to anything," "You've always been selfish. God help the
person you marry." Or "Every man in this family has been a lawyer." Or "No
woman in our family has ever been divorced." Script messages tell us the
way we are or what role we are supposed to play in life. They shame who
we authentically are and create self-rupture.

MODELS

I've already covered the subject of parental models as part of the
dynamics of shame internalization. Script models are not limited to parents.
They could come from fairy tales, movies, TV or other actual cultural or
family models. Women who had nonavailable, abusive fathers might
magically identify with *Beauty And The Beast* and act out the main acts of
that fairy tale over and over in their life by marrying beastly men.

Women are often given the magical belief that if they wait long enough,
their prince will come. Magic plays a part in many shame-based people's
lives. Hiding behind fantasies of "someday", "if only" and "when" — a
person may live out his life waiting for a fairy godmother or godfather. The
fantasy bond sets people up for magical transferences to other fantasy
bonds.

LIFE EXPERIENCES

A person's experiences help share the script. What is happening in the
family is a major factor in script formation. If Mom's an alcoholic, a child
may take on a helper or rescuing role. As the child experiences attention
and praise for this role, it becomes a strong element in sealing the script as
a rescuer. Another child might get lots of attention for being sickly. This may
contribute to a script which embodies life-long sickness. Children growing
up in a shame-based dysfunctional family may learn to experience anxiety
and distress as a way of life. Later they may feel uncomfortable if things are
going too well.

Family System Roles

All families have roles. The father and mother play their roles of modeling
what it is to be a man or woman, father or mother. Parents also model how
to be intimate, have boundaries, cope with problems, fight fair, problem
solve, etc. The role of children is to be curious and to be learners. Members
of a healthy family have flexible roles. Mom may be the heroine because she
baked a special cake. Daughter may take over that role when she volunteers
to do the dishes. Son becomes the hero when he notices smoke coming out

of the stove and prevents a fire. Dad's the hero when he takes the family on a vacation.

I have already described the dysfunctional family system roles in some detail. Ask yourself, "How did I function in my family? What role did I play to keep the family together?"

In our Center For Recovering Families in Houston we have discovered a large number of Family System Roles in addition to the roles I've discussed. Some other roles are Parent's Parent, Dad or Mom's Buddy, Family Counselor, Dad's Star, Mom's Star, Perfect One, Saint, Mom or Dad's Enabler, the Rascal, the Cute One, Athlete, Family Peacemaker, Family Referee, the Family Sacrifice, the Religious One, Winner, Loser, Martyr, Super-Mom, Super-Spouse, Clown, Super-Dad, Chief Enabler, Genius, Mom or Dad's Scapegoat.

We suggest that people really work at getting a feeling of the role(s) they played by putting a name on it. You may find that you played several roles. Each role has a felt sense, and the felt sense of the role will stay with you even if you give it up. You may have been the baby. You were cute and quickly became the family Mascot. Two years later your little brother came along and knocked you out of a job. You will retain the felt sense of being a Mascot. What is important to underscore is that when we play a role, we give up our true and authentic self. *The role is a false self.* In dysfunctional family systems the roles are necessitated by the needs of the family system in its attempt to balance itself in the wake of the primary stressor. The primary distress may be Dad's alcoholism, Mom's pill addiction or eating disorder, Dad's violence, the incest, Mom's religious addiction, etc. Each role is a way to handle the family distress and shame. Each role is a way for each member to feel like he has some control. As one plays the role more and more — rigidity sets in. As one becomes more and more unconscious of one's true self, one's self-rupture increases. The shame which promotes the role is intensified by the role. What a paradox! The roles are necessitated by the family system's shame as ways to overcome the shame, and they in fact freeze and enhance the shame. The old French proverb applies here: The more you try to change, the more it stays the same.

The ultimate issue about the roles is that they don't work. My being a Hero has done absolutely nothing to change my shame-based family system. Max's playing his Scapegoat and Lost Child Role did nothing to change his family system's dysfunction.

The power of these roles for a shame-based person is their rigidity and predictability. Staying in the role gives one a sense of identity. Even the Scapegoat can have predictability, can be somebody. This is why roles are so hard to give up, especially the Hero, Caretaker, Superachiever or Star type of roles. They are mood-altering. One feels good being a caretaker. How could I be flawed and defective when I'm taking care of all these people?

I can remember saying this to myself when I had a counseling load of 50 people a week. *What I couldn't grasp is that there is no way to change your being by your doing.* The shame-based core cries out — you're flawed and defective! There's something wrong with you! All the doing in the world won't change that.

The dysfunctional family system roles are ways we lose our reality. Over a period of time the fact that we are playing a role becomes unconscious. We believe we are the *persona* that the role calls for. We believe the role-designated feelings are our feelings. *The role literally becomes addictive.*

The Characterological Styles Of Shamelessness

A third layer of protection against the felt sense of toxic shame is acting "shameless". This is a common pattern for shame-based parents, teachers, preachers of righteousness and politicians. Acting shameless embodies several behaviors which serve to alter the feeling of shame and to interpersonally transfer one's toxic shame to another person. The transactional theorist call this passing the "hot potato". These behaviors are all strategies of defense against the pain of toxic shame. They are mood-altering and become addictive. These behaviors include perfectionism, striving for power and control, rage, arrogance, criticism and blame, judgmentalness and moralizing, contempt, patronization, caretaking and helping, envy, people-pleasing and being nice. Each behavior focuses on another person and takes the heat off oneself.

Perfectionism

Perfectionism flows from the boundariless core of toxic shame. A perfectionist has no sense of healthy shame; he has no internal sense of limits. Perfectionists never know how much is good enough.

Perfectionism is learned when one is valued only for doing. When parental acceptance and love is dependent upon performance — perfectionism is created. The performance is always related to what is outside the self. The child is taught to strive onward. There is never a place to rest and have inner joy and satisfaction.

Perfectionism always creates a superhuman measure by which one is compared. And no matter how hard one tries, or how well one does, one never measures up. Not measuring up is translated into a comparison of good versus bad, better versus worse. Good and bad lead to moralizing and judgmentalness. Perfectionism leads to comparison-making. Kaufman writes: "When perfectionism is paramount, the comparison of self with others inevitably ends in the self feeling the lesser for the comparison."

Comparison-making is one of the major ways that one continues to shame oneself internally. One continues to do to oneself on the inside what was done on the outside. Judgment and comparison-making lead to a destructive kind of competitiveness. Competition aims at outdoing others and feeling one-up, rather than simply being the best one can be. Competing to be better than others is mood-altering and becomes addictive.

Striving For Power And Control

The striving for power is a way to control others. Power is a form of control. Control is the grandiose will disorder already discussed. Those who must control everything, fear being vulnerable. Why? Because to be vulnerable opens one up to being shamed.

I once heard Terry Kellogg say that he had always lived on guard so that he would never be caught off guard. I identified with that. All my life I used up my energies by always having to be guarded. This was a mighty waste of time and energy. The fear was that I would be exposed. And when exposed, all would see that I was flawed and defective as a person.

Control is a way to insure that no one can ever shame us again. It involves controlling our own thoughts, expressions, feelings and actions. And it involves attempting to control other people's thoughts, feelings and actions. Control is the ultimate villain in destroying intimacy. We cannot share freely unless we are equal. When one person controls another, equality is ruptured.

We need to control because our toxic shame drives us outside ourselves. We are literally beside ourselves. We objectify ourself and experience ourself as lacking and defective. Therefore, we must move out of our own house. It's like living in your front yard — guarding hypervigilantly so that no one will ever come in.

The striving for power flows from the need to control. Achieving power is a direct attempt to compensate for the sense of being defective. When one has power over others, one becomes less vulnerable to being shamed. Power-seeking often becomes a total dedication and life task. In its most neurotic form it is an out-and-out addiction. Individuals spend all their energies planning, scheming, gaming and jockeying for position in order to climb the ladder of success. Power is inherent in certain roles or positions. Such roles are often sought as jobs to cover up shame.

"If I can just gut it out and be a doctor," one client told me, "then no one can ever look down on me again."

Parents, teachers, doctors, lawyers, preachers, rabbis, politicians are roles which carry inherent power.

Those in the power game always attempt to maximize power in relation to others. They often strive for inherent power jobs and secure their position by finding people who are less secure and weaker to work for them. To share power is precisely what such people are unable to do. Sharing power would mean equality — only by being over others can the power pro feel adequate and superior.

For the power addict, power is the way to insulate against any further shaming. One can, through having power over others, reverse the role of early childhood.

The power strategy often includes using power to actively seek revenge. Shame-based parents do to their children what their own parents did to them. They re-enact their own victimization on their own children — this time as offender. Investigation of the parent's own childhood reveals that they were also abandoned and abused, often in exactly the same way.

Rage

Rage is probably the most naturally occurring cover-up for shame. It comes close to being an actual primary ego defense. It would be, except for the fact that not all children rage. Some children will express rage when they are shamed; others will suppress it and sometimes turn it against themselves.

When rage is used as a defense, it becomes a characterological style. Rage protects in two ways: either by keeping others away or by transferring the shame to others. Persons who have held their rage in often become bitter and sarcastic. They are not pleasant to be around.

Although the rage, expressed as hostility or bitterness, was originally intended to protect the self against further experiences of shame, it becomes internalized also. Rage becomes a state of being, rather than a feeling among many other feelings.

Internalized rage foments a deep bitterness within the self. Bitterness destroys the self with its myopic vision and its quest for negativity. Rage often intensifies into hatred. If the person with internalized rage also acquires power, then it can result in violence, revenge, vindictiveness and criminality.

Arrogance

Arrogance is defined as offensively exaggerating one's own importance. The arrogant person alters his mood by means of his exaggeration. The victims of arrogance are those who are unequal in power, knowledge or experience. The victim feels one down and inadequate around the know-it-all, be-all, arrogant person. He believes he is inadequate because of his lack of knowledge, experience or power. Anyone who is on the arrogant person's same level simply sees him as arrogant.

Arrogance is a way for a person to cover up shame. After years of arrogance, the arrogant person is so out of touch, he truly doesn't know who he is. *This is one of the great tragedies of shame cover-ups: not only does the person hide from others, he also hides from himself.*

Criticism And Blame

Criticism and blame are perhaps the most common ways that shame is interpersonally transferred. If I feel put down and humiliated, I can reduce this feeling by criticizing and blaming someone else. As I go into detail about how he has failed, I get out of my shameful feeling (mood alter).

Criticism and blame are strategies of defense against the experience of toxic shame. They are effective mood alterers and become addictive over long periods of continued use. Children subject to criticism and blame are shamed to the core. Children have no way to decode their parents defensive behavior. Mom yelling that you never think of anyone but yourself, is interpreted as I am bad. Mom may be ashamed over the state of her life, marriage and house. Instead of saying, "I feel sad and frustrated over the state of things right now," she says, "You never think of anyone but yourself." While criticizing and blaming, Mom is relieved from her shame. But the child is deeply shamed.

Judgmentalism And Moralizing

Judgmentalness and moralizing are offshoots of perfectionism. Moralizing and judgementalness are ways to win a victory over the spiritual competition. Condemning others as bad or sinful is a way to feel righteous and one up. Such a feeling is a powerful mood alteration and can become highly addictive.

When one is using perfectionism, moralizing, and judgment to mood alter one's own shame, one is acting "shameless". The children who are the victims of perfectionism, judgment and moralizing have to bear their shameless caretaker's shame. This is not only emotionally abusive and soul murdering, *it is spiritually abusive,* since only God is perfect; God alone is shameless . . . *To act shameless is to play God.* Children of shameless parents are given a distorted foundation for experiencing God.

Contempt

In contempt one is intensely conscious of another person who is experienced as disgusting. In contempt, the self of the other is completely rejected.

Parents, teachers and moralizing preachers often act shameless in behaving contemptuously toward children, students and disciples. When a major caregiver or teacher, contempts another person under her tutelage, that person experiences himself as offensive and feels rejected in no uncertain terms.

The child learns to condemn self in introjecting the caretaker's voice and in identifying with the condemning caretaker. The child lacks any means of protection. So identification allows the child to feel protected. The child condemns others as he has been condemned.

Patronizing

To patronize is to support, protect or champion someone who is unequal in benefits, knowledge or power; but who has not asked for your support, protection or championing. It is a way to feel one-up on another person. Being patronizing leaves the other person feeling shame. The interpersonal transfer of shame through patronization is very subtle. On the surface you seem to be helping the other person through support and encouragement, yet in reality the helping doesn't really help. He feels ashamed. Patronizing is a cover-up for shame, and usually hides contempt and passive aggressive anger.

Caretaking And Helping

Strange as it seems, taking care of and helping another person often intensifies her shame. Caretaker is a common family system role. The Caretaker helper actually doesn't help the other person. Helpers are always helping themselves.

A person who feels flawed and defective feels powerless and helpless. Such a person can alter her feelings of defectiveness by helping and taking care of others. When she is caretaking others, she feels good about herself. So the *goal of the caretaker is the caretaking, not the good of the person being cared for.* The caretaking is an activity that distracts one from one's feelings of inadequacy. Distraction is a way to mood alter.

Caretaking and helping as defensive strategies against toxic shame lead to enabling or rescuing. A caretaking spouse of an alcoholic actually enables the alcoholic's disease thereby increasing his toxic shame. Parents often enable or rescue their children, doing for them what they could do for themselves. The children wind up feeling inadequate and defective. Rescuing or enabling is robbery. It robs the other person of a sense of achievement and power, thereby increasing toxic shame.

People-Pleasing And Being Nice

People-pleasing nice guys and sweethearts also act shameless and pass their shame on to others. In their book, *Creative Aggression*, Doctors George Bach and Herb Goldberg have outlined in detail the neurotic behavior of being a nice people-pleaser.

In many ways being "nice" is the official cultural cover-up for toxic shame. The nice guy is as American as motherhood and apple pie. The nice person hides behind a defensive facade of being a friendly well-liked person.

The goal of the nice person is his own image and not the other person. Being nice is primarily a way of manipulating people and situations. By doing so he avoids any real emotional contact and intimacy. By avoiding intimacy, he can insure that no one will see him as he truly is, shame-based, flawed and defective.

Bach and Goldberg sum up the price of being nice. It is self-destructive and indirectly shaming to others because it is hostile. The nice guy:

1. Tends to create an atmosphere wherein no one can give any honest feedback. This blocks his emotional growth.
2. Stifles the growth of others, since he never gives any honest feedback. This deprives others of a real person to assert against. Others feel guilt and shame for feeling angry at the nice guy. The other turns his aggression against himself, generating shame.
3. Nice behavior is unreal; it puts severe limitations on any relationship.

Creative Aggression

Envy

Perhaps Richard Sheridan was right when he observed, "There is no passion so strongly rooted in the human heart as envy." Dante named envy as one of the deadly sins. One classical writer wrote, "Envy is the pain of mind that successful men cause their neighbors."

The most common definition of envy is "discomfort at the excellence or good fortune of another". Such discomfort is frequently accompanied by some verbal expression of belittlement. However the expressions of envy can rage from out-and-out disparagement to subtle innuendo. The latter is what makes envy so mysterious.

Because of this talent for disguise, envy takes forms that are impossible to recognize. An envious person may conceal his envy both from others and himself.

I can remember hearing a public speaker that I have been compared to. I was truly impressed by the power and energy of his delivery and message. Later when recounting this to others, I heard myself say, "I really liked his power and energy . . . although I must admit I was surprised at how often he had to read from his notes." If you had asked me to take an oath pertaining to whether I was envious or not, I would have vowed that I was not envious and passed the oath.

But in fact, I was envious and my nit-picking detail was a way to take back all the positive things that I said. My envy made me oblivious to the content, as I focused on details like his reading from notes. Later when I got honest about this speaker, I thought that his manner was too dramatic and egocentric. What I disliked was his self-assertiveness. This is a common focus when envy comes in the form of disparagement or belittlement. Almost always when envy is disparaging, it is a projection of our own self-assertion.

I have had many people come up to me after giving a lecture and say, "That was a great lecture, but didn't you get your main ideas from such and such a place?" Such praise is really an assertion of the other person's knowledge. Such self-assertiveness is also an attempt at provoking envy in the envied one. But the envious deny self-assertiveness just as they deny envy.

Besides self-assertiveness, envy may disguise itself in admiration or greed. Apropos of admiration, I can remember feeling disgusted with myself as I grandiosely praised a person I actually envied. Upon analysis, I found myself saying almost the exact opposite of what I felt. This is envy's ultimate disguise, to pass itself off as its exact opposite.

As Leslie Farber has beautifully said,

> "True admiration, which, because it is free of conscious will, always has the option of silence. Envy's limitation of admiration clamors for public acknowledgment. The more stinging the envy, the more ardently must the envious one dramatize himself as an admirer whose passion . . . shames the more reticent responses of others."

The most childish form of envy is greed. When I envy someone, I begrudge her of some thing or some qualities she possesses: her wisdom, courage, charisma, etc. The envier magically believes that if he had that quality, he would be okay. Envy in the form of greed is exploited by modern advertising, which offers the posthypnotic suggestion that we are what we possess.

Ultimately self-assertion, admiration and greed are the disguises envy uses to cover up the core issue which is toxic shame. The apprehension of another's superiority forces a critical evaluation of self. To be toxically shame-based is to feel the excruciating depression of self. Another's excellence exacerbates the pain of the ruptured self. In order to avoid the pain of split self, the envy takes the form of self-assertive disparagement. Admiration, in the form of indiscriminating praise, can be more shaming to another than criticism.

As Farber says,

> "It may arouse his own envy toward the exalted image we impose on him and, in his awareness of the immense disparity between it and his own image of himself, remind him even more sharply of his limitations."

Envy as admiration and self-assertive belittlement of another's self-assertiveness are ways that toxic shame is interpersonally transferred. Envy as greed is based on the shame-induced belief that I can only be okay by means of something outside of me.

Compulsive/Addictive Behaviors And Reenactments

Compulsive/Addictive Behaviors

In *Bradshaw On: The Family*, I presented a range of compulsive/addictive behaviors which suggested that there were a lot more addicts than most people realize. We so often limit this area by over-focusing on alcohol and drug abuse. Pia Mellody has defined addiction as "any process used to avoid or take away intolerable reality". Because it takes away intolerable pain, it becomes our highest priority. It does so much for us that it takes time and energy from the other aspects of our life. It thus has life-damaging consequences.

To be shame-based is to be in intolerable pain. Physical pain is horrible, but there are moments of relief. There is hope of being cured. The inner rupture of shame and the "mourning" for your authentic self is chronic. It never goes away. There's no hope for a cure because you *are* defective. This is the way you are. You have no relationship with yourself or with anyone else. You are totally alone. You are in solitary confinement and chronic grief.

You need relief from this intolerable pain. You need something outside of you to take away your terrible feelings about yourself. You need something or someone to take away your inhuman loneliness. You need a mood-altering experience.

There are myriads of ways to mood alter. Any way of mood-altering pain is potentially addictive. If it takes away your gnawing discomfort, it will be your highest priority and your most important relationship. Whichever way you choose to mood alter will be the relationship that takes precedence over all else in your life. Just as with excruciating physical pain, you will do anything to stop it.

Ever had a throbbing toothache? You can't think of anything or anyone else. You become "tooth centered". If the doctor gives you a prescription for medicine to take away the pain, it will take precedence over spouse, work and family. Whatever mood alters our chronic pain will take precedence over everything else. This mood-altering relationship will have to be chronic since the pain is chronic. The chronicity will become life-damaging and pathological. You will do anything to keep mood altered. If someone tries to take this relationship away from you, you will perform mental gyrations to prove to them how much you need it. You will deny it's causing you any harmful consequences. You will believe it is good for you in spite of the fact that it is life-damaging (delusion).

In this way the mood alterers we use to take away our toxic shame become our addictions. If you're shame-based, you're going to be an addict — no way around it. Addictions form the outer layer of our defenses against toxic shame.

As Fossum and Mason have said, "One of the most clearly identifiable aspects of shame is addictive behavior."

The addiction hides the shame and enhances it and the shame fuels the addiction. Furthermore, addiction is always a family disease. We saw that clearly in Max's genogram.

Again Fossum and Mason write, "Addiction is the central organizing principle of the family system — maintaining the system as well as the shame . . . When we address addiction in families, we open the door to the families' shame."

Ingestive Addictions

Some mood-altering phenomena are more inherently addictive than others. This is why chemicals and food have been the focus of compulsive/ addictive behavior.

ALCOHOL AND OTHER DRUGS

Some chemicals have inherently addictive properties. A drug, like alcohol, which affects the electrical activity of the limbic system (the portion of the brain controlling emotional response), has powerful addictive qualities. Alcohol is also a behavioral stimulant since it lowers inhibition. Alcohol is a mind-altering chemical and seriously affects body chemistry and nutrition over long periods of usage. Clear and progressive stages of addiction have been observed and are now unanimously accepted by researchers in the field.

There is some discussion now of two types of alcoholism. One type seems to be the result of a natural genetic weakness and predisposition to alcohol intolerance. Another type seems to be acquired over long periods of chronic use. What all agree on is that children of alcoholics have from five to nine times greater chance of becoming alcoholic than children from non-alcoholic families.

In my own case, my paternal grandmother and my father both seem to have been genetic alcoholics. My dad was in trouble from his first drink. I also believe I'm a genetic alcoholic, i.e., I was in trouble from the first drink. I had my first alcoholic "blackout" at age 15. "Blackouts" are a form of brain amnesia. The memories associated with experiences are erased after a certain threshold of tolerance is reached. "Blackouts" are a powerful warning about genetic alcoholism.

The genetic data would seem to refute the position that toxic shame is the core of addiction. While I would never want to say that there has never been a case of purely genetic alcoholism, I would honestly have to say I've never seen one. I've been an active part of the recovering community for 22 years. I've counseled some 500 alcoholics and run the Palmer Drug Abuse Program in Los Angeles for four years, having been a consultant to that program for ten years prior to that. In all those years I've never seen anyone who did not have abandonment issues and internalized shame, along with their physical addiction. My guess is that the same is true for other depressant drugs, like tranquilizers and sleeping pills, likewise for stimulants, hallucinogens, nicotine and caffeine. I believe with Fossum and Mason that addiction is much more than one single identifiable "disease".

EATING DISORDERS

Eating disorders or food addictions are likewise a combination of genetic factors coupled with distorted emotional coping. Food addictions are clear syndromes of toxic shame. Clinicians usually divide eating disorders into four categories: obesity, anorexia nervosa, bulimia and what is referred to as the fat/thin disorder.

Food Addiction: Obesity

Figures range from 34 million, with 60% of women and 50% of men being overweight. Fossum and Mason define obesity as being 15 pounds overweight. Generally strong defensive rationalizations are used to "excuse" obese behavior and deny its life-damaging consequences. These include glandular disorders, heredity, aging, childbearing, lifestyles, necessary social eating and what I was often told, having big bones. There is no doubt that there is some genetic predisposition for obesity. No one seems to know

Figure 3.3. The Shame-Bound Control — Release Triggers

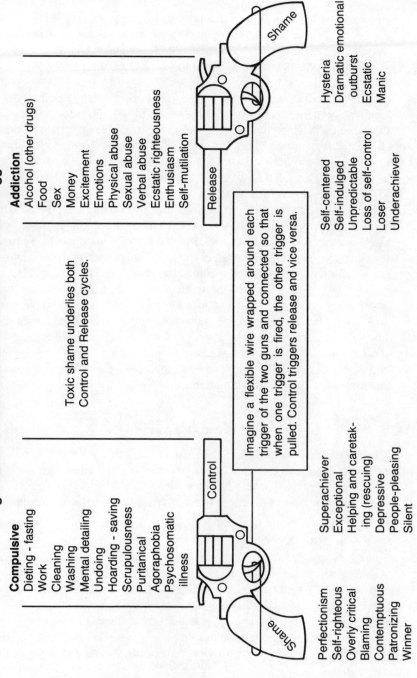

Compulsive
Dieting - fasting
Work
Cleaning
Washing
Mental detailing
Undoing
Hoarding - saving
Scrupulousness
Puritanical
Agoraphobia
Psychosomatic
    illness

Addiction
Alcohol (other drugs)
Food
Sex
Money
Excitement
Emotions
Physical abuse
Sexual abuse
Verbal abuse
Ecstatic righteousness
Enthusiasm
Self-mutilation

Toxic shame underlies both
Control and Release cycles.

Imagine a flexible wire wrapped around each trigger of the two guns and connected so that when one trigger is fired, the other trigger is pulled. Control triggers release and vice versa.

Control

Release

Shame

Shame

Perfectionism
Self-righteous
Overly critical
Blaming
Contemptuous
Patronizing
Winner

Superachiever
Exceptional
Helping and caretak-
    ing (rescuing)
Depressive
People-pleasing
Silent

Self-centered
Self-indulged
Unpredictable
Loss of self-control
Loser
Underachiever

Hysteria
Dramatic emotional
    outburst
Ecstatic
Manic

exactly what portion of the problem is genetic. My discussion will be limited to the emotional components of the problem.

Jane Middelton-Moz, a brilliant clinician in the Seattle area, tells of watching the origins of a possible eating addiction while sitting in an airport. A mother and father were having a verbal fight. Their 18-month-old child was lying on a seat next to them. They were paying no attention to the child. Each time the child made any noise, the mother thrust a juice bottle in her mouth. A person sat down next to the child and startled her. She began to cry in alarm. The mother looked in her purse and found another bottle filled with milk and thrust it into the child's mouth. The mom and dad were both 20 plus pounds overweight.

This child is going to see overeating modeled for her. She is also learning to repress emotional expression and to stuff her feelings with food. (*Children of Trauma: Rediscovering The Discarded Self*, Jane Middelton-Moz)

As least one part of the dynamics of obesity is the result of a self-indulging and abusing pattern of survival learned in a dysfunctional family. Obese people have been shame-bound in either their angry or sad feelings. They feel empty and lonely and eat to be full and filled (fulfilled). Anger manifests in the gut (a tight gut), and eating and being full take away the feeling of anger by deluding persons into believing that their tight gut is about being full, rather than about the anger that needs to be expressed. Obese people often act jolly and happy to cover up their fear of the potential shame if they expressed deep sorrow or anger.

For the most part diets are the greatest hoax ever perpetrated on a suffering group of people. Ninety-five percent of the people who diet gain the weight back within five years. Diets underscore one of the most paradoxical aspects of toxic shame. In dieting and losing weight, one has the sense of controlling and fixing the problem. As you saw earlier, control is one of the major strategies of cover-up for shame. All the layers of cover-up are attempts to control the outside so that the inside will not be exposed.

One of the landmarks for me in the naming of the demon I'm calling toxic shame was the outline of the control/release dynamics by Fossum and Mason in their book *Facing Shame*.

Figure 3.3 is an adaptation of their work. Control and release are natural polarities in human activity. You had to learn to hold on and let go as a child learning muscle balance. Later on you learned more sophisticated balance, as in dancing (some of us that is). In dancing you let go within a learned structure. At first you learned the individual dance steps. They were awkward and you did them with conscious control. Soon you forgot the instructions and just danced. The steps were now unconscious. The control and release fused together in an unconscious two-step or waltz.

When healthy shame is internalized, it becomes toxic and destroys all balance and boundaries. You become grandiose: either the best, or the "best-worst". With toxic shame, you are either more than human (superachieving) or less than human (underachieving). You are either extraordinary or you are a worm. It's all or nothing. You either have total control (compulsivity) or you have no control (addiction). They are interconnected and set each other up.

Fossum and Mason write,

> "When shame underlies the control and release it seems to intensify both sides of the tension . . . Shame makes the control dynamic more rigidly demanding and unforgiving and the release more dynamic and self-destructive. The more intensely one controls, the more one requires the balance of release and the more abusingly or self destructively one releases, the more intensely one requires control."

Diets follow this control and release cycle. An addiction is an addiction. The word means to give oneself up (from Latin *addicere*). To be addicted is to surrender oneself to something obsessively. The answer for addicts is not trying to control the addiction. The answer is to be aware of powerlessness and unmanageability and surrender. *Surrender means facing up to the fact that one can't control it. That's why it is an addiction.*

Fat/Thin Disorder

Many eating addictions are not visible. In the fat/thin disorder one obsesses on food constantly. The mental obsession is the mood alteration. It is really a mental distraction. By being in your mind and constantly thinking about eating or not eating, you can distract yourself from your feelings.

I've personally groped with this disorder for years. I go through cycles of exercise, good nutritional non-sugar diets and then (usually after months of control) I eat a donut or a piece of carrot cake. Usually I do this while traveling. It is then that my loneliness and vulnerability are most exposed. I usually reward myself for all the hard work I've done.

Once I eat the sweets, then the release phase starts. I start obsessing on what I've done. I've blown it now. I might as well eat some more. I'll binge just for today and start my control tomorrow. Ah! But tomorrow never comes! The sugar craves sugar. The mental obsessing keeps me thinking about sweets, and I'm off and running into the release cycle.

This cycle usually lasts *until I start developing breasts!* Then I know it's time to diet, exercise and give up sugar. Here, as in all compulsive/addictive behavior, there is no balance. It's all or nothing.

Anorexia Nervosa

The numbers of fasting, self-starving women grow steadily in our culture. Anorexia is certainly one of the most paradoxical and life-threatening of all the eating disorders. It is most dominant in affluent families with daughters ages 13 to 25. It is almost epidemic in some affluent private schools.

Anorexics most often come from affluent families which are dominated by perfectionism. Affluent families are often focused on self-image actualizing. Respectability and upper class have a very special look and image to keep up. The following patterns predominate: perfectionism; non-expression of feelings (no talk rule); a controlling, often tyrannical and rigid father; an obsessive mother, completely out of touch with her sadness and anger; a pseudo-intimate marriage with great pretense at looking good; great fear of being out of control in the whole family system; enmeshment and cross-generational alliances. These factors appear in various combinations.

The anorexic person takes control of the family with her starving and weight loss. She is a metaphor of what's wrong with the family. She is rigidly controlled, denies all feelings, is superachieving and is encrusted in a wall of pretense. She becomes the family system Service Bearer and Scapegoat. Mom and Dad become more intimate as their fears for her life intensify.

The addiction usually begins with feeding/fasting cycles and strong craving for sweets. It is often accompanied by excessive exercise and depression. The use of laxatives and forced vomiting usually accompany starvation as the disease progresses. There is intense mood alteration and altered states of consciousness accompanying the stages of starvation.

Anorexics dramatically underscore the refusal to be human which lies at the heart of toxic shame. This includes a disdain for, and denial of, their bodies. Such disdain extends to renouncing their instinctual and emotional life. Anorexics renounce their sexuality by literally refusing to develop the signs of genital womanhood (menstruation and breast development). They renounce their emotions by refusing to eat. For anorexics food seems to equal feelings. Since all their feelings are shame-bound, refusing to eat is a way to avoid feeling toxic shame.

There is also enmeshment and boundary confusion between the daughter and mother. The daughter is often carrying the mother's repressed anger and sadness about the father. This feels overwhelming since these are deeply repressed emotions (remember our hungry dogs). Therefore, to starve and avoid eating is a protection against feeling these overwhelming emotions.

Anorexia is complicated and I certainly don't believe the foregoing does it clinical justice. My wish is that you see this addictive disorder as rooted in the mood alteration of the family shame. Believing that you can live while refusing the nourishment of food is the ultimate rejection of one's humanity. It is an attempt at being more than human.

Bulimia

Anorexics often solve their starving problem through the binge/purge cycle of bulimia. Bulimia can also be developed without any preceding anorexic condition. It is not limited to females, since many males become bulimic out of their addiction to physical fitness. In order to keep their youthful bodies, many male "fitness addicts" begin vomiting.

Kaufman definitely sees bulimia and bulimarexia as well as anorexia as shame-based syndromes. He sees toxic shame as present in both the binging and the purging cycle. Following Tomkins he sees binging on food as a substitute for interpersonal needs which are shame-bound.

> "When one feels empty inside, hungry to feel a part of someone, desperate to be held close, craving to be wanted and admired — but these have become taboo through shame — one turns instead to food."

Food can never satisfy the longing and as the longing turns into shame, then one eats more to anesthetize the shame. The meta shame, the shame about eating in secret and binging, is a displacement of affect, a transforming of the shame about self into the shame about food. The same dynamic takes place in obesity.

In bulimia the binging cycle intensifies the shame which then triggers the purge cycle which adds self-disgust and self-contempt. Vomiting is a disgust reaction. A disgusting emotional situation often elicits the feeling of nausea. We say, "That makes me sick to my stomach" or "I can't stomach that" or "That's hard to swallow". Vomiting may consciously be a behavior to keep the weight down, but unconsciously bulimics resort to vomiting as a way to cleanse themselves of the shameful amount of food they just devoured. By vomiting one literally bathes in shame.

Tomkins describes bulimic vomiting as affect magnification. Magnifying something will bring it to its peak intensity which allows it to discharge. The vomiting intensifies humiliation and self-disgust. This brings the toxic shame to a peak and there is an exploding effect wherein one feels cleansed and purified.

Kaufman writes, "By magnifying feelings of humiliation in intensity and duration, they are finally spent, their fire burned out."

Many shame-based people seem to be in touch with their feelings because they express intense emotions. But as Cermak has pointed out, the emotional outbursts are a way to get over the feelings. This is the exact same thing as Tomkin's affect magnification. It's a masochistic strategy of reduction through intensification. Magnification can also go in just the opposite direction. Feelings can be intensified to the point of explosion, or they can be diminished to the point of numbness.

Feeling Addictions

There are other ways to mood alter without using chemicals or food. I have already described feeling rackets, whereby one undesirable feeling is replaced by a family-authorized feeling. Any emotion can be addictive. The most common addiction to an emotion is that form of intensified anger we call rage.

Rage is the only emotion that can't be controlled by shame. Actually the intensified anger we call rage is anger that has been shamed. Anger like sexuality is a preserving emotional energy. Anger is the *self*-preserving feeling. Our anger is an energy by which we protect ourselves. Our anger is our strength. When anger is shamed, it is a hungry dog that cannot be kept in the basement. Once our identity has become shame-based, we use our anger in an abortive way. When our shame is hooked, the shamed anger now becomes rage, breaks out of the basement to protect us, and does its job. Rage frightens those around us.

RAGE ADDICTION

When we are raging, we feel unified within — no longer split. We feel powerful. Everyone cowers in our presence. We no longer feel inadequate and defective. As long as we can get away with it, our rage becomes our mood alterer of choice. We become rage addicts.

In the early days of my marriage I was a rageaholic. In my toxic shame, I had no boundaries. My primary mood alteration was being a nice guy caretaker Daddy. I let my children run all over my boundaries. I gave up my needs for their needs, with the exception of my need to appear as wonderful and good guy Dad. Finally something would happen, the last straw. I'd start raging, yelling and screaming at my wife or children.

As I write this now it astounds me that at the time I didn't see this behavior as abusive and dysfunctional. It was the only way I knew to protect my boundaries, my shame-based inner core. My raging began to stop when my wife and children stood up to me. This is not always a stopper. Be careful of it if the offender is also physically violent. But it stopped me. I've been working on rage for ten years now. I can assure you it can be changed.

I've seen families demolished by rage. In one family I worked with the mother was a rageaholic. She tyrannized her family and used her rage to manipulate and get her own way. The father had allied in a Surrogate Spouse relationship with the oldest daughter. The daughter, victimized by this emotional incest, had never had a healthy sexual relationship. She was 29 years old. There were many other dysfunctions in this family. They looked structurally the same as an alcoholic family. All the dysfunctional family system roles were present.

Addiction To Sadness, Fear, Excitement, Religious Righteousness And Joy

Any emotion can be addictive. Most of us can think of a person who is addicted to melancholy or to anxiety and fear. I frequently encounter what I call "joy" addicts. They wear a frozen smile on their faces. They are never angry. They laugh at inappropriate times and only speak about happy and joyful things.

The feeling of righteousness is the core mood alteration among religious addicts. Religious addiction is a massive problem in our society. It may be the most pernicious of all addictions because it's so hard for a person to break his delusion and denial. How can anything be wrong with loving God and giving your life for good works and service to mankind?

As I write, I think of the daughter of a minister I counseled. She was shame-based to the core. She thought of herself as the 'Whore of Babylon'. She had been abandoned by her shame-based, self-righteous minister father. He was so busy saving souls and being Mr. Wonderful, he had no time for her. I remember being at a conference years later and seeing this man and his obese wife. He was still pompous and passive aggressive. Such men are dangerous. They hide their shame with patronizing self-righteousness, and transfer it to their children and disciples.

If you're anger phobic, i.e., terrified of your own anger, then you can be sad all the time. Your sadness will mood alter your rage.

If you come from a dysfunctional family and you never knew what to expect, you may have come to believe that life is one unexpected excitement after another. You may have learned to constantly seek out new and unexpected things in order to create excitement (addiction to excitement).

Addiction To Shame

Shame-based people are always addicted to their toxic shame. It is the source and wellspring of all their thoughts and behavior. Everything is organized around preventing exposure. You can't ever give up your mask and defenses against exposure. Toxic shame is far worse than the hungry dogs in the basement. It's like a herd of charging rhinos — a school of hungry man-eating sharks. You cannot let your guard down for one second.

Addiction To Guilt

You can also be addicted to toxic guilt. Toxic guilt says you have no right to be unique — to be the very one you are. To stay in toxic guilt forces you into constantly taking self-inventory. *Life is a problem to be solved, rather than a mystery to be lived.* Toxic guilt keeps you endlessly working on yourself and analyzing every event and transaction. There is never a time for rest because there is always more you need to do. Guilt puts you in your head a lot. Guilt is also a way to feel powerful when you are really powerless. "I've made my mother mad" or "I'm responsible for her sickness" are statements of grandiosity.

Thought Addictions

Thoughts and mental activity are also potentially addictive. Thought processes are part of every addiction. Mental obsession, going over and over something, is a part of the addictive cycle. It is also addictive in itself. I mentioned earlier the ego defense called "isolation of affect". By focusing on a recurring thought you can avoid painful feelings. You can also avoid feelings by ruminating, turning thoughts over and over in your head. You can be addicted to abstract thinking.

One of my degrees is in philosophy. I spent years of my life studying the great philosophers. In itself this is not harmful. For me, the reading and teaching of philosophy was a way out of my feelings. When I was reading the *Summa Theologiae* of Thomas Aquinas or Emmanuel Kant's *Critique of Pure Reason* or Wittgenstein's treatise on logical positivism, I could completely mood alter my toxic shame.

Intellectualizing is often a way to avoid internal states which are shame-bound. One's very way of intellectualizing can be addictive. Generalizing and universalizing keep one in categories so broad and abstract that there's no contact with concrete specific sensory-based reality. Abstract generalizing is a marvelous way to mood alter.

DETAILING

Detailing is another thought process which mood alters. Many obsessive/compulsive types use this form of mental activity.

An example comes to mind from my client file. I once had a person whose presenting problem was that people found her boring. I asked her to tell me about it. What follows is an adapted version of her report. She said,

"Well, when I started to come to this appointment, I wanted to wear my blue silk dress. But I forgot that I sent it to the cleaners. I'm very disappointed with our cleaners. They used to do such good work and have such good prices. They've actually ruined two of my son Bobby's good jackets. Although it's hard to get Bobby to take care of his clothes. He's just like his dad. They like to be comfortable and both of them are sloppy. I don't mind that as long

as they pick up in the kitchen. That is my one bug-a-boo, keeping the kitchen clean. Cause I spend so much time there. This morning my husband left the top off the yellow corn meal. He likes stone-ground corn meal but Bobby likes that old Weingarten corn meal . . . you know you used to get . . ."

If I haven't lost you, I will if I go on. After 15 minutes, I was starting to doze off. I was bored!!! I stopped her and gently began to point out her obsession for detail. She was a detail addict.

I learned in the course of our time together that her father was absolutely crazy. He had kept her home at gunpoint until she was 32 years old. She had grown up in West Texas in a small town where her dad was the Sheriff. He could get away with anything. He was violent and verbally abusive. His classic line to her was, "Women should keep their mouths closed and their legs open."

My client was a victim of physical, emotional and sexual violence. When she got away from him, she never stopped talking. But her talking and detailing was a way to avoid her excruciating shame and loneliness.

Mental obsessing is a common element in all co-dependent relationships. Obsessing on one's alcoholic spouse or lover or children or parents, is a way to stay in your head and out of your feelings. Relationships can be tremendously addictive. People go from one bad relationship to another or stay in one that is destructive and life-damaging. The feeling and experience of *love* is a powerful mood alterer and can be an addiction.

Activity Addictions

Another form of mood alteration is through behavior or activity. I've already described the ritual and magical behavior that constitutes the ego defense of undoing. Certain obsessive/compulsive ritualized behaviors have the goal of taking one away from one's fears of certain shameful desires, feelings or impulses.

The more common forms of activities which mood alter are working, buying, hoarding, sexing, reading, gambling, exercising, watching sports, watching TV, having and taking care of pets. No one of these activities is an addiction if it has no life-damaging consequences. But all of these activities can be full-fledged and life-damaging addictions. Each is a way to get so involved in an activity that one is mood altered by doing the activity.

Work addiction is a serious addiction. The work addict, who spends thousands of hours at work, can avoid painful feelings of loneliness and depression. I know of an experimental retreat that was done with ten CEOs of companies. These people were asked to avoid anything during a four-day week-end which would take them out of their feelings. They were not to read, drink, smoke, watch TV, talk about business, use the telephone, exercise, etc. By the third afternoon, this troop of dynamic, high-rolling superachievers were all depressed. They were in touch with their emptiness and loneliness. In many cases their children were in serious trouble with drugs or the law. Their children were often carrying their loneliness and pain.

The same dynamic is true for the other activity addictions. They are all ways to cover up the loneliness and pain nestled in the underbelly of toxic shame. The toxic shame is the villain, the black hole sucking up their life, driving them to more and more accomplishments.

Will Addiction

The human will loses its cooperative relationship with the intellect because of the contaminations resulting from the shame-bound emotions.

The intellectual operations of perception, judgment and reasoning are crucial to the will in its choicemaking duties. Perception, judgment and reasoning allow the will to see the available alternatives when making choices. As one's emotional energy is frozen and shame-bound, the intellect is seriously biased and impaired. The will loses its power to envision alternatives; the will loses its eyes, as it were. Without eyes the will is blind. It no longer has resource data from which to make choices. Without resource data, the will has no content outside of itself. With only itself as content, *the will can only will itself.* This affects *a pathological relationship to one's own will.* Such a relationship is "mood-altering".

In moments of self-willed impulsiveness, one no longer feels split or self-ruptured. In those moments one feels self-connected, powerful and whole. As Leslie Farber points out, "The will becomes a self." This willing for the sake of willing leads to life-damaging willfulness. To be willful is to be full of will. This willfulness leads to self-centeredness, control madness, dramatic extremes and to willing what cannot be willed (unreality). Willfulness has 'no boundaries'.

Such willfulness is the core of all addictions. All addicts are ultimately addicted to their own wills. In AA this is expressed as "I want what I want when I want it". It is also referred to as "self-will run riot".

Addiction to one's own will is the way that toxic shame causes spiritual bankruptcy. This is why spiritual healing is necessary when it comes to healing the syndromes of toxic shame.

One may wonder after an exposition like this whether everyone isn't an addict. Stanton Peele called addiction, "Mankind's great unifying experience." But if everyone is an addictive/compulsive and everything is addictive, then the word addiction loses all meaning. My answer is that what we have to understand is the toxic shame that fuels the addictive/

compulsive behavior. Not everyone uses substances, feelings, thought processes, activities addictively, because not everyone is shame-based. However, when I look at our culture, schools, religions and our family systems, my belief is that massive numbers do carry toxic shame. Who knows the percentage and what does it really matter?

Maybe obsessing on such a detail is a way to avoid our shame. In *Bradshaw On: The Family* I quoted Satir and Wegscheider-Cruse who estimate that 96% of families are dysfunctional. Such a statistic is not intended to be accurate. (How could anyone know?) It is intended to get our attention; to grab us at the level of surprise or even horror. The statistics I gave earlier on the extent of addiction do seem to be fairly accurate. They are the kind of stats that if we had them for polio or smallpox, we would call it an epidemic. The Black Plague was Mickey Mouse compared to our addiction stats.

Reenactments

Another way toxic shame is covered up is through a paradoxical phenomena called reenactment or "acting out". Examples of such behavior are: Repeatedly entering into destructive and shaming relationships which repeat early abusive trauma; some criminal behavior; doing to your children what was done to you as a child and "panic attacks".

In order to grasp these types of behavior, it's important to review the nature of human emotions. E-motions are energy in motion. *They are the energy that moves us — our human fuel.* Our emotions are also like the red light oil gauge on our car signaling us about a need, a loss or a satiation. Our anger is our strength; our fear is our discernment; our sadness is our healing feeling; our guilt is our conscience-former; our shame signals our essential limitation and is the source of our spirituality.

When our emotions are shamed, they are repressed. Repression involves tensing muscles and shallow breathing. One set of muscles is mobilized to block the energy of the emotion we're ashamed to feel. Sadness is commonly converted into a false smile (reactive formation).

I have often smiled when I felt sad. Once the energy is blocked, we no longer feel it. However, it is still a form of energy. It is dynamic. I already gave you the example of how repressed anger intensifies. How anger is like Virignia Satir's example of the hungry dogs in the basement. In that example, the anger explodes because it cannot be repressed anymore. In reenactment, the emotional energy is "acted out". The behavior which set up the shaming event.is repeated with surrogates who reenact the original shaming scene.

REENACTING VICTIMIZATION

Incest victims often continue to reenact their earlier sexual violation in one relationship after the other. In being violated such a person is used and then abandoned. The abuse is often translated into the message that sex is the only way I'm desirable or worthwhile. I have to be sexy and sexual or else I'm nothing.

Leander was 30 years old. She had already established herself as a businesswoman. She had her own ad agency. Her husband wanted her to quit her job to have children. He was verbally shaming to her and threatening to destroy her business. She hated her husband who demanded oral sex four times a week. Leander was having an affair. When I talked to her husband, I determined quickly that he was an offender. He talked about her like she was an object. He told me he didn't care what she did as long as she took care of his sexual needs four times a week and gave him a baby.

Leander's affair was with a well-known womanizer. Over the course of the therapy, she had the baby, gave up her career and had several more affairs. She finally divorced her husband and continued to have one affair after another. Each time she chose a high-rolling, wealthy male with a history of womanizing (a Level I Sex Addict). Each time she was showered with gifts, used sexually and abandoned. And each time she was reenacting the sexual abuse she had experienced from her alcoholic father.

From age 5½ until age 10 she had frequently performed fellatio on her father. She was his favorite; he showered her with gifts. He gave her the only love she got in her childhood. Leander was extremely seductive. She wore clothes that made a man immediately look at her sexually. She came to see that her seduction was a way to act out her shame. It was a way to gain control over the situation she had previously been powerless in. It was a way to try to work out her unresolved grief.

In every single case when the man left her, she could have the feelings she was forbidden to have in the original situation. She would fear abandonment; she would cry; she would be angry and rage at him. Each reenactment was an abortive attempt for her to act out the feelings she had dissociated from. In her normal dissociated state, she was out of touch with these feelings. She often felt like she was crazy. In acting out the feelings, she felt less crazy.

This repetition compulsion, this urge to repeat, is referred to by Alice Miller as the "logic of absurdity". It happens in less cruel ways to many people.

I know a man who grew up with an emotionally unavailable mother. He was married four times, all to emotionally unavailable women. The best selling book, *Women Who Love Too Much,* by Robin Norwood, describes variation after variation of this reenactment.

CRIMINAL BEHAVIOR

In Alice Miller's work on criminality, she presents the case of Jurgen Bartsch, who was a child murderer. He murdered four boys between 1962-1966. With some minor deviations his modus operandi was the same. After he enticed a boy into a former air-raid shelter not far from his home, he beat the child into submission, tied him up with butcher's string, manipulated his genitals while he masturbated, killed the child by strangulation or by blows, cut open the body, emptied out the stomach and buried the remains. Bartsch testified that he would achieve sexual climax while he was cutting up the corpses.

Reading the details of this account are truly nauseating. One feels outrage and horror. Surely such a person has criminal genes, or some pathological sexual drive and perversion. However, as Alice Miller outlines the details of Jurgen's childhood, one cannot easily dismiss her thesis that there is a direct relationship between Jurgen's criminality and his early childhood. She writes,

> "Every crime contains a concealed story which can be deciphered from the way the misdeed is enacted and from its specific details."

The specific details are beyond the scope of my purpose here. Bartsch was an orphan, who was adopted after his parents made a careful search to find the right child. Jurgen would spend hours, ritually looking for the right boy to murder. Jurgen was beaten as a baby. On many occasions he was found black and blue and bruised. He was beaten in the same room that his father, who was a butcher, was cutting up carcasses. Later, as the beatings continued he was locked in an old underground cellar. This went on for six years. He was forbidden to play with any other children. He was sexually abused by his mother. She bathed him until he was 12 years old, manipulating his genitals. At the age of eight he was seduced by his 13-year-old cousin, and later at 13, by his teacher. His crimes bore the imprint of each detail of his life. He "acted out" his pent-up hatred on the little boys who all wore lederhosen (just as Jurgen had done as a child). He butchered them with a butcher knife as he'd seen his father do while Jurgen was being whipped, beaten and abused by his mother. She would often give him wet kisses on the mouth after she had beaten him. Jurgen also kissed his victims.

Jurgen was a victim who became an offender. He awakens our outrage and horror. "But," as Alice Miller writes, "the horror should be directed at the first murder, which was committed in secret and gone unpunished."

When a child is being violated, his normal reaction is to cry out in anger and pain. The anger is forbidden because it would bring more punishment. The expression of pain is also forbidden. The child represses these feelings, identifies with the aggressor and represses the memory of the trauma. Later disconnected from the original cause and the original feelings of anger, helplessness, confusion and pain, he acts out these powerful feelings against others in criminal behavior, or against himself in drug addiction, prostitution, psychic disorders and suicide.

Again Alice Miller writes, "Someone who was not allowed to be aware of what was being done has no way of telling about it except to repeat it."

In a lesser way all parents who have not worked through their own childhood trauma will reenact it on their own children.

A slogan we use in our Center For Recovering Families is, "You either pass it back or you pass it on."

PANIC ATTACKS

The compulsion to repeat shows us clearly that people's behavior makes sense, no matter how dehumanizing and bizarre. Every detail of behavior that is ungrieved and unfinished will be acted out. This can be seen clearly in panic attacks.

Jane Middelton-Moz calls panic attacks the window of the frightened child's. She gives two examples of panic attacks as reenactments of earlier childhood trauma.

In one instance a woman would go into "panic" if she increased her heartbeat to a certain point while she was jogging. She had tried many things to control these states of panic. Middelton-Moz was able to help her find the unresolved childhood trauma that was at the bottom of her panic attack.

As a young child growing up in a poor district she and her brother played a lot in the streets. This was risky because there were gangs who roamed these areas. On one tragic occasion she and her brother were chased by one of these gangs. She remembered running fast and escaping her attackers but her brother did not make it and was killed.

The past terror and unresolved grief was being triggered and reenacted whenever she reached the same speed in jogging as she reached in her runaway escape. (*Children of Trauma: Rediscovering The Discarded Self,* Jane Middelton-Moz)

Middelton-Moz tells of another woman who had been divorced by three husbands because of her insane jealousy. She was normally not a jealous type of person. Her attacks would occur around occasions of separation. If one of her husbands had to go back to work at night or go on a business trip, she would go into a panic attack, sweating, trembling and being terrified. When the husband would return home, she would go into a hysterical tirade. She would have great remorse the next day, realizing how completely over-reactive her behavior was. As Middelton-Moz helped her connect the panicky feeling with an episode from the past, she found the early scene that her panic reenacted.

She had lived in a town in the midwest. Her father worked across the river which separated this town from another town. One day when he left for work, a storm came up. It flooded the river and her father could not return for a week. Her mother was an alcoholic, and her father was Mom's supplier! At six years old this child and her four-year-old brother went through delirium tremors with their mother for a week! Each time one of her husbands started to leave her, this unresolved trauma was triggered. (*After The Tears,* Jane Middelton-Moz, Lorie Dwinell)

From this section, you can see the extent and life-damaging power of internalized shame. Its power lies in its darkness and secrecy. By exposing this demon, we can begin to set up educational programs and therapeutic approaches to prevent shame from being internalized in families.

We can find creative ways our society, schools and religions can counteract the dynamics of shame-based identity formation. Such a search is crucial. It moves us in the direction of *actually* finding a way to *prevent* addiction.

PART II
THE
SOLUTION

Introduction —
The Externalization Process

To heal our toxic shame we must come out of hiding. As long as our shame is hidden, there is nothing we can do about it. In order to change our toxic shame we must embrace it. There is an old therapeutic adage which states, "The only way out is through."

Embracing our shame involves pain. Pain is what we try to avoid. In fact, most of our neurotic behavior is due to the avoidance of legitimate pain. We try to find an easier way. This is perfectly reasonable. However, as Scott Peck has said, "The tendency to avoid emotional suffering . . . is the primary basis for all human mental illness."

In the case of shame, the more we avoid it, the worse it gets. We cannot change our "internalized" shame until we "externalize" it. Doing the shame-reduction work is simple but difficult. It mainly involves what I call methods of *externalization*. Externalization methods include the following:

1. Coming out of hiding by social contact, which means honestly sharing our feelings with significant others.
2. Seeing ourselves mirrored and echoed in the eyes of at least one non-shaming person who is part of our new family of affiliation. Re-establishing an "interpersonal bridge".
3. Working a 12-Step program.
4. Doing shame-reduction work by "legitimizing" our abandonment trauma. We do this by writing and talking about it. (Debriefing). Writing especially helps to externalize the past shaming experiences.

115

We can then externalize our feelings about the abandonment. We can express them, clarify them and connect with them.

5. Externalizing our lost inner child. We do this by making conscious contact with the vulnerable child part of ourselves.
6. Learning to recognize various split-off parts of ourselves. As we make these parts conscious (externalize them), we can embrace and integrate them.
7. Making new decisions to accept all parts of ourselves with unconditional positive regard. Learning to say, "I love myself for . . ." Learning to externalize our needs and wants by becoming more self-assertive.
8. Externalizing old unconscious memories from the past, which form collages of shame scenes, and learning how to heal them.
9. Doing exercises to externalize our self-image and change it.
10. Externalizing the voices in our heads. These voices keep our shame spirals in operation. Doing exercises to stop our shaming voices and learning to replace them with new nurturing and positive voices.
11. Learning to be aware of certain interpersonal situations most likely to trigger shame spirals.
12. Learning how to deal with critical and shaming people by practicing assertive techniques and by creating an externalization shame anchor.
13. Learning how to handle our mistakes, and having the courage to be imperfect.
14. Finally, learning through prayer and meditation to create an inner place of silence wherein we are centered and grounded in a personally valued Higher Power.

All of these externalization methods have been adapted from the major schools of therapy. Most all therapies attempt to make that which is covert and unconscious, overt and conscious.

These techniques can only be mastered by practice. You must *do* them, and reinforce them by doing them again. *They will work if you will work.*

A Parable:
The Prisoner In The Dark Cave

There once was a man who was sentenced to die. He was blindfolded and put in a pitch dark cave. The cave was 100 yards by 100 yards. He was told that there was a way out of the cave, and if he could find it, he was a free man.

After a rock was secured at the entrance to the cave, the prisoner was allowed to take his blindfold off and roam freely in the darkness. He was to be fed only bread and water for the first 30 days and nothing thereafter. The bread and water were lowered from a small hole in the roof at the south end of the cave. The ceiling was about 18 feet high. The opening was about one foot in diameter. The prisoner could see a faint light up above, but no light came into the cave.

As the prisoner roamed and crawled around the cave, he bumped into rocks. Some were rather large. He thought that if he could build a mound of rocks and dirt that was high enough, he could reach the opening and enlarge it enough to crawl through and escape. Since he was 5'9", and his reach was another two feet, the mound had to be at least 10 feet high.

So the prisoner spent his waking hours picking up rocks and digging up dirt. At the end of two weeks, he had built a mound of about six feet. He thought that if he could duplicate that in the next two weeks, he could make it before his food ran out. But as he had already used most of the rocks in the cave, he had to dig harder and harder. He had to do the digging with his bare hands. After a month had passed, the mound was 9½ feet high and he could

117

almost reach the opening if he jumped. He was almost exhausted and extremely weak.

One day just as he thought he could touch the opening, he fell. He was simply too weak to get up, and in two days he died. His captors came to get his body. They rolled away the huge rock that covered the entrance. As the light flooded into the cave, it illuminated an opening in the wall of the cave about three feet in circumference.

The opening was the opening to a tunnel which led to the other side of the mountain. This was the passage to freedom the prisoner had been told about. It was in the south wall directly under the opening in the ceiling. All the prisoner would have had to do was crawl about 200 feet and he would have found freedom. He had so completely focused on the opening of light that it never occurred to him to look for freedom in the darkness. Liberation was there all the time right next to the mound he was building, but *it was in the darkness.*

4

Coming Out
Of Hiding And Isolation

"One Man Is No Man"
Ancient proverb

"We Are As Sick As Our Secrets"
Program Saying

The excruciating loneliness fostered by toxic shame is dehumanizing. As a person isolates more and more, he loses the benefit of human feedback. He loses the mirroring eyes of others. Erik Erikson has demonstrated clearly that identity formation is always a social process. He defines identity as "an inner sense of sameness and continuity which is matched by the mirroring eyes of at least one significant other". Remember, it was the contaminated mirroring by our significant relationships that fostered our toxic shame.

In order to be healed we must come out of isolation and hiding. This means finding a group of significant others that we are willing to trust. This is tough for shame-based people.

I remember frantically looking for a hypnotist when I was told I needed to go to a 12-Step program. It terrified me to think of being exposed to the scrutiny of other people.

Shame becomes toxic because of premature exposure. We are exposed either unexpectedly or before we are ready to be exposed. We feel helpless and powerless. No wonder then that we fear the *scrutinizing eyes of others.* However the *only* way out of toxic shame is to embrace the shame . . . we *must* come out of hiding.

Finding A Social Network

The best way to come out of hiding is to find a nonshaming intimate social network. The operative word here is *intimate.* We have to get on a core gut level because shame is core gut level stuff. Toxic shame masks our deepest secrets about ourselves; it embodies our belief that we are essentially defective. We feel so awful, we dare not look at it ourselves, much less tell anyone. The only way we can find out that we were wrong about ourselves is to risk exposing ourselves to someone else's scrutiny. When we trust someone else and experience their love and acceptance, we begin to change our beliefs about ourselves. We learn that we are not bad; we learn that we are lovable and acceptable.

True love heals and affects spiritual growth. If we do not grow because of someone else's love, it's generally because it is a counterfeit form of love. True love is unconditional positive regard. Unconditional positive regard allows us to be whole and accept all the parts of ourselves. To be whole we must reunite all the shamed and split-off aspects of ourselves.

Virginia Satir speaks of the five freedoms which accrue when one is loved unconditionally. These freedoms involve our basic powers. These are the power to perceive; the power to love (choose and want); the power to emote; the power to think and express and the power to envision or imagine.

When we are whole and fully self-accepting, we have the freedom to see and hear what we see and hear, rather than what we should or should not see and hear; the freedom to think and express what we think, rather than what we should or should not think or express; the freedom to feel what we feel, rather than what we should or should not feel; the freedom to love (choose and want) what we want, rather than what we should or should not love (choose or want); the freedom to imagine what we imagine, rather than what we should or should not imagine. When we are loved unconditionally, i.e., accepted just as we are, we can then accept ourselves just as we are.

Self-acceptance overcomes the self-rupture of toxic shame. Self-acceptance is equivalent to personal power. Self-acceptance means we are unified; all our energy is centered and flows outward. Nonself-acceptance creates an inner rupture and inner warfare. In nonself-acceptance we are beside ourselves. We use our energy to hide our self from our self. As a result, we have less energy left for directly coping with the world. Self-acceptance makes us fully functional.

Since it was personal relationships that set up our toxic shame, we need personal relationships to heal our shame. This is crucial. We *must risk reaching out and looking for nonshaming relationships if we are to heal our shame. There is no other way.* Once we are in dialogue and community, we will have further repair work to do. But we can't even begin that work until affiliative relationships are established.

12-Step groups have had far and away the greatest success in healing shame-based people. Remember, that toxic shame is the root of all addiction. 12-Step groups literally were born out of the courage of two people risking coming out of hiding. One alcoholic person (Bill W.) turned to another alcoholic person (Dr. Bob) and they told each other how bad they really felt about themselves. I join with Scott Peck in seeing this dialogue coming out of hiding as one of the most important events of this century. 12-Step programs are always worked in the context of a group. The group comes first.

Because we are essentially social, we cannot live happily and fulfilled without a social context. Another way to say this is that we humans need to love and be loved. We need and need to be needed. These are basic. We cannot be fully human unless these needs are met.

To heal our shame, we have to risk joining a group. We have to be willing to expose our essential selves. AA teaches alcoholics to introduce themselves at meetings with — "My name is X. I am an alcoholic." Identification of the core problem is essential to recovery. It verbally states one's acceptance of powerlessness and unmanageability. It is indicative that one has embraced one's shame by surrendering.

This surrendering is the core of the spiritual paradox that tells us we can only win by losing. This is hard for any hard-driving American. As with most spiritual laws — it is paradoxical. To find one's life, one must lose one's life. This is a literal truism for shame-based people. We must give up our delusional false selves and ego defenses to find the vital and precious core of ourselves. In our neurotic shame lies our vulnerable and sensitive self. We must embrace the darkness to find the light. Hidden in the dark reservoirs of our toxic shame lives our true self.

There is no life without death, no sound without silence, no holding without letting go and no light without darkness. Nothing is more spectacular than watching an ocean roaring onto a pure white sand beach at high noon on a sunny day. We can look out on the horizon and be enthralled. Yet if this were all there was, we would miss out on something spectacular. We would miss ever seeing a heaven filled with twinkling lights on a starry night. Because to see the stars, we need darkness.

The parable at the beginning of this section is an adaptation of a story told in therapeutic circles. The story is typical of human endeavor. We always look for our solutions in the obvious places. It never occurs to us that there is a way out in the darkness. This is the only way with toxic shame.

Guidelines For Selecting A Group

There are certainly other intimate groups other than 12-Step groups. One might find such a group in one's church or synagogue. Many have found non-shaming intimacy in psychotherapy groups or with individual therapists. Several things are crucial to look for:

- The group must be nonjudgmental and nonshaming. As you risk being in a group, be aware that you can leave it if you feel unduly exposed or shamed.
- The group should be democratic and noncontrolling. Each person can be real in such a group. Each person can be different. This is what no shame-based person has ever experienced.
- The leader of the group needs to model healthy shame. This means he or she will not act "shameless" (controlling, perfectionistic, rigid). The leader will be a person who is walking the walk as he talks the talk. The leader will be like a guide who has gone ahead of the group and can tell them what's in the next valley.
- Most shame-based people need a group that touches and hugs in a respectful way. What this means is that no one just comes up and hugs you. Boundaries need to be respected. If it's too threatening to be physical, you can abstain without any explanation. You will be taught to ask if you want a hug and you will be asked before someone hugs you.
- For many of us, we were shamed in our preverbal life by not being touched and held. Before language, the interpersonal bridge is built through touch and holding. Infants who are not touched and interacted with die of a kind of stroke deprivation called "mirasmus". Marcel Geber, who went on a UN commission to study protein deficiency in Ugandi children, found their infants and toddlers to be the most advanced children in the world. It seems that the infants were continually held by the Ugandi mothers. Their bodies were in continuous contact and movement.
- Finally the group must allow for the full expression of all emotions. This is the most crucial dynamic of the group process. One must be able to express feelings openly and freely. Shame is the master emotion because it binds all the other emotions except anger. But as we have

seen, it turns anger into rage and feels overwhelming. Freely expressing our feelings is like thawing out. As shame binds all our feelings, we become psychologically numb. Getting in touch with our feelings is difficult at first. You may feel overwhelmed at times. You may also feel confused. Sometimes we feel worse before we feel better. The important thing is to feel. Our feelings are who we are at any given moment. When we are numb to our emotions, we lose contact with who we are.

My advice is to go slowly in learning to identify and express emotions. This is what we never learned because of the "no talk" rules and poor modeling in our dysfunctional families. Emotions will feel strange and scary at first. We will fear being overwhelmed by our emotions. Some will have to do more intense work with their emotions. *In the beginning just to be feeling our emotions is shame-reducing.* Sharing emotions with another is to be vulnerable. It is to externalize and come out of hiding.

Robert Firestone in his book *The Fantasy Bond* stated that we are not functioning in a fully human fashion until we have true friendship and are living in community. The opposite is to live our life in a fantasy bonded illusion of connectedness. All addictions and enmeshed relationships are fantasy bonds, creating a life of inner withdrawal and self-indulging gratification. Such a life is inhuman. Only in the life of dialogue and community can we truly live and grow.

5

12 Steps For Transforming Toxic Shame Into Healthy Shame

*"Perhaps the fastest-growing spiritual movement in
the world today is the 12-Step Program."*

Keith Miller
Sin: Overcoming The Ultimate Addiction

I owe my life to the participation in a 12-Step program. Therefore, it is impossible for me to be unbiased concerning its ability to heal the shame that binds you. No one argues with the fact that 12-Step programs have a proven record for dealing with addictions. I will describe my understanding of how the steps work to heal toxic shame. Since toxic shame is the fuel of addiction, I think it will be apparent why 12-Step programs do so well with toxic shame.

Step 1 states, "We admitted we were powerless over (whatever the addiction) and our lives had become unmanageable." This step acknowledges the most powerful aspect of any shame syndrome — its functional autonomy.

An old adage about alcohol illustrates this.

Man takes a drink.
Drink takes a drink.
Drink takes a man.

Alcohol has its own inherent chemical properties of addiction. Toxic shame is an internalized state, which once internalized, functions the same way as a chemical. The second sentence of the First Step underscores the functional autonomy of the compulsive/addictive disorders. In my own compulsivity support group, we often speak of toxic shame as an entity in itself with its own power.

In the face of it, we are powerless. All recovering persons come to a turning point in their lives precipitated by the pain of their addiction.

Pain made me aware of my powerlessness and unmanageability. The only way out of the pain was to come out of hiding — I had to surrender. I had to embrace my shame and pain. In my own case the pain had become so agonizing that I was ready to go to any length. Embracing my pain led me to expose my pain, sorrow, loneliness and shame. This is what I had feared doing for so long. As I confessed how bad I really felt, I saw acceptance and love in the mirroring eyes of others. As they accepted me, I began to feel like I mattered. I began to accept myself. *The interpersonal bridge was being repaired.*

The Second Step asks us to reach out to something greater than ourselves. It states, "We came to believe that a Power greater than ourselves could restore us to sanity."

I've spoken earlier of the Genesis account of the Fall. Genesis suggests that four relationships were broken by Adam's toxic shame: the relationship with God; the relationship with self; the relationship with brother and neighbor (Cain kills Abel); and the relationship with the world (nature). The 12 Steps restore those relationships. The Second Step starts by accepting something greater than ourselves. The Third Step says, "We made a decision to turn our will and our lives over to the care of God as we understand God." While there is conscious mention of God as the Higher Power, it is left to each person to decide how he understands God.

I remember a guy who made an oak tree his Higher Power. I remember his running into a meeting one day and saying, "They just cut down my Higher Power!" 12-Step groups do not impose any notion of God onto their members.

The restoration of a bond of mutuality with God has enormous power to heal toxic shame. Toxic shame is a disorder of the will. As disabled, the will becomes grandiose. As a shame-based persons gets entrenched in their cover-ups, they become more 'shameless'. They hide their mistakes with perfectionism, control, blame, criticism, contempt, etc. . . . To be shameless is to play God. This grandiose God-playing is a spiritual disaster. It is spiritual bankruptcy. Steps 2 and 3 reconnect the essential bond of dependence in man with a Higher Power.

Shame-based people also do not believe that *they have the right to depend on anyone*. This is a consequence of the violated dependency needs which were ruptured through the abandonment trauma. To turn one's will and life over to God is to restore a right relationship of dependence. To go to meetings and trust other people is to risk depending again.

Healthy shame is the permission to be human. To be human is to be essentially limited. It is to be finite, needy and prone to mistakes. Healthy shame lets us know that we are not God and that we truly need help.

The first three steps restore the proper relationship between ourselves and the source of life. Admitting powerlessness and unmanageability, having faith that a greater power can restore us to sanity, making a decision to give up control and submit our will to the care of God as we understand God restores us to our healthy shame and grounds us in our fundamental humanness. The shamelessness and grandiose control madness and God-playing are given up.

With Steps 1 through 3 we rejoin the human race; we accept our need for community and the essential limitations of our human reality. Scott Peck once defined emotional illness as avoiding reality at any cost and mental health as accepting reality at any cost. Steps 1 through 3 restore us to reality.

Step 4 states, "We made a searching and fearless moral inventory of ourselves."

In this step we begin the restoration of our relationship with ourselves and our neighbor (the second and third broken relationships suggested in the story of the Fall). Our shame defenses kept us from showing ourselves to anyone else. More tragically these defenses kept us from looking at ourselves. As I've suggested, to be shame-based is not to be in one's self. It is to make oneself an object of alienation.

By restoring a relationship of trust with God as we understand God, and by sharing honestly and vulnerably with our group, we come to have a relationship with ourselves. Being mirrored by the loving and honest eyes of others allows us to accept ourselves. The process of self-reunion takes place slowly and gradually.

I didn't write a Fourth-Step inventory for two years after entering a 12-Step program. This is not right or wrong. The taking of the steps is an individual process.

Most 12-Step programs strongly advise that new members get a sponsor. A sponsor is a person who hopefully has some quality emotional health and is working a healthy program. A sponsor serves as a model and offers firm guidance in helping one work her own program.

In my own case, writing my inventory needed to wait while I struggled with the first three steps. My intellectual cover-ups were very strong. I had been a professor and had degrees in psychology, philosophy and theology.

I had taught all these subjects at the university level. I struggled with the simplicity of the 12-Step program. Part of my facade was the act of being a sensitive intellectual who saw the awesome complexity of human suffering and pain. I drank because I bore so much awareness of human suffering. As I suggested elsewhere, this was all hogwash. It was a subtle way to maintain my delusion and denial.

One of the significant lessons in my life was given me by Abraham Low, the founder of Recovery, Inc. He said that intellectualizing about our problems is complex but easy, while doing something about them is simple but difficult. Shame-based intellectuals love to discuss and complexify.

When I did write out my Fourth Step, I found that much of my wrongdoing resulted from my drinking and my fear. I came to see that the core of all my problems was my sense of inadequacy. At that time I didn't understand shame. Toxic shame was the inner core of all my wrong-doing.

I realized in taking my inventory that my core problem was moral rather than immoral. In fact, my first attempts at inventory were long lists of immoral behavior. What my sponsor helped me see was that I was involved in continuous moral failure. In my grandiosity I was either superhuman (exceptional) or inhuman (wormlike). I was never first human. I tried to be more than human (shameless). I wound up less than human (shame-full).

To be in the arena of morality one must have a fully functioning will, the choice-making faculty. Moral acts require judgment, reason and ability to choose. I think shame-based people are premoral because of the disabled will. It's hard to attribute full human power to a false self. This does not mean that real wrongs have not been done to others by shame-based people. They certainly were in my case. In this step I took responsibility for the wrongs I had done, but I got in touch with the core problem. Some years later I took this step again in the light of my understanding of toxic shame. Then I clearly saw that 95 percent of the shame I bore was a result of my abandonment issues. Once I could see this, I was willing to do something about it. For a shame-based person to see that most of the shame he bears is "carried shame" is hope-giving. Remember, internalized shame feels hopeless and irremedial. If we are essentially a mistake, flawed and defective then there's nothing we can do about it.

The Fourth Step helps one focus on one's wrong-doings in such a way as to open the possibility of remedy. In Step 4 one begins a process of transforming toxic shame into healthy shame, which developmentally is the foundation for healthy guilt.

Steps 5, 6 and 7 state, "We admitted to God, to ourselves and to another human being the exact nature of our wrongs" (Step 5). "We were entirely ready to have God remove all these defects of character" (Step 6). "Humbly asked God to remove our shortcomings" (Step 7). I group these together because each is a part of the process of surrendering the controlling and grandiose will. Each is a step of owning responsibility for our life and giving up control. Each is an act of hope.

In Step 5, we come out of hiding. We talk about our shame. We tell God and another human being about our shame (the exact nature of our wrongs). In my opinion, this step not only helps one focus on one's wrongs as mistakes and sometimes awful acts; but helps one see that these acts flowed from character defects which were used as defenses for shame. By telling another human being, we embrace the pain of our shame, and expose ourselves to the eyes of another. We let another see how bad we have really felt about ourselves. There is no pretense or cover-up.

Step 6 is an act of faith and hope. We feel good enough about ourselves to believe that God will remove these defects of character. At least we are willing to ask and believe that we do have the right to depend on someone or something greater than ourselves. Grandiose control and God-playing are over. We need God's help. We need help and we know it and we ask for it. The presumption in asking for the removal of these defects is the belief that we are worthy of their being removed.

In Step 7 we humbly ask God to remove our shortcomings. To humbly ask is to be restored to our healthy shame. We know we have failed. We are human and we've made mistakes (like all humans). But we also believe we can be helped. We can change and grow. We can learn from our pain and misfortune.

With this step I was restored to my healthy shame. Out of this healthy shame, I felt my guilt. Guilt is the emotion which forms our conscience. To be shameless is to have no conscience. Our conscience tells us that we have failed. We have transgressed our own values. The emotion of guilt moves us to change. A *guilty person fears punishment and wants to make amends. A shame-based person wants to be punished.* As I connected with my guilt and my conscience I was moved to make amends.

Step 5, 6 and 7 restore us to ourselves. We accept ourselves enough to be willing to talk about our wrongs. We have enough hope about ourselves that we can ask our higher power for help. We are ready to be responsible, to remedy our wrongs, to move on and grow.

Steps 8 and 9 are the remedial steps. They state, "We made a list of all the persons we had harmed, and became willing to make amends to them" (step 8). "We made direct amends to such people wherever possible; except when to do so would injure them or others" (step 9).

Now we turn to the third broken relationship outlined in the story of the Fall, our relationship with other people. Perhaps the greatest wound a shame-based person carries is the inability to be intimate in a relationship. This inability flows directly out of the fundamental dishonesty at the core of toxic shame. To be a false self, always hiding and filled with secrets, precludes any possibility of honesty in relationships. And as I've suggested elsewhere, shame-based people always seek out relationships with shame-based people. Hockey players don't usually hang out with professional bridge players. They don't know each other's rules. We tend to find those who play by the same rules.

Secretiveness, dishonesty and game-playing were certainly the substance of my relational history. I hurt women by treating them like objects and playthings that I could lie to, love and leave.

I remember being told how cruel I was in relation to women by members of my 12-Step group. They had told me not to date women in the program. This is a guideline in most 12-Step groups. It's not an absolute rule and many good relationships have come from meeting someone in a 12-Step group. But there is grave danger because of the shame base. Usually several years of recovery are suggested before 12-Step members start coupling.

I immediately started dating women in the program. And as I was a fully dysfunctional adult child of an alcoholic, I always picked women who were very sick. I usually pitied them and could feel powerful and strong as they immediately enmeshed with me. Then as the burden of their desperate dependence became more and more painful, I'd let them down easy. This was also very dishonest and cruel. A gentle cut makes a stinking wound. When I was confronted with my cruelty and passive aggressive rage toward women, I was totally incensed! It took me years to see how I was reenacting my anger toward my own mother in very devastating passive aggressive ways. My hero, good guy, ex-seminarian role always confused me. After years of playing these roles, I could pass a lie detector concerning them.

There were also the victims of my patronizing and enabling behaviors. There were the students who had to carry my shame as I hid under the black robes of perfectionism, holiness and sanctity. My brother especially bore the fruits of my patronizing holiness. I was a rigid seminarian during the time I studied to be a priest. In the early days of my training I would sometimes kneel for six hours trying not to move a muscle. I was internally extremely judgmental and that was passed on to my neighbors and family.

During my drunken episodes, I raged and became violent. I destroyed property and violated people's boundaries and their rights. Being moved to take action to remedy the wrongs done, is the purpose of guilt. Guilt is the "conscience former" and it moves us to repair our damages, to move on and to grow.

Steps 10, 11 and 12 are the steps which help us maintain these restored relationships. Step 10 says, "We continued to take personal inventory and when we were wrong, promptly admitted it." Step 11 says, "We sought through prayer and meditation to improve our conscious contact with God, as we understand God, praying only for knowledge of God's will for us and the power to carry that out." Step 12 says, "Having had a spiritual awakening as a result of these steps, we tried to carry this message to others, and to practice these principles in all our affairs."

Step 11 continues and deepens our bond of mutuality with God. It promotes a relationship of conscious contact. This is a true relationship, We've come full circle, starting from the broken and abandoning source relationships that set us up to internalize our shame, and ending with a friendship with God as we understand God.

Step 10 is the maintenance step for our relationship with ourself. It keeps us in touch with our healthy shame, the emotion that tells us we can and will make mistakes. By continually being in touch with our fundamental humanness and our essential limitations, we can accept ourselves. To acknowledge our mistakes is to embrace and express our vulnerability and our finitude. Such a consciousness keeps tab on our tendency to become grandiose and shameless.

Step 12 announces that a spiritual awakening is the goal and product of the 12 Steps. It underscores the fact that toxic shame and all its cover-ups end in spiritual bankruptcy. Toxic shame is soul murder. Because of it we become other-ated human doings, without an inner life and without inner peace. Shame-based people long for true inner silence and solitude.

Silence and solitude are the marks of spiritual maturity. They lead to peace and bliss. The spiritual life is an inner life. It cannot be attained on the outside. The spiritual life is its own reward and seeks nothing beyond itself. Once we achieve inner peace and conscious contact, we want to overflow. It is the mark of truth and love to move toward goodness and transcendence.

The ancient philosophers called goodness, truth, beauty and love the transcendental properties of Being.

Step 12 moves us to carry the message to our brothers and sisters who are still hidden behind the masks of toxic shame. This step calls us to practice the spiritual principles of rigorous honesty and service toward others in all our affairs. It asks us to put our bodies where our mouths are, to practice what we preach and to walk the walk as we talk the talk. It asks us to attract others by modeling a life of self-disciplined love and respect. As we model our restored relationships with God, self, our neighbors and the world, we can show others that there is a way out. There is hope.

CHAPTER

6

Liberating Your Lost Inner Child

Probably I, too, would have remained trapped by this compulsion to protect the parents . . . had I not come in contact with the Child Within Me, *who appeared late in my life, wanting to tell me her secret . . . now I was standing at an open door . . . filled with an adult's fear of the darkness . . . But I could not close the door and leave the child alone until my death . . . I made a decision that was to change my life profoundly . . . to put my trust in this nearly autistic being who had survived the isolation of decades.*

Alice Miller, Pictures of Childhood

Bradshaw On: The Family describes three distinct phases of my own shame reduction and externalization process. Figures 6.1 gives you a visual picture of these phases.

The first phase is the recovery phase. Through the group's support and mirroring love, I recovered my own sense of worth. I risked coming out of hiding and showing my shame-based self. As I saw myself reflected in the non-shaming eyes of others, I felt good about myself. I reconnected with myself. I was no longer completely alone and beside myself. The group and significant others restored my sense of having an interpersonal bond.

The recovery process is a first-order change. What that means is that I changed one kind of behavior for another kind of behavior. I quit drinking and isolating. I shared my experiences, strength and hope. I started talking and sharing my feelings. I started feeling my feelings again. I shifted my dependency to the new family I had discovered. There was still a dependent and shame-based child in me who made the new group into my parents' safeguarding security.

My shame was reduced but still active. This was evidenced by the fact that I was still compulsive and having trouble with intimacy. I chose women who I felt needed me, confusing love with pity. I set up rescuing-type relationships where others became dependent upon me and saw me as all-powerful. I started working 12-hour days, including Saturday. I smoked more and started eating lots of sugar. Indeed I had stopped a life-threatening disease called alcoholism; I had reduced my shame; I felt better about myself, but I was still compulsive and driven. I was not yet free.

In order to get free I had to do my family-of-origin work. I still needed to grow up and truly leave home.

Fritz Perls once said, "The goal of life is to move from environmental support to self-support." The goal of life is to achieve undependence. Undependence is grounded in a healthy sense of shame. We are responsible for our own lives.

Our source relationships were bathed in poor modeling and abandonment. This created our shame-based identity. Because we had no authentic self, we either clung to our caregivers in a fantasy bond or built walls around us where no one could hurt us. These earliest imprints colored all our subsequent relationships.

I once heard Werner Erhard, the founder of *est*, say, "Until we resolve our source relationships, we are never really in another relationship." Leaving home means breaking our source relationships. And since we carry much of our shame as a result of those relationships, leaving home is a powerful way of reducing shame.

Leaving Home

What does leaving home involve? How do we do it?

Leaving home is the second phase of the journey to wholeness. I call it the Uncovery Phase. What it involves is making contact with the hurt and lonely inner child who was abandoned long ago. This child is that part of us that houses our blocked emotional energy. This energy is especially blocked when we have experienced severe abuse. In order to reconnect

Figure 6.1.

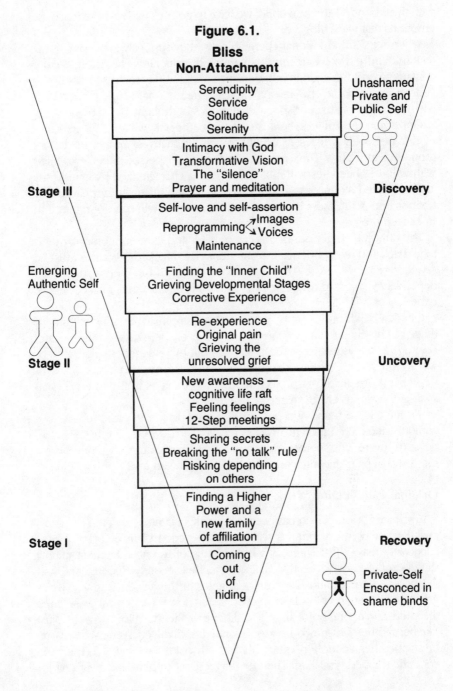

Bliss
Non-Attachment

| | Unashamed Private and Public Self |
| Serendipity
Service
Solitude
Serenity | |

Stage III — Intimacy with God / Transformative Vision / The "silence" / Prayer and meditation — **Discovery**

Self-love and self-assertion
Reprogramming ⟨Images / Voices⟩
Maintenance

Emerging Authentic Self — Finding the "Inner Child" / Grieving Developmental Stages / Corrective Experience

Stage II — Re-experience / Original pain / Grieving the unresolved grief — **Uncovery**

New awareness —
cognitive life raft
Feeling feelings
12-Step meetings

Sharing secrets
Breaking the "no talk" rule
Risking depending
on others

Stage I — Finding a Higher Power and a new family of affiliation — **Recovery**

Coming
out
of
hiding

Private-Self
Ensconced in
shame binds

with the wounded and hurt child, we have to go back and re-experience the emotions that were blocked.

When we form emotional energy blocks, they seriously affect our ability to think and reason. Our mind is narrowed in its range of vision. We are contaminated in our judgment, perception and ability to reason about the concrete personal events in our life. (Such emotional blockage does not seem to impair abstract or speculative modes of thought.)

Once our practical judgment is shut down, the will, which is the executor of our personality, loses its ability to see alternatives, and is no longer grounded in reality. The emotionally shut-down person literally is filled with will, i.e., becomes will-full. Willfulness is characterized by grandiosity and unbridled attempts to control, and is the ultimate disaster caused by toxic shame. Willfulness is playing God; it's the self-will run riot referred to in 12-Step programs.

The only way to get our brains out of hock and cure our compulsivity is to go back and re-experience the emotions. The blocked emotions must be re-experienced as they first occurred. The unmet and unresolved dependency needs must be re-educated with new lessons and corrective experiences.

Our lost childhood must be grieved. Our compulsivities are the result of those old blocked feelings (our unresolved grief) being acted out over and over again. We either work these feelings out by re-experiencing them, or we act them out in our compulsivities. We can also act them in as in depression or suicide, or project them onto others as in the interpersonal strategies for transferring shame.

We must leave home and become our own person in order to cure our compulsivities. Even though I was in recovery, I had never left home. I had never uncovered the sources and set-up for my toxic shame. I had never done the "original pain" feeling work. I had never dealt with my family of origin.

Original Pain Feeling Work

Any shame-based person has been in a family of trauma. Children of trauma experience too much stimulus within a short period of time to be able to adequately master that stimulus. All the forms of the abandonment trauma stimulate grief emotions in children and then simultaneously block their release.

I watched a man and his young daughter in the airport recently. I was getting a haircut and he was sitting two chairs down. He constantly scolded the child, and at one point angrily told her that she was a lot of trouble, just like her mother. I assumed he was separated or divorced. As he walked out, he slapped her a couple of times. It was really painful to watch. As the child cried, he slapped her again. Then he dragged her into the ice cream parlor and bought her ice cream to shut her up. This child is learning at a very early age that she's not wanted, that it's all her fault, that she's not a person, that her feelings don't count and that she's responsible for other people's feelings. I can't imagine where she could find an ally who would sit down with her and validate her sadness and allow her to grieve.

In a healthy respectful family a child's feelings are validated. Trauma is bound to happen somewhere along the way in any normal childhood.

As Alice Miller has repeatedly written, "It is not the traumas we suffer in childhood which make us emotionally ill but the inability to express the trauma."

When a child is abandoned through neglect, abuse or enmeshment, there is outrage over the hurt and pain. Children need their pain validated. They need to be shown how to discharge their feelings. They need time to do the discharge work and they need support. Each abandoned child would not become shame-based if there was a nourishing ally who could validate his pain and give him time to resolve it by doing his grief work.

I think of a healthy family I know in which the father was severely injured in a home accident. The six-year-old son was playing outside when he heard an explosion. He was shocked to find his father bleeding and apparently crippled. The father directed him to call an ambulance. A neighbor kept him until his mother returned from work. The boy was in a state of shock. The mother took him to a child play-therapist. He was afraid to go into the basement of the house (where the heater was). He was angry with his mother for not being home and his father for going away (being taken to the hospital).

Over the next months the boy worked his feelings out in the context of symbolic play. His mom and dad were both happy that he was able to express his anger toward them. (Shame-based parents would have guilted him for expressing anger.) They gave him support as he worked through his fears of going into the basement where the new heater was. They shared their own feelings with the child.

VALIDATION

In order for grief to be resolved several factors must be present. The first factor is validation. Our childhood abandonment trauma must be validated as real or it cannot be resolved. Perhaps the most damaging consequence of being shame based is that *we don't know how depressed and angry we really are.* We don't *actually feel* our unresolved grief. Our false self and ego defenses keep us from experiencing it. Paradoxically, the very defenses which allowed us to survive our childhood trauma have now become barriers to our growth. Fritz Perls once said, "Nothing changes 'til it becomes what it is." We must uncover our frozen grief.

I remember my paternal grandmother ridiculing me because I was in hysterics over my dad going out to get drunk. He had just had a fight with my mom and left the house in anger, vowing to get drunk. I began to cry and was soon out of control. I was ridiculed and shamed by this grandmother. I was told that I was a "big sissy" and to get hold of myself. I've never forgotten this experience. Years later I still carried the unresolved grief.

SUPPORT

The greatest tragedy of all of this is that we know grief can naturally be healed if we have support. Jane Middelton-Moz has said, "One of the things we know about grief resolution is that grief is one of the only problems in the world that will heal itself with support." (For a clear and concise discussion of unresolved grief read *After the Tears* by Jane Middelton-Moz and Lorie Dwinell.)

The reason people go into delayed grief is that there's nobody there to validate and support them. You cannot grieve alone. Millions of us adult children tried it. We went to sleep crying into our pillows or locked in the bathroom.

Delayed grief is the core of what is called the posttraumatic stress syndrome. As soldiers come back from the war, they have common symptoms of unreality: panic, being numbed-out psychically, easily startled, depersonalization, needing to control, nightmares and sleeping disorders. These same symptoms are common for children from dysfunctional families. They are the symptoms of unresolved grief.

"GRIEF WORK" FEELINGS

After validation and support one needs to experience the feelings that were not allowed. This must be done in a safe non-shaming context. The feelings involved in "grief work" are anger, remorse, hurt, depression, sadness and loneliness. Grief resolution is a kind of "psychic work" that has to be done. It varies in duration depending upon the intensity of the trauma. One needs enough time to finish this work. In dysfunctional families, there is never enough time.

At our Center for Recovering Families in Houston we do a four-and-one-half-day "original pain" workshop. We use the family system roles as a way for people to see how they lost their authentic selves and got stuck in a false self. As a person experiences how he got soul murdered, he begins his grieving. Often the therapist facilitator has to help him embrace the feelings because they are bound in shame. As a person connects with his true and authentic feelings, the shame is reduced. This work continues after the workshop. It may go on for a couple of years.

There are many other methods for doing this original pain work. It must be done if the grief is to be resolved and the re-enactments and compulsive lifestyle stopped.

Corrective Experience

The unresolved grief work is a re-experiencing process, liberating and integrating your lost inner child.

Since the neglect of our developmental dependency needs was a major source of toxic shame, it is important to reconnect. Each developmental stage was unique with its own special needs and dynamics. In infancy we needed a mirroring of unconditional love. We needed to hear words (nonverbal to an infant) like "I'm so glad you're here. Welcome to the world. Welcome to our family and home. I'm so glad you're a boy or girl. I want to be near you, to hold you and love you. Your needs are okay with me. I'll give you all the time you need to get your needs met." These affirmations are adapted from Pam Levin's book *Cycles Of Power,* soon to be published by Health Communications.

I like to set up small groups (six to eight people) and let one person sit in the center of the group. The person in the center directs the rest of the group as to how close he wants them to be. Some people want to be cradled and held. Some want only light touching. Some who were stroke-deprived don't feel safe enough for such closeness. Each person sets his own boundary.

After the group is set, we play lullaby music and each person in the group communicates one of the verbal affirmations while touching, stroking or just sitting near the subject.

Those who have been neglected will start sobbing when they hear the words they needed to hear, but did not hear. If a person was a Lost Child, he will often sob intensely. These words touch the hole in his soul.

After the affirmation the group discusses their experience. I always try to have a mixed group so that a person hears male and female voices. Often a person will report that he especially loved hearing the male voice or the female voice, since he never heard it as a child. Sometimes if a person has been abused by a parent, he will not trust the voice that corresponds to that parent's sex. The group sharing, hearing the affirmations, being touched and supported, offers a corrective kind of experience.

I also suggest other ways people might get their infancy needs met as those needs are recycled in new experiences. They usually need a friend who will give them physical support (lots of touching), and who will feed them (take them out to eat). They need lots of skin satisfaction. They may need a nice warm bath, or wrap up in a blanket. They may want to try a body massage.

We go on to toddler needs, repeating the group process. Since the toddler needs to separate, we let the person sit near but separate from everyone. I usually do an age-regression type meditation, in which I ask the one in the middle to experience himself as a toddler. I give affirmations like, "It's okay to wander and explore. It's okay to leave me and separate. I won't leave you. It's okay to test your limits. It's okay to be angry, to have a tantrum, to say no. It's okay for you to do it and to do it your way. I'll be here. You don't have to hurry. I'll give you all the time you need. It's okay to practice holding on and letting go. I won't leave you."

Again the group shares after each person has heard these affirmations several times. Frequently people express deep emotions as they share. Often they remember an episode of abandonment that was long forgotten. Some get into more unresolved grief-work.

We go through all the developmental stages through adolescence. Adolescence is important because many people went through painful abandonment and shaming incidents during adolescence. Remember Arnold?

I usually ask each person to write a letter to his parent(s) telling them the things he needed that he didn't get.

Wayne Kritsberg has them write the letter with the nondominant hand. I sometimes follow his lead. Writing with the nondominant hand helps create the feeling of being a child. Great emotion is discharged as the person reads his letter to the group. After the letter is read, I ask the group to give the person the affirmations that correspond to the unmet needs that he described in his letter to his parents.

Toward the close of the workshop I have each participant encounter his Lost Child. I cannot describe the power of this exercise. I have put it on several of my cassette tapes. There's no way to convey its power through the written word. I'll outline the meditation. You can put it on a tape recorder and listen to it. I recommend using Daniel Kobialka's "Going Home" as background music.

Meditation: Embracing Your Lost Inner Child

Sit in an upright position. Relax and focus on your breathing . . . Spend a few minutes becoming mindful of breathing . . . Be aware of the air as you breath it in and as you breath it out . . . Notice the difference in the air as it comes in and as it 'goes out. Focus on that difference . . . (one minute). Now imagine that you're walking down a long flight of stairs. Walk down slowly as I count down from ten. Ten . . . (ten seconds) Nine . . . (ten seconds) Eight . . . (ten seconds), etc. When you reach the bottom of the stairs, turn left and walk down a long corridor with doors on your right and doors on your left. Each door has a colored symbol on it . . . (one minute). As you look toward the end of the corridor there is a force field of light . . . Walk through it and go back through time to a street where you lived before you were seven-years-old. Walk down that street to the house you lived in. Look at the house. Notice the roof, the color of the house and the windows and doors . . . See a small child come out the front door . . . How is the child dressed? What color are the child's shoes? Walk over to the child . . . Tell him that you are from his future . . . Tell him that you know better than anyone what he has been through . . . His suffering, his abandonment . . . his shame . . . Tell him that of all the people he will ever know, you are the only one he will never lose. Now ask him if he is willing to go home with you? . . . If not, tell him you will visit him tomorrow. If he is willing to go with you, take him by the hand and start walking away . . . As you walk away see your mom and dad come out on the porch. Wave goodbye to them. Look over your shoulder as you continue walking away and see them getting smaller and smaller until they are completely gone . . . Turn the corner and see your Higher Power and your most cherished friends waiting for you. Embrace all your friends and allow your Higher Power to come into your heart . . . Now walk away and promise your child you will meet him for five minutes each day. Pick an exact time. Commit to that time. Hold your child in your hand and let him shrink to the size of your hand. Place him in your heart . . . Now walk to some beautiful outdoor place . . . Stand in the middle of that place and reflect on the experience you just had . . . Get a sense of communion within yourself, with your Higher Power and with all things . . . Now look up in the sky; see the purple white clouds form the number five . . . See the five become a four . . . and be aware of your feet and legs . . . See the four become a three . . . Feel the life in your stomach and in your arms. See the three become a two; feel the life in your hands, your face, your whole body. Know that you are about to be fully awake — able to do all things with your fully awake mind — see the two become a one and be fully awake, remembering this experience . . .

I encourage you to get an early photo of yourself. Preferably a photo of you before you were seven years old. I suggest you put it in your wallet or purse. Put the picture on your desk so that you can be reminded of this child that lives in you.

Much data supports that the child lives within us in a fully developed state. This child is the most vital and spontaneous part of us and needs to be integrated into our life.

Getting Child Developmental Needs Met As An Adult

We recycle our developmental needs all through our lives. Each time we start something new we trigger our infancy needs. After we are secure and trust our new environment, our toddler part wants to explore and experiment. Our own children trigger our needs as they go through their various developmental stages. We have an opportunity as an adult to care for ourself at each of these stages.

As adults we can create a context where we can get our needs met. I was neglected in fathering. I've created a group of men who serve as supporting friends who give me feedback. I've learned that as an adult I can make what I get from others serve my needs. Children never get enough. Adults learn as they mature to make what they get be enough. So I can take an event of sharing in my group and make fathering out of it. If one of the members is especially nurturing to me, I can allow that to be fathering. I can also let other events in my life serve as fathering and mothering. I can also learn as an adult to get the things I specifically need. I can be good to myself and treat myself with nurturing respect and kindness.

The Universal Quest For The Inner Child

It is important to note that the need to find the Inner Child is part of every human being's journey toward wholeness. No one had a perfect childhood. Everyone bears the unresolved unconscious issues of his family history.

The Inner Child journey is the hero's journey. Becoming a fully functioning person is a heroic task. There are trials and tribulations along the way. In Greek mythology, Oedipus kills his father, Orestes kills his mother. Leaving one's parents are obstacles one must encounter on one's hero's journey. To kill our parents is a symbolic way to describe leaving home and growing up.

To find our Inner Child is the first leap over the abyss of grief that threatens us all. But finding the Inner Child is just the beginning. Because of his isolation, neglect and neediness, this child is egocentric, weak and frightened. He must be disciplined in order to release his *tremendous spiritual power*.

7

Integrating
Your Disowned Parts

*"The course of our life is determined . . . by an array of selves
that live within each of us. These selves call out to us constantly
— in our dreams and fantasies, in our moods and maladies
and in a multitude of unpredictable and inexplicable reactions
to the world around us."*

Hal Stone and Sidra Winkelman

*"These transformations cannot be gained without cost. They
required my learning to live the rest of my days in the ambiguity
of knowing that of all that I am, I am also the opposite. I cannot
rid myself of my demons, without risking that my angels will flee
along with them."*

Sheldon Kopp

As a formerly shame-based person, I have to work hard at total self-acceptance. Part of the work of self-acceptance involves the integration of our shame-bound feelings, needs and wants. Most shame-based people feel ashamed when they need help; when they feel angry, sad, fearful or joyous; and when they are sexual or assertive. These essential parts of us have been split off.

143

We try to act like we are not needy. We pretend we don't feel what we feel. I think of all the times I've said I feel fine when I was sad or hurting. We either numb out our sexuality and act very puritanical, or we use sexuality to avoid all other feelings and needs. In all cases we are cut off from vital parts of ourselves. These disowned parts appear most commonly in our dreams and in our projections. This is especially true of our sexuality and natural instincts.

Here are some examples:

- A man dreams he's in a classroom. A group of women are undressing him. One of them touches him sexually and he's fully aroused.
- I dream a wild animal is chasing me.
- I dream a black-hooded burglar is trying to break into my home.
- A woman dreams that she's driving along and Black Muslim men are leering at her.

Each dream represents instinctual energy that has been disowned. Dreams are a wonderful way to get in touch with those disowned parts of ourselves. These parts are trying to get our attention. The disowned part of self is an energy — an emotion or desire or need, that has been shamed every time it emerged. These energy patterns are repressed but not destroyed. They are alive in our unconscious.

Jung called these disowned aspects of ourselves our shadow side. Without integrating our shadow, we cannot be whole.

The Voice Dialogue Work Of
Hal Stone And Sidra Winkelman

In their book, *Embracing Our Selves,* Hal Stone and Sidra Winkelman have developed a powerful approach for overcoming the self-alienation that results from toxic shame. Their work is based on the premise that our personality is constituted by an array of selves that live within each of us. These selves are the result of the self-splitting that happens naturally in the process of growing up. Since our caretakers are imperfect, no one of them could have accepted us with perfect unconditional love. Each in his own way put conditions of worth on us and measured us according to his map of the world. In so doing they naturally rejected the parts of us that did not measure up to their way of viewing things. These parts were split off and over a long childhood become somewhat autonomous.

Each split-off part became a little self. These selves call out to us constantly. They are "manifested in our dreams and fantasies, in our moods and maladies, and in a multitude of unpredictable and inexplicable reactions to the experiences of our lives". These inner selves are experienced as inner voices. The more we can become conscious of these inner voices, the greater is our range of freedom. While everyone has these voices, shame-based people have them in spades, so they have greater need than others to integrate their many selves.

As forms of energy, the disowned parts of us exert considerable influence on us. Shame-based people tend to be exhausted a lot of the time. They spend a lot of energy holding on to their false self-masks and hiding their disowned parts. I have compared it to holding a beachball under water. Virginia Satir compares it to keeping guard over hungry dogs. The repressed parts exert lots of pressure by forcing us to keep their opposites going.

While we tend to be repelled by our disowned selves, they also hold a certain fascination for us. The underlying premise of Stone and Winkelman's work *is that all of our parts are okay.* Nothing could be more affirming and less shaming. Every aspect of every person is crucial for wholeness and completeness. There is no law which says that one part is better than another part. Our consciousness with its many selves needs to operate on principles of social equality and democracy.

Voice dialogue work requires lots of commitment and practice. I can only give you a bare outline of its rich structure.

Voice dialogue posits consciousness as a process, rather than an entity. Consciousness is not something we strive to achieve; it is a process that must be lived out. It is an evolutionary process continually changing, fluctuating from one moment to the next.

There are three distinct levels of consciousness: (1) Awareness, (2) Experience of the sub-personalities or inner voices, and (3) Ego. The awareness level is a witnessing capacity that does not judge what it witnesses. The sub-personality is the experience of a part of self-manifesting as an energy pattern. This could be physical, emotional, mental or spiritual.

A raging man, for example, could be experiencing his shame-bound anger which he has repressed for years. His rage overwhelms him so that he is identified with his anger. There is no awareness. Once he becomes aware that he is raging, he can experience his anger. Then he can use his Ego to become more aware of his experience. The Ego is the executive of the psyche — the choicemaker. The Ego receives its information from the awareness level and from the experience of the different energy patterns. As Stone and Winkelman say, "As one moves forward in the consciousness process, the Ego becomes a more aware Ego. As a more aware Ego, it is in position to make real choices."

This is the needed direction for healing the shame that binds us. The grandiose and disabled will I spoke of earlier is mired in the shame-bound and disowned emotions. As we developed our false perfectionistic, controlling, people-pleasing parts, our Ego lost its authentic executive power and became identified with what Hal and Sidra call the Protector/ Controller.

The Protector/Controller often appears as the Perfectionistic, Inner Critic or the Pleaser sub-personalities. Once the Ego is identified with these sub-personalities, it loses its ability to have real choice.

This identification of the Ego with the Perfectionistic, Protector/ Controller, Inner Critic or Pleaser is what I called the False Self. The crucial issue is to distinguish each of these sub-personalities from Ego, which is the authentic Executor of Personality.

Once we've identified with any one individual sub-personality, we've lost any real choice. The goal is to get in touch with the energy we are experiencing and see it as one of many energy patterns that must be integrated in order to affect conscious choice leading to integrated action. All sub-personalities are parts of us — to be valued and accepted. All of us is okay. We just need to be aware that the voice we hear is only a voice. Awakening the consciousness process and expanding it is the desired goal.

Stone and Winkelman sum up voice dialogue as follows:

1. **Exploration of Sub-Personalities or Energy Systems**

   The sub-personalities are also referred to as Voices. Voice Dialogue directly engages the sub-personalities in a dialogue without the interference of a critical, embarrassed or repressive Protector/ Controller. Each sub-personality is addressed directly with full recognition of both its individual importance and its role as only a part of the total personality. Each sub-personality experiences life differently. The frightened Inner Child for example is experienced as a queasy feeling.

   These sub-personalities can also be viewed from the outside. As energy patterns they can be seen in bodily manifestations. I have seen executives in my Inner Child workshop become transformed before my eyes: furrowed brow, taut cheeks and jaw, narrowed lips can become a wide-eyed, grinning and relaxed child.

2. **Clarification of Ego**

   Voice Dialogue separates the Ego from the Controller/Protector and the entourage of sub-personalities that work with this dominant energy pattern. *Remember control is one of the hiding places for shame-based people.* Developing the Protector/Controlling sub-personality is universal for all people. It was developed to take care of the vulnerable child. In shame-based people the Protector/Controller is rigidly identified with Ego. The Protector/Controller energy pattern is the Boss. The Boss works with other sub-personalities like the Pusher, the

Critic, the Perfectionist, Power Brokers and Pleasers. Any of these sub-personalities can exist separately or they can be part of a general Protector/Controller pattern. This will vary from one person to the next.

When any one sub-personality begins to take over the function of Ego, the facilitator will point out this takeover. He will ask the subject to move to another physical space and will engage this sub-personality directly in dialogue. In this way the Ego becomes more and more differentiated, i.e., becomes a more aware Ego.

What it means is that we begin to be aware of all the hiding places of shame. The Protector/Controller, the Critic, the Perfectionist, are what I've called the masks of the false self. They are a false self in the sense that the Ego is identified with them. To see that these parts or sub-personalities were frozen in order to survive the shame we've internalized is to realize that these parts are not who we essentially are. We make no judgment that they are bad parts. They are simply parts, not the whole of us.

3. Enhancement of Awareness

The most crucial part of Voice Dialogue is Awareness. The context of voice dialogue provides a physical space for each sub-personality, the Ego who coordinates and executes for Awareness. The physical space of awareness is separate from the other two. It is a point where one can witness and review all that is going on in a nonjudgmental way. Awareness is not about decisions or action. Nothing is to be changed. Awareness is the still point where everything is noted and accepted. In awareness one clearly observes the drama played out by the sub-personalities in relation to the Ego.

One cannot do Voice Dialogue alone. In the beginning, one needs a facilitator. Actually it is a mutual process and a joint venture. The facilitator and the subject cooperate in the search for the sub-personalities and in the attempt to understand their functions. As one becomes more adept at facilitation, his sensitivity to changing energy patterns is more highly developed. This means that his awareness is in a constant state of expansion.

(Anyone finding this work interesting can contact Doctors Stone and Winkelman, P.O. Box 604, Albion, California 95410-0604. The book *Embracing Our Selves* can be ordered from the same address.)

What you can do for yourself is the following exercise. I have adapted it from the work of Hal Stone and Sidra Winkelman. I call the exercise "Making peace with all your villagers". This title was suggested by the Reverend Mike Falls, the Episcopal Chaplain at Stephen F. Austin College in Nacogdoches, Texas.

MAKING PEACE WITH ALL YOUR VILLAGERS

1. Think of people you dislike. Rank order them according to the intensity of your feelings. The number one person being the most reprehensible and the most worthy of contempt. Write a line or two under each person specifically outlining the character and moral defects that repel you.
2. Read over each name on your list. Pause and reflect on the reprehensible aspects of that person. Be aware of your own feelings as you do this. Which one trait brings out your feeling of righteousness and goodness most intensely?
3. Reduce the people to their one most reprehensible character trait. For example on my list:

   a. Joe Slunk — Grandiose egomaniac
   b. Gwenella Farboduster — Aggressive and rude
   c. Maximillian Quartz — Hypocrite (Pretends to help people; does it for the money.)
   d. Farquahr Evenhouser — Uses Christian facade to cover-up phoniness
   e. Rothghar Pieopia — A wimp; has no mind of his own

4. Each of these personality traits represent one of your disowned parts — an energy pattern that you do not want to integrate into your life under any circumstances. You have now externalized a personality trait that you disown.
5. Every disowned part has an opposite energy with which your Protector/Controller is identified. It takes lots of energy to keep this part disowned. This explains the intense energy we feel about our enemies. Hal Stone compares this energy to a dam that has been built to stop the flow of this energy. Behind the dam there is an accumulation of dirty water and all kinds of debris. It is important to integrate this energy and use it more creatively.

   Ask yourself this question about each person on your list. How is this person my teacher? What can I learn by listening to this person? This person whom you feel averse toward can help you look at the parts of you that you are overidentified with.

   On my list Joe helps me to see that I'm overidentified with being humble. In my case it is really more like appearing humble. Gwenella helps me to see that I'm overidentified with people-pleasing. Maximillian helps me see that I'm overidentified with being a total helper without wanting anything in return. Such helping is inhuman. It's a product of toxic shame trying to be more than human. Farquahr helps me see that I'm overidentified with having to be a perfect Christian (which at times keeps me from being one at all) and Rothgahr helps me to see that I'm overidentified with my "be strong" driver. Being strong is a way I try to be more than human — refusing to accept normal human weakness. This is the way I reject my healthy shame.

6. As you go through your list — talk to the disowned part directly. Ask it what it thinks. Ask it how it would change your life if you owned it. Let this part talk to you. Listen to what it has to say. See the world through its perspective. Feel any new energy that it brings you. It's bound to be a source of new ideas. Maybe it can offer new solutions to old problems. "After all," Sidra Winkelman writes, "its views have never been available before."

You may be surprised at the new energy you receive from this exercise. You are bringing a part of you out of hiding and secrecy. You are turning your shadow into light. You do not have to become the disowned self. That would be doing the same thing you did before — identifying with one part to the exclusion of another. In this exercise you learn to speak to and listen to a shamed and disowned part of you. By so doing, you free up an energy that has been bound in shame.

The Parts Party

The Work Of Virginia Satir

Perhaps no one has done more pioneering work in healing toxic shame than Virginia Satir. I remember the first time I saw her work with a family. Her validation and nurturing of each person was something to behold. As she performed her mighty mirroring, I could see each person accept herself a little better. As that happened, the family moved closer together. The work was so beautiful, I actually wept while watching her work.

In her book, *Your Many Faces,* Virginia presents the core theory of a technique that is used by therapists all over the country. It is commonly called the Parts Party. I've seen this exercise adapted in various ways by different schools of therapy. In what follows I will give you my own variation of this very powerful exercise. My belief is that this work is best done with a group of people. It has more impact. I would especially recommend the work done by Joe Cruse and Sharon Wegscheider-Cruse.

The Parts Party Meditation

Exercise — Put the following instructions on your tape recorder.

Close your eyes . . . Let your mind focus on your breathing. Spend two or three minutes just becoming mindful of your breathing. As you breathe in

and out, begin to see the number seven appear on a screen. It can be a black
number seven on a white screen or a white number seven on a black screen.
Focus on the number seven. If you can't see it clearly, imagine that you
finger paint it or hear a voice say seven in your mind's ear, or do all three
if you can. Then see, finger paint, hear, the number six; then five; then four,
etc., down to the number one. As you focus on the number one, let it slowly
turn into a stage door and see it slowly open. Walk through the stage door
and see a beautiful little theater. Look at the walls and the stage . . . (pause).
Look at the closed curtain (pause). Sit down in a front row seat and feel the
fabric of the seat . . . Make it your favorite fabric. Feel it as you sit down. Get
comfortable . . . (pause) . . . Look around again and make this theater be
any way you want it to be. Then see the curtain beginning to open . . . Let
yourself feel the excitement that goes with such an opening. As the curtain
opens see a large sign covering the wall of the stage. It reads *The (put your
name) Parts Review.* Think of some part of yourself that you really like and
see some famous person or someone you know well who represents that
part walk out on the stage. I like my humor and I see Johnny Carson walk
out . . . Hear a sounding applause. Then think of another part of you that
you really like and repeat the process. I like my charismatic speaking ability
and my honesty and I see John F. Kennedy walk onto the stage. Repeat this
until five people are on the right hand side of the stage. Then think of a part
of yourself you don't like and see that part walk onto the stage as personified
by a famous person or someone you know. I don't like my sloppiness and
disorganization and I see a very unkempt friend of mine walk onto the stage.
Hear a resounding boo as if there was an audience there. Then think of
another part that you don't like. I don't like the part of me that is cowardly
and afraid and I see a person whom I imagine to be Judas Iscariot walk onto
the stage. Finally, after five parts you hate or dislike or reject are standing on
the left side of the stage, imagine that a wise and beautiful person walks to
the center of the stage. This person can look like an old man with a beard
or a radiant youth like Jesus or a warm nurturing mother or whatever . . .
Just let your wise person appear . . . Then see her walking off the stage and
coming to get you . . . As she approaches, notice whatever strikes you about
her . . . Then hear her invite you to come up on the stage and review your
many parts. Walk around each person who represents a part of you; look her
in the face. How does each part help you? How does each part hinder or
limit you, especially your undesirable parts? What can you learn from your
undesirable parts? What can they teach you? Now imagine they are all
interacting. Imagine them at a table discussing a problem. Think of a current
problem you have. What does your humor say about it? How is that helpful?
How does it hinder you? How does your disorganization help you? What
would happen if you simply didn't have this part? What would you lose?

How would you like to change the part you want to reject? Modify that part in the way it would be more beneficial . . . How does it feel to modify that part? . . . Now go around and repeat that procedure with every single part. Modify it until it feels right for you. Then walk up to each part and imagine that part melting into you. Do this until you are alone on the stage with your wise person. Hear the wise person tell you that this is the theater of your life. This is the place you can come and review your many selves from time to time. Hear your wise person tell you that all these parts belong to you, that each has its own complementariness in your psychic balance. Make a decision to embrace your selves; to love and accept and learn from all your parts . . . See your wise person walk away. Thank her for the lesson. Know that you can call on her again . . . Walk down off the stage. Be aware of yourself sitting in the theater looking at the stage whereon you play out your life. Let your mind see each of your newly modified parts float by and feel yourself as one whole organism with many aspects and interdynamic parts. Speak out, hear yourself saying, "I love and accept all of me." Say it again. Subvocalize it as you get up to walk out of your theater. Walk through the theater doors. Turn around and see the number one . . . a black number one on a white curtain or a white number one on a black curtain. Finger paint it and hear it if you can. Or do any of these. Then see the number two and do the same thing. Then the number three, start feeling the life in your fingers and toes. Let it come up through your legs. See the number four and feel your whole body becoming alive. Then see the number five and know that you are coming back to your normal waking consciousness. See the number six and say I am becoming fully conscious — feel the place where you are and when you see the number seven, be fully restored to your present waking consciousness.

Dream Work

Another way to work on your shamed unacceptable parts is to learn how to integrate and interpret your dreams. A full presentation of dream work is too much to undertake in this chapter or in this book. But I want to say enough to make you aware of dream work as a powerful tool for self-integration.

You dream every night. Current studies suggest that each of us dreams from one and one half to four hours each night. We dream in order to keep our lives up to date. Each night our dreaming is like the workers at the bank who are getting all the accounts up to date. The parts of our life that we've rejected clamor for us to notice them in our dreams. Our dreams are telling us about these parts. They are trying to get our attention so that we will integrate them. Our dreams may also be telling us about a part of ourselves that needs to be actualized. Sometimes our dreams of death and dying are telling us of something or some behavior that we've given up. Such dreams may be signaling a new beginning and a new and creative stage in our lives.

Everyone can remember his dreams. Most of us have not been told that we can. Take a 3x5 card and write, "I will remember a dream tonight". Put it in your pocket or purse. Look at the card three or four times during the day, and right before going to sleep at night.

Keep a diary or note pad or tape recorder by your bed. When you wake up and the dream is fresh, write it down or record it quickly. Record every detail of the dream, as details are crucial parts of the dream. The language of dreams is the language of imagery, not the language of logical thoughts. The dream is always trying to tell us something that our conscious mind does not know.

The Talmud says, "A dream is an unopened letter to yourself."

Dream work is work. The great error is to think it can be done quickly. The dream images have associations. These associations are parts of ourselves. They need to be integrated and owned. Some dream work errs in trying to be too interpretative. For instance, believing that every time you dream of a gun, it signifies the male sex organ. There are whole books of dream symbols. They can be useful but should not be taken rigidly. One can also err on the side of dream integration. In that case one assumes that there are no symbolical associations and that every part of the dream is a disowned or unrealized part of oneself. Good dream work involves both interpretation and integration.

One needs to truly commit to dream work and one needs a guide in doing it. My favorite guide is a Jungian by the name of Robert A. Johnson. His helpful book is called *Inner Work*, (Harper and Row). The subtitle is "Using Dreams and Active Imagination For Personal Growth".

Step One: Making Associations

After you have written your dream down as carefully as you can including all the details, you are ready to do step one. Write down the first image that appears in the dream. Remember that the language of dreams is different than the language of our ordinary logical mind. I had a dream about flying an airplane. I write:

"I am flying a single engine airplane. I am at Hobby Airport. I take off one way but I can't get off the ground. I try taking off another way. It is clear to me that I keep going from south to north and then east to west — I make a perfect cross with equal lines (+). No matter what I do I can't take off."

I write down the first image. Flying an airplane (single engine). For every symbol in a dream the unconscious has an association. The language of the unconscious can be decoded. The task is to let the associations come spontaneously.

Ask yourself, "What feeling do I have about this image? What words or ideas come to mind when I look at it?" This means that you literally write anything that you spontaneously associate with the image. Usually an image will inspire several associations as in Figure 7.1.

Figure 7.1. Dreamwork Worksheet

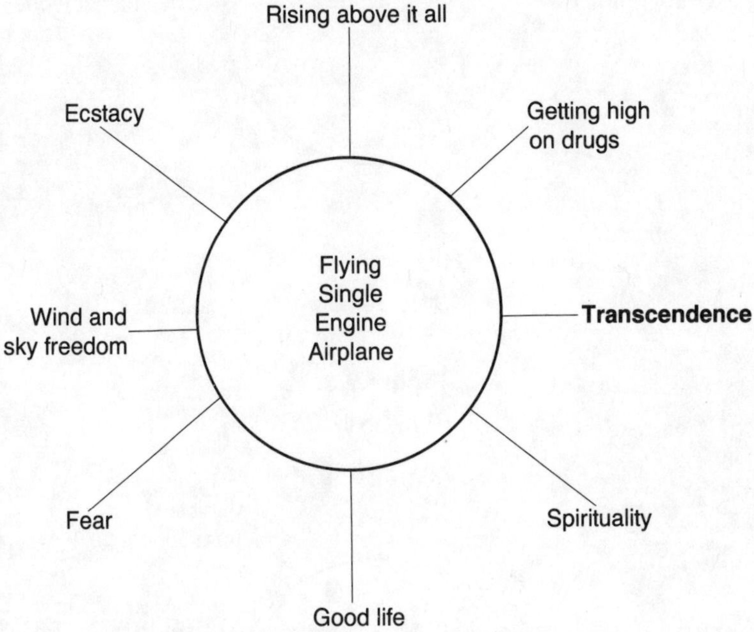

Rising above it all

Ecstacy

Getting high on drugs

Wind and sky freedom

Flying Single Engine Airplane

Transcendence

Fear

Spirituality

Good life

After you've exhausted your associations, go on to the next image. My next image was Hobby Airport. An image is a person, object, situation, color, sound or speech. I write down the image in the center of a circle as in Figure 7.2. When I've exhausted my associations I move on to the next image. I do the same with it as in Figure 7.3, where I use the image of criss-crossed runways. For me the action of not being able to take off had only a few associations. I just couldn't get off the ground. I just couldn't do what I wanted to do. I also got the feeling of "being in a rut" of being stuck.

To choose one of these associations we look them over and wait until one "clicks". The "it clicks" method has to do with waiting for one of the associations to have some voltage or energy.

Figure 7.2.

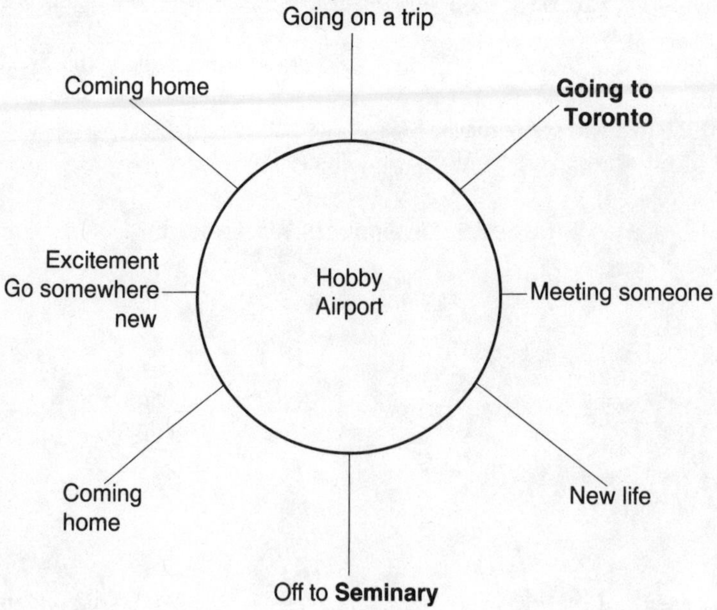

Going on a trip

Coming home

Going to
Toronto

Excitement
Go somewhere
new

Hobby
Airport

Meeting someone

Coming
home

New life

Off to **Seminary**

Figure 7.3.

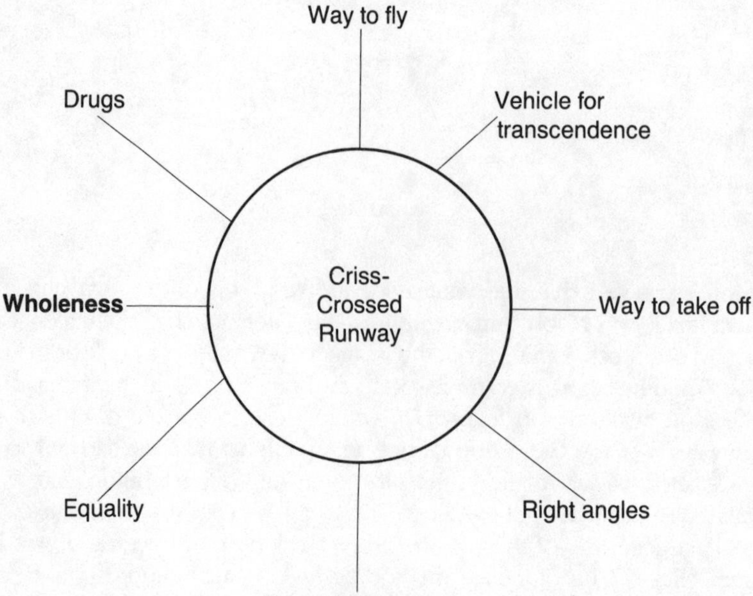

Way to fly

Drugs

Vehicle for
transcendence

Wholeness

Criss-
Crossed
Runway

Way to take off

Equality

Right angles

Mandala balance

Robert Johnson says, "One way to find the essence of the dream is to go to where the energy is — go to the associations that bring a surge of energy." Remember the split parts of ourselves are full of energy. Likewise with the symbols of the unconscious they are full of energy. Sometimes it's not totally clear which association has the most energy. In that case leave it alone for a while. The energy is often there when you come back to it.

In my dream the associations with the most energy were Transcendence, Seminary, Toronto, Mandala and Being Stuck. Now we go to step two.

Step Two: Connecting Dream Images To Inner Dynamics

In this step we attempt to connect the dream image to inner parts of ourselves. To perform this step we go to the dream image again. We ask the following: "What part of me is that? Who is it inside me who feels or behaves like that? Where do I find that trait in my personality?" Then write down each example you can think of.

Most but not all dreams are expressive of the dreamer's inner life. So we write out examples from our life that correspond to the events in this dream.

In my case I felt stuck. I was about 45 years old when I had this dream. I was stuck in my life. I needed some kind of balance. The Mandala is a symbol of balance and completeness. I was stuck. I didn't know where to go. I had recently had some financial success but it was unfulfilling. I was at a high point in my career but something was missing. The dream was a read-out of my inner condition. It also held a clue to a solution for me. The word Toronto was a puzzle to me. Toronto is where I studied for the priesthood. There was the obvious association of spirituality with Toronto. And I did feel spiritually stuck in my life.

Step Three: Interpreting

My interpretation was that this dream was a deep corroboration of the lack of fulfillment in my current spirituality. Even though I lectured in Christian Theology, something in me was unsatisfied spiritually. I was stuck and out of balance.

Step Four: Doing Rituals To Make The Dream Concrete

I honored this dream by talking to my best friend about my spiritual barrenness. I allowed my mind to focus on Toronto. I just embraced the word and let my thoughts flow back to my seminary days in Toronto. I got no answer to the riddle for some time.

One night I dreamed that I was in the same single engine airplane. This time I took off with ease. I flew to Toronto. The first thing that hit me as I got out of the plane was the memory of an abbot whom I had met 20 years before in a Trappist Monastery in New York.

I worked on this dream and found that my unconscious was telling me. that *meditation* was the key to unlock my blocked spirituality. I had been deeply moved by that Trappist monk years before. I had spent hours in meditation when I studied to be a priest. But I was never able to benefit from it. Later when I read Robert Johnson's book, *He,* I realized that I was too young and inexperienced to be able to meditate then.

In the book *He,* Robert Johnson writes about the Percival Myth. He interprets the quest for the Holy Grail as a myth describing masculine development. He suggests that all men, like Percival, are in the Grail Castle in their teens. All young men have a mighty vision — but they are too young to know how to actualize it.

In Toronto I had studied to be a priest. I had spent my first monastic year in Rochester, New York. During that year I had met the Trappist abbot. He was the most powerful spiritual figure I had ever met. As the years went by I forgot all about him. Now here I was 45 years old in my middle-aged crisis and my dreams led me back to Toronto and to the abbot of the Trappist Monastery.

I had a couple of intervening dreams which helped me arrive at full awareness of the meaning of all of this. Over the next few months I became fully aware that my life was a dead end if I only pursued money and worldly prestige. It became clear to me that I had to begin meditating if I wanted to move on and expand my consciousness and my creativity.

One of my current achievements had been being on the Board of Directors of an Oil Company. One part of me — a very shame-based part of me — loved being on the Board of Directors. But the other parts of me felt out of place. These dreams helped me to start meditating.

Almost coincidentally I met Dennis Weaver in Los Angeles. Kip Flock and I were doing a Training for Drug Counselors. Dennis was our guest lecturer on 'Meditation'. Dennis had been meditating since 1959 — sometimes several hours a day. He was a leader in the Self-Actualization Movement in Los Angeles. I was deeply impressed by his depth and the inner peace which he exuded. I began meditating shortly afterward. It has made a great difference in my life.

I honored this dream sequence by going back to Toronto. I walked around the places I had been before. I prayed and meditated in the same chapel in which I had prayed and meditated before. There was an incredible difference. My dreams had led me to a new place in my life. My dreams had gone far in healing my shame.

8

On Loving Yourself

"You do not need to be loved, not at the cost of yourself. The single relationship that is truly central and crucial in a life is the relationship to the self . . . Of all the people you will know in a lifetime, you are the only one you will never lose."

Jo Courdet, Advice From A Failure

Toxic shame's greatest enemy is the statement I love myself. To say "I love myself" can become your most powerful tool in healing the shame that binds you. To truly love yourself will transform your life.

Choosing To Love Yourself

Scott Peck has defined love, "As the will to extend myself for the sake of nurturing my own and another's sprititual growth." This definition sees love as an act of the will. This means that love is a decision. I can choose to love myself, no matter what the past has been and no matter how I feel about myself.

Exercise: The Felt Sense Of Self

Try this experiment. Imagine you are sitting in your favorite chair. Get really comfortable and relaxed. Now close your eyes and imagine that the person you currently love and respect the most is sitting across from you.

(Don't pick someone you're in emotional pain about.) The person can be a spouse, lover, child, parent, friend, hero, etc. Close your eyes and see that person now. Take three or four minutes . . .

Now get in touch with the feelings you have when you experience that person with you. I felt warm and vitalized and appreciative when I saw my best friend. This is my felt sense of that relationship.

Now close your eyes and see yourself sitting across from you. Stay in the experience three or four minutes . . .

The first time I did this experiment, I felt myself begin to criticize myself. This happens to me occasionally even now when I look at myself in the mirror. Just notice what you felt when you looked at yourself. One person I was working with recently saw her cheeks as too fat, and felt bad about her posture. Most of us have some negative feelings about ourselves. If you're shame-based and you've done nothing to heal your shame, you will probably feel intense feelings of rejection. The rejection of self is the core of toxic shame.

Accepting Yourself Unconditionally

To counteract these negative feelings about yourself, make a decision to accept yourself unconditionally. You do this by an act of choice.

"I love myself. I will accept myself unconditionally."

Say this out loud and often. What this amounts to is unconditional love.

I can remember vividly the first time I truly accepted and loved myself unconditionally. It was awesome! I later read a book by Gay Hendricks where he talked about the same thing. (See *Learning To Love Yourself* by Gay Hendricks.) He described how he would confront people in his workshops with the simple statement, "Will you love yourself for that?"

At first when I read the dialogue of one of his therapeutic interventions with a group member, I was taken aback. Surely there are things we do that are unworthy of love. As Gay went on and on, asking the person if he could love himself no matter what he did or didn't do, I realized that our love needs to be for who we are, not for what we do. You are lovable, period.

Remember that toxic shame turns you into a human doing because toxic shame says your being is flawed and defective. If your being is flawed and defective, nothing you do could possibly make you lovable. You can't change who you are.

Understanding the distinction between being and doing is one of the great learnings of my life. I tried so hard to achieve and do better and better. But no matter what I did, I still felt that deep sense of defectiveness that is the mark of internalized shame. Saying "I love myself for *whatever* . . ." is a powerful counteraction to the voice of shame. Saying "I accept myself unconditionally" can transform our lives.

One of the best successes I ever had therapeutically was dealing with a lady's weight problem. The success came as a result of this exercise. She felt she was 25 pounds overweight. She was contemptuous of her body and put herself down with comparisons and self-labeling. I worked with her for several months, continually challenging her comparisons and put-downs. I'd ask her, "Will you love and accept yourself for that?"

No matter what she said, I'd challenge her with that statement. Gradually she began to accept herself just as she was. I refused to talk about diets or exercise. I knew that until she accepted herself exactly as she was, she would never change. She couldn't lose weight by continually shaming herself. How can a problem which is organized and motivated by toxic shame be cured by increasing the toxic shame? Every time my client compared herself or put herself down with a negative label, she started a shame spiral. The shame spiral intensified the toxic internalized shame, and that set her up to eat more as a way to mood alter the pain of the shame. So self-labeling and odious comparisons are the way to stay overweight, not the way to lose weight.

In order to heal the shame that binds you, you have to begin with self-acceptance and self-love. Love creates union. When we make the decision to love ourselves unconditionally, we accept ourselves unconditionally. This total self-acceptance creates at-one-ment. We are at one with ourselves. Our full power is available to us because we are not dissipating our power by having to guard our hungry dogs in the basement (our split-off parts).

Choosing to love ourselves is possible, even if we have negative feelings about ourselves.

I have often disliked one of my children, but that didn't mean I stopped loving him or her. If we make the decision to love ourselves unconditionally, we will start feeling differently about ourselves.

As we choose to love ourselves, our self-value will be enhanced. Years ago Sidney Simon and Kirschenbaum wrote a book called *Values Clarification.* They suggested that a value is not a value unless it has seven factors in it. The seven factors are:

> It must be freely chosen.
> It must be chosen from a consideration of alternatives.
> It must be chosen with clear knowledge of the consequences.
> It must be prized and cherished.
> It must be publically proclaimed.
> It must be acted on.
> It must be acted on repeatedly.

Choosing to love yourself is a free choice. It is a simple decision. The alternatives are a shame-based lifestyle with disastrous consequences. I'm encouraging you to say, "I love myself," out loud, to proclaim that you love and accept yourself unconditionally. If you act on such a belief repeatedly, you will grow more deeply self-loving and self-valuing.

Giving Yourself Time And Attention

If you decide to love yourself, you will be willing to give yourself time and attention.

Scott Peck's definition of love implies that love is hard work. It involves expansion; it means we have to extend ourselves. To extend yourself requires work.

The work of love involves giving yourself time. How much time do you spend with yourself? Do you take time for proper rest and relaxation or do you drive yourself unmercifully? If you're a "human doing", you drive yourself. You need more and more achievement in order to feel okay about yourself. If you're willing to love and accept yourself unconditionally, you will allow yourself time to just be. You will set aside times when there's nothing you have to do and nowhere you have to go. You will allow yourself solitude, a nourishing time of aloneness. You will take time for hygiene and exercise. You will take time for fun and entertainment. You will take vacations. You will take time to work at your sex life. You will be willing to give yourself pleasure and enjoyment.

The work of love is the work of listening to yourself. You listen to yourself by monitoring your feelings, needs and wants. You need to pay attention to yourself. This may mean learning techniques for getting in touch with your feelings. It may mean joining a share group where you get feedback. The work of paying attention to yourself requires discipline.

Again, as Scott Peck has pointed out, discipline allows us to enhance life's pleasure. If you love yourself, you're willing to delay gratification so that something else more conducive to your growth might take place.

When I was a shame-based drinking addict, I could not even think of delaying gratification. Like most children of trauma and dysfunction I never thought there was going to be enough. I wouldn't delay gratification because my shame-based self didn't trust that I could get anymore.

Discipline demands telling the truth and being responsible for my own life. If I love myself, I will live in reality. I will commit to telling the truth and being responsible. Those behaviors increase my self-esteem. I love those behaviors in others, why wouldn't I love them in myself?

We have a saying in the Recovery Community — "Fake it 'til you make it." Sometime we must just decide to act ourselves into a right way of feeling, rather than trying to wait 'til we feel like changing. This applies to loving yourself. Make the decision. Say it aloud. Act like you love, value and accept yourself unconditionally, and you will begin to feel more self-loving and accepting.

Self-Assertion

Another action and work of love that will enhance your self-love and heal your toxic shame is to become more assertive. Assertiveness is based on self-love and self-valuing. This is different from aggressiveness. Aggressiveness is usually shame-based behavior. To become aggressive is to win at any cost. It often involves shaming another person. Shaming someone else cannot enhance one's self-love.

I consider self-assertion and assertiveness training to be one of the powerful ways to heal the shame that binds you. As the shame internalization process took place in your dysfunctional family, your needs became bound by shame. After a while you no longer knew what you needed. There was no way to learn how to ask for what you wanted. As your dependency needs were violated, you came to believe that you couldn't depend on anyone. You lost all sense of your human rights as an utterly unique and unrepeatable human being.

Assertiveness Training is a way to learn how to get those needs met. In Assertiveness Training you learn how to say no and ask for what you want. You learn to build new physical, emotional, volitional and intellectual boundaries.

Books like, *When I Say No, I Feel Guilty* by Manuel Smith, *Do You Say Yes When You Want To Say No?* by Fensterheim, and *Your Perfect Right* by Alberti and Emmons, are all useful ways to learn how to stand your ground and get your legitimate needs met. The methods presented in these books require practice.

Each of us needs to create his own Bill of Rights. We need to have total permission for our rights. Manuel Smith sets forth the following List of Rights. You may add your own to these.

- You have the right to judge your own behavior, thoughts, emotions, and to take responsibility for their initiation and consequences upon yourself.
- You have the right to offer no reasons or excuses for justifying your behavior.
- You have the right to judge if you are responsible for judging other people's problems.
- You have the right to change your mind.
- You have the right to make mistakes and be responsible for them.

- You have the right to say, "I don't know."
- You have the right to be independent of the goodwill of others before coping with them.
- You have the right to be illogical in making decisions.
- You have the right to say, "I don't understand."
- You have the right to say, "I don't care."

When I Say No, I Feel Guilty

In loving yourself, think about how you loved that person in the beginning exercise. If someone was hurting him or hassling her, what would you do? If you saw him hurting or shaming himself, what would you do to take care of him? Think of the work and energy you have exerted in loving your children. Will you love yourself the same way? You really are worth it. There has never been anyone like you. Nor will there ever be anyone like you again. You are unique, unrepeatable and of precious worth.

Reframing Mistakes *

A shame-based person tries desperately to present a mask to the world that says, "I'm more than human," or "I'm less than human." To be more than human is to never make a mistake. To be less than human is to believe that you are a mistake. Dealing in a healthy manner with our mistakes is crucial for the maintenance of self-love. Reframing our mistakes is a way to handle them.

Reframing, as I'm using the word, means changing your interpretation or point of view. You put a new frame around a picture or an event to change the way you look at it. This new frame will change its meaning for you. Reframing mistakes means learning to think about them in ways that remove their catastrophic qualities. Instead of awful catastrophes, you view your mistakes as natural and valuable components of your life. This is exactly the purpose of your healthy shame. When you are connected with your healthy shame, you know you can and will make mistakes and use your mistakes as occasions for new learnings or as warnings to slow down and look at what you're doing.

Mistakes As Warnings

Mistakes are like the buzzer in your car that warns you of the dangers of driving without a seatbelt. If you get a speeding ticket, it can be a warning

---

* Much of material in this section was inspired by the book *SELF-ESTEEM* by Matthew McKay and Patrick Fanning.

to drive more slowly and to concentrate on your driving. Such a mistake could ultimately save your life.

Toxic shame with its mask of perfectionism changes the warning into a moral indictment. You become so preoccupied with defending yourself against the inner critical voices that you miss the opportunity to heed the warning of the mistake. Get into the habit of reframing the mistake as a warning. Focus on the warning, rather than the culpability.

Mistakes As Allowing Spontaneity

To know you can and will make mistakes allows you to live your life with vitality and spontaneity. Healthy shame is a condition of creativity. Knowing you will make mistakes allows you to seek new information and new solutions. It keeps you from believing that you know it all.

The fear of mistakes kills your creativity and spontaneity. You walk on eggs, always afraid to say what you think or feel. McKay and Fanning write,

> "If you're never allowed to say the wrong thing, you may never feel enough to say the right thing, to say you love someone or that you hurt or want to give comfort."

Mistakes As Teachers

There is no way you can learn any task or skill without errors. The process of learning has been defined as "successive approximation". Watch children learning to walk. They literally learn to walk by falling down. Each time they fall, they adjust their balance and try again. Each failure creates a successive approximation. Finally they can walk.

Mistakes are a form of feedback. Every error tells us what we need to correct. As we correct each mistake, we get nearer to the behavioral sequence that works best.

As a teacher I know that students who fear making mistakes have trouble learning. They are scared to tackle new material because of the possibility of not understanding it. Such students go on to take the first job they are offered. They often stay in that job for a lifetime. They are too scared to get a new job because they would be faced with new procedures and challenges. They won't get new and advanced training because the inevitable mistakes are just too painful.

Again McKay and Fanning say it beautifully,

> "Framing mistakes as necessary feedback for the learning process frees you to relax and focus on your gradual mastery of the new task. Mistakes are information about what works and what doesn't work. They have nothing to do with your worth or intelligence. They are merely steps to a goal."

Common Categories Of Mistakes

There are common categories of mistakes. Ten of the most common are:

1. **Errors of Data.** You write down a phone number as 529-6188 when it was actually 529-6185.

2. **Errors of Judgment.** You decide to buy the cheaper shoes and they lose their form in six months.

3. **White Lies.** You say you're sick and you run into your boss at the grocery store.

4. **Procrastination.** You keep putting off the visit to the dentist. Now it's the weekend and you have a raging toothache.

5. **Forgetfulness.** You go out for a fun shopping trip and forget your money.

6. **Missed Chances.** The gold you decided not to buy at $48 an ounce is now $432 an ounce.

7. **Overindulgence.** You ate the whole thing and you're sick all night.

8. **Wasted Energy.** You work on a manuscript entitled *Places In The Heart* and a movie comes out with that exact title. (It happened to me.)

9. **Failure To Reach A Goal.** You're on the summer trip to the beach and you're still fat.

10. **Impatience.** You try to flip the fish over the side of the boat and it spits out the hook.

Many more categories could be added to the list. These are human issues. They are natural to homo sapiens. The common thread running through all of these examples is this. A mistake is always the product of hindsight. McKay and Fanning write,

> "A mistake is anything you do that you later, upon reflection, wish you had done differently. This applies to things you didn't do that you later, upon reflection, wish you had done."

Hindsight is what you see so clearly later on. The keyword is "later". It is the later interpretation that turns the action into a mistake. A mistake is a label you apply in retrospect.

At the time you always choose the action that seems most likely to meet your needs. The benefits seem at the time to outweigh the disadvantages. The action in any given moment depends on our awareness. McKay and Fanning define awareness as follows,

> "Awareness is the degree of clarity with which you perceive and understand, consciously or unconsciously, all the factors relating to the need at hand."

Mistakes are the result of a later interpretation. Hence, mistakes have nothing to do with self-esteem. If you label your choice "bad" because it was a mistake in the light of later awareness, you end up punishing yourself for actions you couldn't help performing. Better labels for your past mistakes would be "unwise", "not useful" or "ineffective". These terms are a more accurate assessment of your judgment.

Expanding awareness is an obvious corollary to the problem of mistakes. If you are mistake-prone, you might consider expanding your awareness as you approach a course of action. This is the most useful solution. Vowing never to make the same mistake again is not useful because you will make the same mistake again if you do not expand your awareness.

Saying that you have always made the best decisions available to you does not relieve you of being responsible for your mistakes.

Responsibility means accepting the consequences for your actions. There is a consequence for every action. Becoming more responsible means expanding your awareness to be more aware of the consequences of your choices.

As you externalize your shame, your awareness increases. A shame-based person has a very low level of awareness because the blocked and bound emotions bias one's ability to think and be aware. Internalized shame creates a kind of tunnel vision, which in turn narrows awareness and is manifested in distorted thinking. As one heals one's shame through the various externalization processes, awareness increases. You start getting your "brains out of hock".

The Habit Of Awareness

McKay and Fanning describe a simple procedure they call "The habit of awareness". They suggest certain questions that you ask yourself when considering the likely consequences, both short- and long-term, of any significant decision you are to make. Here are the questions:

- Have I experienced this situation before?
- What negative consequences came or might be expected to come from the decision I plan to make?
- Are the consequences worth it, given what I expect to gain?
- Do I know any alternative with less negative consequences?

The chief ingredient of the habit of awareness is to make a commitment to yourself. You commit to examining the probable consequences of every significant act that you do. This is a decision to love yourself. It is a decision to take the time to weigh and evaluate the consequences of your choices. After all, your choices are the fabric of your life!

9

Healing Your Memories And Changing Your Self-Image

"One day it will be realized that men are distinguished from one another as much by the forms their memories take as by their character."

Andre Malraux

"Our best feelings will come from memories of times we felt lovingly accepted no matter what we had done."

S. Kopp
Mirror, Mask and Shadow

"Now I'm going to show you how you can change your personal history," exclaimed the trainer David Gordon. I gulped and thought to myself, "Wait a minute. I know we can change the future with new choices, but change the past? Come on!"

Changing Your Personal History

David Gordon was my primary trainer in what is an exciting new model of change called Neuro-Linguistic Programming (NLP). A technique called changing your personal history was one that I learned then and have used and adapted over the last six years. Of all the techniques in this book, I consider this to be one of the most powerful for healing the shame that binds you.

What follows is my adaptation of the NLP technique. I call this process "Giving Back the Hot Potato". It works best with a memory involving a caretaker (parent, minister, teacher, priest) who shamed you by using one of the interpersonal strategies for transferring felt shame.

The Nature Of Anchors

The technique itself is based on a phenomena of human programming which the NLP people call *anchoring*. An anchor is like the "on" button of a stereo that plays an old recorded memory. An anchor triggers the sounds, sights (images), feelings and even tastes and smells of an old recorded memory. Words themselves are anchors. Words are triggers which stimulate the images and feelings of old memories.

In fact, if you look at Figure 9.1 you can see that the reality we experience can only be re-presented as we talk about it. What I mean is that we can never convey our lived experience exactly as it happens. When we talk about it, we talk about the way we interpreted the experience by means of our two representational systems — our sensory perceptual and intellectual ways of knowing.

The sensory perception is our first and most immediate way of knowing. Our intellectual knowing is always two degrees removed from reality. The philosopher Gottfried von Leibniz taught us that concepts (intellectual knowledge) are always based on precepts (sensory knowledge). Every thought we think carries sensory data with it. Every thought we think was first perceived, seen, heard, touched, tasted, smelled. Concepts trigger sensory images — either visual images, auditory self-talk or feelings (kinesthetic) responses.

When we talk about toxic shame, many memories are elicited unconsciously. These shame memories are often enmeshed in collages of imagery. When shame has become internalized, these images are often triggered and send the shame-based person into shame spirals. These spirals seem to operate independently of us. They seem to have a life of their own.

Shame spirals are also triggered by internal self-talk. Such inner talk is based on old beliefs we have about ourselves and the world. These beliefs were fostered by our shame-based caretakers. Auditory shame spirals result from introjected parental voices which were originally the actual voices of our shaming caretakers. They play like stereo recordings in our head. The Transactional Analysis therapists estimate there are 25,000 hours of these recordings.

Figure 9.1. Represented Reality

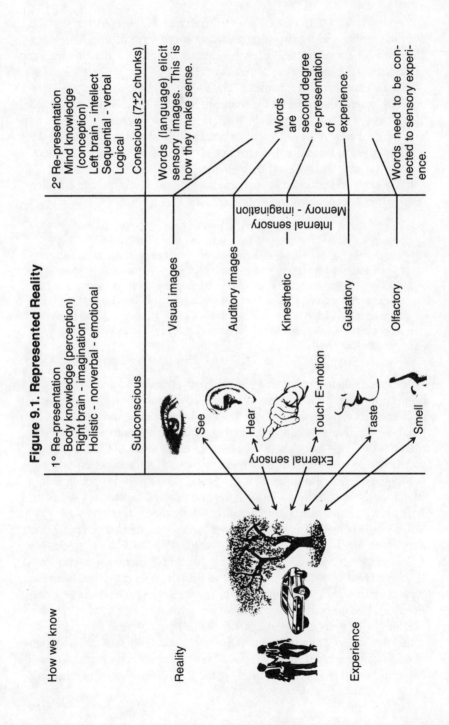

"Giving Back the Hot Potato" is a way to change old imagery through the use of kinesthetic anchors (touch anchors). It is a form of re-experiencing the past with corrective resources. It is also a way of giving back what Pia Mellody calls the induced or carried shame.

When a caretaker acts "shameless" by raging, condemning, criticizing or being judgmental, we take on the shame they are avoiding. While they avoid their shame, we have to carry it. In actual fact it is our shame, i.e., we actually experience being shamed by their acting in a shameless manner. We accepted their judgment as being about us, when it was really about them. It is in this sense that we carry their shame.

In order to understand this technique, let me quote from Leslie Bandler, one of the early pioneers and creators of NLP.

> "A basic premise of my work is that people have all the resources they need to make the changes they want and need to make . . . The resources I am speaking of . . . lie in each of our personal histories. Each and every experience we have ever had can serve as an asset. Most every one has had the experience of being confident or daring or assertive or relaxed at some time. The therapist's task is to make those resources available in the contexts in which they are needed. Bandler, Grindler, Delozier and I have developed a method called *anchoring* which does just that."
>
> *They Lived Happily Ever After*

Leslie goes on to explain that just as certain stimuli, like an old song, can bring back past experiences, we can learn to deliberately associate a memory to a specific experience. We can do this by accessing the memory and touching our thumb and finger together while we are re-experiencing that memory. Once the association has taken place, the touch of thumb to finger will then trigger the experience. We can then retrigger the experience at will.

Language works the same way. I remember sitting in a meeting with a friend some ten years ago. I looked over and saw that he was crying. I asked him what was the matter and he said, "Bluffy died." Bluffy was his dog. When I heard this, I thought it was weird for a grown man to be crying over the death of a dumb animal. The word dog had no first degree representation associated with it for me. I had no experience of owning a dog. As a child I was afraid of dogs. I had been a paper boy! Dogs were our natural enemy. It didn't make sense to me for someone to cry over a dog, because I had no sensory memories of warmth with a dog.

Some eight years ago I bought my son a little Shetland sheepdog. We called him Cully. When I come into the house and Cully sees me, he jumps two feet off the ground and tinkles on himself. (I never had a friend do that.) No matter when or how many times I come in, Cully goes crazy because he's so glad to see me. I have become very attached to Cully. I now have the sensory experience to know why someone would cry if he lost his dog. It makes sense to me now. If someone told me his dog died, the word "dog" would immediately trigger my experience with Cully. So words are anchors which trigger past sensory experience. Again, as Leslie Bandler writes:

> "If I ask you to remember a time when you felt truly satisfied with yourself, my words send you on a search through your past experiences . . . you know how you can become angry again by remembering a past argument or frightened again by remembering a terrifying movie or incident. Thus by bringing up a memory (an internally generated experience) we re-experience many of the same feelings which occurred when that memory was formed."

In my version of the NLP technique, I would have you select a past shame memory and anchor it. This is done by simply closing your eyes and letting your memory take you back to a time when Mom or Dad or a teacher or preacher was laying their shame on you.

One of my clients remembered being shamed in the second grade. He was at a Catholic parochial school, and the priest who was in charge of the church handed out the children's report cards. It was this priest's custom to throw the cards on the ground if a child got a D or an F. My client was an undiagnosed dyslexic and was having a terrible time learning to read. He got an F in reading and the good priest threw his card on the ground. My client was ashamed and humiliated and somehow couldn't pick the card up. (He was a fingernail biter.) Everyone laughed, as this child suffered an excruciating moment of being shamed. This memory, as with most nondissociated painful memories, was easy to anchor. He anchored it with the thumb and finger of his left hand.

I then asked him what resource(s) he now had, which if he had had them then would have helped him handle that experience better. He thought for a moment. Then he said firmly, "I'm articulate now and I've learned to be assertive."

I said, "Close your eyes and think of a time when you were being articulate. The memory can come from any time in your life. You are speaking firmly and clearly, saying exactly what you want to say."

As my client searched for that past experience, I saw his face begin to change. His jaw loosened and he looked more confident. I asked him to touch his right thumb to a finger on his right hand. I had him hold the touch for 30 seconds as he re-experienced being articulate. Then I had him take a deep breath and relax. I suggested that he think of a pleasant memory from the past in order to separate the experience of being verbally expressive from the next anchor we were going to make — the assertiveness anchor.

After a moment I said, "Now think of a time when you were actually being assertive." I took some time to let him get fully into the details of the memory. I asked him, "Who was there? What did they have on? How were you dressed?" When he was re-experiencing being assertive, I had him touch his right thumb to the same right finger and make the assertive anchor exactly in the same way he did for the anchor associating verbal expression. I had him hold it for 30 seconds and then I asked him to take a deep breath, and go back to the pleasant memory he had accessed earlier. Up to this point we had:

1. Made a shame anchor (X) of the second grade report card scene with the touch of his left thumb to one of his left fingers.
2. Made a resource anchor (Y) with the touch of his right thumb to one of his right fingers. This anchor embodied two strengths which my client now had that he did not have in the second grade, viz., verbal expressiveness and assertiveness.

Now we were ready for the redoing of the old memory. It may help you understand this process if you think about a premise used in cybernetics. That premise states that the brain and central nervous system cannot tell the difference between real and imagined experience if the imagined experience is vivid enough and in detail.

Most people can achieve sexual arousal by using their *imagination*. This means that there is full kinesthetic response without another real person being there. Paranoid personalities live in a threatened and hypervigilant universe by virtue of fantasies and hallucinations that they themselves create. Normal people often create terrible stress and anxiety by worrying about the future — something that hasn't even happened yet. These are all ways that behavior is programmed by simply using one's imagination.

In step three of the process I asked my client to go back into the shame scene with the new resources of verbal expressiveness and assertiveness. This is accomplished by touching the two anchors X and Y simultaneously. I tell my client not to change anyone else's behavior in the scene. He is to focus only on his own responses to the report card throwing. He is free to respond any way he wants to with his assertiveness and verbal expression. I encourage him to really tell the priest what he feels. I may even suggest things like — "How awful for you to bully and humiliate a child like me. I'm doing the best I can. You're a poor model of the love of God, etc."

It's best when the words come spontaneously. They can be actually said out loud or subvocally. What I look for is good energy in expressing the anger about the shame.

Finally I ask the person to give his shameless caretaker back the shame that he has been carrying for him for years. I like to symbolize it as a black soggy bag. The symbolic giving back is important. Once the experience feels better internally, I ask the person to take a deep breath, relax and open his eyes.

WELL-FORMED ANCHORS

This work can be done without anyone else. And each scene can be done several times. I've personally worked on over 100 shame memories. Some scenes I've done ten times. The key to this work is making good resource anchors. The shame anchors are usually easy because of the high voltage of the pain. Achieving well-formed resource anchors will require time, practice and patience. The conditions for well-formed anchors are:

1. **Pure access state** — This means that the best anchor is the one with the highest energy voltage . . . when you're feeling the feeling most intensely.
2. **Well-timed application** — We need to set the anchor (thumb and finger) when the energy is at or near its apex.
3. **Can be duplicated** — We can check as to whether we've made a good anchor by testing it. When we touch our thumb and finger, the past experience is triggered. If we've made a good anchor, it will have high voltage.

The last point is a crucial one. Always check your resource anchor at least once before doing the corrective experience to be sure you have a good anchor.

A couple of things excite me about this method. The first is that *the person using it uses his own actual resources.* This is crucial for shame-based co-dependents who have such poor awareness of their own inner strengths and believe that they must be helped from the outside. Using a person's own strengths and resources is what good therapy is all about. The power is in the one we're trying to help. All of us already have all the resources within ourselves that we need in order to change, but toxic shame blocks our awareness of our strengths.

The second thing I like about this technique is that *it can be tested.* Toward the end of my work with the aforementioned client, I asked him to relax, close his eyes and go to that second grade classroom on report card day. I had him touch the first anchor he had made with his left thumb and finger. I let him feel that previously anchored shame experience and asked him to pay attention to any changes in the experience. I noticed his face, and calibrated it with what I remembered before. My client reported significant change in the experience. I noted it also.

When we first made the anchor, his head dropped down, he furrowed his brow, his breathing was rapid and his cheek color reddened. When he tested it two sessions later, he held his head upright, his breathing was more relaxed and his skin color stayed the same. These are neurological cues that match his reported re-experience of the old pain. This technique can be summarized as follows:

Giving Back The Hot Potato

1. Take three to five minutes, close your eyes and just focus on your breathing. Be aware of the differences in how the air feels as you breathe in and out. Let yourself totally relax.
2. Let your mind drift back in time to a shame experience with someone. As you feel the upset or distress of that experience touch your left thumb to one of your left fingers. Hold it for 20 seconds . . . Take a deep breath, let your thumb and finger relax. Shift your awareness to something familiar, like the house you live in.
3. After focusing on something familiar, think of a resource or several resources you now have that if you had had during the shame experience, you could have handled it differently. (For example, you are more articulate now. You are more assertive now. You have a resource group now.)
4. Think of a time when you were using the needed resource (an actual experience from any time in your life) and go into that memory in as much detail as possible. What did you have on? What color was the other person's hair, eyes, etc?
5. When you feel that resource (you feel assertive — you are being assertive), touch your right thumb to any finger on your right hand. Hold for 30 seconds . . . Take a deep breath and let your thumb and finger relax. Repeat the above with any other resource you feel would have helped you in the past shame experience.
6. Let your awareness return to some current familiar scene (like your bedroom or the car you drive).
7. Now imagine that you are preparing to return to the past shame theme. Imagine you could go back in time with the present resources you have just anchored. Imagine you are going to redo the experience in a way that uses the resources you just anchored.
8. Now touch your two anchors (your left thumb and finger and your right thumb and finger) simultaneously. Go back into the shame memory and redo it. Tell the shaming person how angry you are and whatever else you want to say and do. *(Do not change any of their behavior — only your own)*. Stay in the experience until your internal experience feels different. If you have difficulty doing this, come back to the present and anchor more resources. Then go back and change

the memory, using the new resources. Remember to give him back his shame — the shame that they avoided by acting shameless.

9. Wait a minute or two and then remember the past experiences with no anchors to discover by your own sensory experience if indeed this memory has been subjectively changed.

10. When the past experiences have been changed, future pace them. Imagine the next time a situation or context will arise which is similar to the above past experiences. As you imagine the future context, imagine yourself having the resources in this context. Use no anchors.

I recommend that you either memorize this sequence of instructions or put them on a tape recorder.

Changing Your Self-Image

Another very powerful technique I have used for years is a technique called Self-Image Thinking. I'm indebted to Stephen and Carol Lankton for the core of this process. They are brilliant proteges of Milton Erickson and give Erickson credit for being the inspiration behind this technique.

In their book, *The Answer Within: A Clinical Framework Of Erickson Hypnotherapy,* the Lanktons present their process for changing one's self-image. What follows is my adaptation of their work.

Our self-image is like the lens of a camera. It conditions how we view and interact with the world. It is the filter which sets the limits for our experience and choices. Shame-based people have a negative self-image. They see themselves as defective. Often a shame-based person is not aware of his negative self-image because of his false self cover-up. We become so identified with our Role or Script, we are no longer aware of our deepest feelings about ourself.

Learning to change your self-image will require hard work. Think of it as a work of love. It will demand practice and real commitment. The basic process involves using visualizations.

I've already suggested how visualization works. Your brain and central nervous system cannot tell the difference between real and imaginary experiences if the imaginary experience is vivid enough and in detail. Visualization will work no matter whether you believe it or not. Your scepticism may keep you from trying visualization, but it won't stop the technique from working once you do try it.

A word of warning before we begin. Everyone is able to internally *perceptualize,* but not everyone can *visualize.* Some people must learn to visualize. The ability to visualize seems to be related to how your mental map got set up. If your parents used a lot of rich imaginative language, you learned to visualize.

So the first step in using visualization to change our self-image is to learn how to visualize. What follows is a preparation for using the exercise of self-image thinking.

Preliminary Warm-Up

The first thing that must be done is to get relaxed. The most effective visualizations occur while your brain is producing alpha waves. Alpha waves result from complete relaxation. When you are in the relaxed alpha state, your brain power is in a heightened state of suggestibility.

Put the following instructions on your tape recorder:

Sit down in a comfortable place. Be sure your head has support and that it is not too hot or too cold. Begin by focusing on your breathing. At first just be aware of breathing. Normally you are unaware of breathing, so by focusing on breathing you are making your unconscious conscious. Be aware of what happens in your body when you breathe . . . Be aware of the air as it comes in and as it goes out . . . Pay attention to the difference. Focus on the difference . . . Now imagine that you can see a white vapor as you breathe out — like seeing your breath on a cold day . . . Starting with your forehead, notice any tension there and breathe into it. If there is tension, breathe it out. See the tension as black dots in the white vapor as you breathe out. Breathe in and out until the vapor is pure white . . . Next focus on the area around your eyes. Notice any tension and breathe it out . . . Next focus on your facial muscles . . . breathe out any tension . . . Next focus on your neck muscles . . . breathe out any tension . . . Next focus on your shoulders . . . breathe out the tension. Next focus on your hands and arms . . . breathe out the tension. Next focus on your chest . . . Take several deep breaths and breathe out any tension. Next your stomach . . . breathe out the tension . . . Next focus on your buttocks . . . breathe out any tension . . . Next on your knees . . . breathe out any tension . . . Next on your calves and ankles . . . breathe out any tension. Next on your feet . . . breathe out any tension.

Now just allow your whole body to relax. Imagine that you've become like a hollow bamboo shoot. A warm golden energy is coming in through the top of your head and going out through your toes. Allow every cell in your body to relax . . .

Now as you breathe in and out begin to see a black number seven on a white canvas or a white number seven on a black canvas . . . You choose the one that's easiest for you . . . If you have trouble seeing this — draw it ahead of time before beginning this exercise. Practice looking at the drawing and then closing your eyes and seeing it on your internal screen. After you've mastered the seven, you can . . .

Start by breathing out the number seven . . . Now breathe out a six, then a five, four, three, two, one. Focus on the number one. Let the one become a candle flame. See the orange, red, yellow, blue aspects of the flame . . . Look into the center of the flame; feel its warmth and hear the crackling of a fire. Let the flame become a warm fire in the fireplace . . . Feel the warmth; smell the fire . . . hear it crackle . . . Imagine you are toasting marshmallows . . . Taste a toasted marshmallow . . . Let your tongue and taste buds relish the taste . . . Now let your imagination take you to a summer day . . . You are walking along a path . . . (10-second pause) . . . You can feel a warm wind touching your face . . . (10 seconds) . . . On your left are apple trees loaded with big red apples . . . (10 seconds) . . . You walk over and pick an apple . . . (10 seconds) . . . You bite into it . . . and taste its delicious juices . . . Next you see an orange tree . . . (10 seconds) . . . You pick an orange. You peel it, rubbing your thumb and fingers on the inside of the skin . . . (10 seconds) . . . You smell it and taste its delicious juices . . . (10 seconds) . . . Up ahead are rows of yellow flowers . . . (10 seconds) . . . You can smell them as you draw near . . . buttercups, honeysuckle . . . (10 seconds) . . . your favorite flowers . . . Continue walking until you reach a white sandy beach . . . (10 seconds) . . . Take your shoes off and let your feet touch the clean white sand. Feel it run through your toes. Pick up a handful of sand and let it run through your fingers . . . (10 seconds) . . . Look to your left and see a path . . . (10 seconds) . . . Start walking down the path . . . There are trees on each side of the path . . . (10 seconds) . . . There are birds in the trees . . . hear them singing and chirping . . . (10 seconds) . . . Hear the wind blowing through the leaves of the trees . . . At the end of the path, there is a small lake . . . You can hear the water lapping . . . (10 seconds) . . . Fish are jumping from time to time . . . (10 seconds) . . . Across the lake a herd of cows are coming toward the lake. You can hear the cows mooing . . . (10 seconds) . . . Sit down by the side of the lake . . . Just relax and imagine you could see yourself walking up to you . . . Look at yourself. Your hair . . . what color is it? Look at your eyes . . . ears . . . nose . . . Look at your . . . whole body . . . Imagine you have turned around . . . Look at the back of you . . . Turn to the side . . . Look at your profile . . . Allow yourself to slowly walk away . . . Sit there by the lakeside and reflect on your own image . . . Slowly count back from seven . . . Allow yourself to come back to your normal waking consciousness as you come back to the number one . . .

As you reflect on this experience, you may have had trouble seeing your own body image. Most shame-based people do. If you did, you can work on it by doing the following:

Body Image Exercise

Part one of this exercise is an eyes-open exercise you can do any time. Stand in front of a full-length mirror: Examine your face, forehead, eyebrows, eyes, cheeks, smile, mouth, moles, marks, ears, hairstyle and color. Practice smiling and looking serious. Practice becoming an expert on your own face.

Now do the same for the rest of your body. Scan downward and study your neck, shoulders, arms and hands. Check out your chest and stomach, your hips and legs. Turn around and see as much as you can of your backside. Notice your posture. Stand up straight and slowly slump down. March in place and swing your arms. You might get some photos of yourself and look at yourself in different poses. This is not a critical appraisal. Nor is it the time to take an inventory of what you'd like to change.

Once you've become an expert on your own appearance, you're ready for step two. Do this in bed before you get up in the morning. Visualize yourself waking up. Hear the alarm clock. Feel the warm bed. Start to get up and then get back under the warm covers. Then get out of bed. Feel the cold floor against your bare feet. Look around at your room: your furniture, your belongings, your windows. Put your clothes on. Feel the fabric on your body as you dress. See the colors of your clothes. Do whatever grooming you normally do — brushing teeth, washing face, shaving, combing your hair. Notice the feel of the water, the smell of your cosmetics or shaving lotion. Notice any aches or pains in your body. Make the scene as vivid and detailed as possible.

Remind yourself that you are still lying in bed. Open your eyes and actually do all the activities you just imagined. Be aware of the actual sensations and compare them with your visualizations. Carefully note any differences in your imagination from your real experience. Do this visualization exercise every morning for one week. Each time you do it, add the details you left out the day before. A week of this exercise will greatly enrich your visualizations.

Once you've mastered this, you've arrived at a Central Self-Image (CSI). Practice closing your eyes and seeing your CSI. You can practice all during the day: at work, riding the bus, at lunch, whenever you have a minute or two. (But never do it while driving your car.)

Self-Image Thinking

STEP ONE: INTEGRATING NEW STRENGTHS INTO YOUR CSI

Step one involves looking at your CSI. If there is something you think can be different (your posture, your energy, your clothes, your facial expression), be sure it is something you can change. Think of someone who smiles the way you'd like to. As you see his smile, anchor it as we did in the exercise on giving back the hot potato. After you've anchored it, close your eyes and see your CSI. As you look at your face, fire the anchor of the desired smile. Keep holding it until you see that smile on your face. You can practice this many times. Soon you should be able to close your eyes and see yourself smiling in the more desirable way. You can do the same with posture, confidence, eye contact, the way you walk and talk. You can also see yourself as you would like to be. You can see yourself ten pounds heavier or lighter. You can see yourself behaving in desired ways. What's most important is to seek those traits and behaviors in a nonjudgmental or noncritical way. If you are seeking a radical change, you should see your new image as an ideal image.

STEP TWO: ADDING A SIGNIFICANT OTHER

Step two involves adding significant relationships. Your shame-based identity resulted from the breaking of the interpersonal bridge with significant others. Good identity demands the mirroring eyes of at least one significant other. Therefore, you need to have your new self-image mirrored by someone you trust, whose opinion means something to you.

Close your eyes and see your CSI with the new trait of warm personable confidence. As you look at yourself, float into your own body. Stand in your own shoes; look out of your own eyes; feel the touch of your clothes on your body. As you look out of your own eyes, see a trusted, loving, nonjudgmental friend coming toward you. Be sure she is the kind of friend who will always tell you the truth (not a people-pleaser). Interact with your friend and hear her giving you feedback about your smile and your new confidence. Dialogue with her. See her true appreciation of you in her eyes. Tell yourself, "I love my new smile and my new sense of confidence. I enjoy being with my friend and my friend enjoys being with me." Affirmations are excellent supportive material for self-image work.

STEP THREE: PRACTICING SCENARIOS

In step three you go through various scenarios relating to behaviors you'd like to change. For example, I've worked hard on changing my people-pleasing act. I've done it as follows:

Imagine you are talking to a good friend. Your friend invites you to go out to eat at the new Thai restaurant. He's raving about how great the food is. Feel the urge in yourself to say yes and please your friend. Pay attention to your own body. You are tired and you have no taste for Thai food. You remember how you almost threw up eating some exotic Thai dish. You hear your voice as you tell your friend, "No, I'm tired and I don't like Thai food. I'd probably like to go out tomorrow night but not for Thai food. You'll have to find another buddy for that kind of food." Hear your friend's disappointment. Square your shoulders; take a deep breath and tell your friend that you hear his disappointment, and you look forward to some other types of meals together. As you look him in the eyes, tell him you wouldn't want to lie to him or pretend while you're with him . . . Later see him leaving. As you close the door say, "I can be truthful in relationships. I can say what I want and feel. I have a right to my own likes and dislikes. I love myself when I tell the truth."

You can practice many other types of scenarios. Some examples are saying, "I love you" to someone you've wanted to express love to; saying "No" to someone; asking for a raise; applying for a job; returning unwanted merchandise to a store; asking someone for a date; meeting new people; successfully handling a speech you have to make. Pick situations which have been infected by your toxic shame.

The Lanktons suggest using positive scenarios along with a strong CSI to build new habit patterns for overcoming stressful psychic states as they arise. Suppose you started thinking that you have to go to the bank on Monday to ask for a loan. As you think about it your muscles tense; your throat gets tight and you get butterflies in your stomach. At the first sign of the stress, you can get into the habit of consciously focusing on your strong confident CSI and one of your successful scenarios. The Lanktons suggest that you repeat the process with six or more other successful scenarios. As the habit patterns are built up, they become unconscious. You begin to automatically respond with confidence and positive expectation.

I want to remind you that our shame-based identity has been formed by negative shame scenes and language imprints. The collages of shame memories connect with each other and function unconsciously. In like manner (now positive) self-image thinking involves building up a positive internal map which will guide our actions. Researchers have shown convincingly that our performance follows our internal imagery.

Step Four: Emanated Images

The purpose of step four is to create new and positive developments out of our imagined positive goals. The Lanktons call this "Emanated Images". You are to step inside a picture of yourself enjoying a desired goal and have a new fantasy which "emanates" from the first one. In my example of refusing to be a "people-pleaser", I imagined that my friend called me that night to tell me how he appreciated my honesty for my refusing to go somewhere I really didn't want to go. I could hear the respect in his voice. I felt good about it.

STEP FIVE: FUTURE PACING

A final step of self-image thinking is to "future pace". This is achieved by pretending that the desired future goal has already arrived. The Lankton's write:

> "In the present tense of the future the client is directed to really enjoy the associated feelings of accomplishment, pride, intimacy, etc., which are present, and then to fall into a daydream and look back at all those steps taken in arriving at this dream come true."

This is a way to look back from the fantasized future and learn something important about making that dream come true.

These techniques are very powerful and will work whether you believe in them or not. All you have to do is commit yourself to practicing them. It takes so much energy to hide our shame. If you will use a tiny part of that energy, these imagery techniques can change your life.

10

Confronting And Changing Your Inner Voices

"We are all in a post-hypnotic trance induced in early infancy."
Ronald Laing

"We either make ourselves miserable or we make ourselves strong.
The amount of work is the same."

Don Juan
Journey To Xtlan

I looked at her face. It was almost shining. She was radiant, perhaps the most beautiful woman I had ever counseled. When she walked down the hall towards my office, I was moved by her petite femininity and elegance. She was the kind of woman that Fra Angelico said you could not lust after. Her beauty was too stunning. As she began to talk about herself I thought she was putting me on, the way someone might downplay herself in order to get compliments or praise.

"I'm a terrible mother. My child deserves better. I'm about to lose my job. I can't seem to catch on to the computer system. I've always been sorta stupid. I don't blame my husband for divorcing me. I should have married

Sidney. He was blind. He wouldn't have had to look at my body." She went
on and on seemingly unable to stop. Her voice tone changed two distinct
times. One tone was gutteral and raspy. The other was sort of whiny and
weak. The most powerful impression I had was that of a recording that
couldn't stop.

I worked with her for about a year. Her name was Ophelia. A clear picture
of abandonment emerged. Her real father was an alcoholic. He had left her
mother when Ophelia was three years old. Her first stepfather burned her
with matches on several occasions, telling her that this was a sample of what
the fires of hell felt like. Another man, the stepfather's brother, used to take
her for rides and do "funny things" with her. She said he was the only one
who ever really paid any attention to her. He once gave her a puppy. This was
one of her rare pleasant childhood memories. Her mother was a waitress in
a bar, and used to yell at Ophelia a lot in her rough raspy voice. Her mother
was voted the sexiest girl in her senior year of high school and constantly
compared Ophelia to herself. When Ophelia was 13, she told her things like,
"You better work on getting some tits and ass if you want the boys to take you
out. I was a 36C at your age." One of her mother's boyfriends got into bed
and made her do sexual things to him. Ophelia reported this with obvious
pain, but also as if it were a triumph over her mother. All in all, this woman
was severely violated. She was deeply shame-based and maintained the
shame through negative self-talk which triggered continuous shame spirals.

The "Inner Voice"

This negative self-talk is the internal dialogue that Robert Firestone calls
the "inner voice". The inner voice has been described by others in different
ways. Eric Berne referred to it as a set of parental recordings that are like
cassette tapes. Some have estimated that there are 25,000 hours of these
tapes in a normal person's head. Fritz Perls and the Gestalt school call these
voices "introjected parental voices". Aaron Beck calls them "automatic
thoughts". Whatever we call them, all of us have some voices in our heads.
Shame-based people especially have dominant negative shaming, self-
depreciating voices. Robert Firestone writes:

> "The 'voice' may be described as the language of an insidious self-
> destructive process existing, to varying degrees, in every person. The
> voice represents an external point of view toward oneself initially
> derived from the parents' suppressed hostile feelings toward the child."
>
> *The Fantasy Bond*

The voice basically tells a shame-based person that they are unlovable,
worthless and bad. The voice supports the bad child image.

The voice may be experienced consciously as a thought. Most often it is partially conscious or totally unconscious. Most of us are unaware of the habitual activity of the voice. We become aware of it in certain stressful situations of exposure when our shame is activated. After making a mistake, one might call oneself a "stupid fool". Or say, "There I go again. I'm such a blundering klutz." Before an important job interview, the voice might torment you with thoughts like, "What makes you think you could handle the responsibility of a job like this? Besides, you're too nervous. They'll know how nervous you are."

Actually getting rid of the voices is extremely difficult because of the original rupturing of the interpersonal bridge and the resulting fantasy bond. As children are abandoned, and the more severely they are abandoned (neglected, abused, enmeshed), the more they create the illusion of connection with the parent. The illusion is what Robert Firestone calls the "Fantasy Bond".

In order to create the fantasy bond the child has to idealize his parents and make himself "bad". The purpose of this fantasy bonding is survival. The child desperately relies on his parents. They can't be bad. If they are bad or sick, he can't survive. So the fantasy bond (which makes them good and the child bad) is like a mirage in the desert. It gives the child the illusion that there is nourishment and support in his life. Years later when the child leaves the parent, the fantasy bond is set up internally. It is maintained by means of the voice. What was once external, the parent's screaming, scolding and punishing voice, now becomes internal. For this reason the process of confronting and changing the inner voice creates a great deal of anxiety. But as Firestone points out, "There is no deep-seated therapeutic change without this accompanying anxiety."

In beginning this work of confronting and changing our inner voices, it's imperative that you realize how powerful these voices can be. The child, by incorporating the parent's voice, is taking on the parent's subjective, and in the case of a shame-based parent, distorted viewpoint toward him or herself. And as Firestone has pointed out, the child incorporates "the attitudes the parents held when they felt the most rejecting and angry. The daughter or son incorporates feelings of loathing and degradation that lie behind their statements."

As children in shame-based families we could not help but believe that we were bad and unlovable. We simply were not capable of grasping that our parents were shame-based, needy or in some cases downright emotionally ill. The voice also has a tendency to generalize, moving from a specific criticism to other areas of our own life. If Mom transferred her shame by means of compulsive perfectionism about neatness and cleanliness, that critical perfectionism will be generalized to all other bad habits and personal defects. Children will treat themselves and others with the same ridicule, sarcasm and derision that their parents fostered onto them.

The voice is not a positive system of values. "Rather", says Firestone, "it interprets and states an external system of values in a vicious manner of self-attack and castigation." The voice can be out and out contradictory by both initiating actions and condemning them later.

Firestone has offered evidence that "in their most pathological form patients, who are suicidal or homicidal, report experiencing 'voices' as actual hallucinations instructing them to act out destructive impulses." In less pathological form when the voices appear to represent a parental value system, the tone is most often vindictive and leads to self-hatred rather than corrective behavior. Even when a person acknowledges a mistake or error in judgment, i.e., actually admits that she is at fault, the voice is self-righteous and punitive. The voice might say, "Sorry is not enough! You're never going to learn. You're so weak and clumsy. Face it, you're just no damn good. This proves it." The voice makes the categorical judgment that one is defective and flawed and is never going to change.

The voice is mostly constituted by the shame-based shut-down defenses of the primary caretakers. Just as the shame-based parents cannot accept their own weakness, wants, feelings, vulnerability and dependency needs, they cannot accept their children's neediness, feelings, weakness, vulnerability and dependency. Firestone writes that the voice is the result of the "parents' deeply repressed desire to destroy the aliveness and spontaneity of the child whenever he or she intrudes on their defenses."

We must remember that the shame-based caregivers were once hurting children themselves. Their pain, humiliation and shame were repressed. Their anger toward their shaming parents could not be expressed for fear of losing the parent. That anger was turned inward against self and became self-hatred. The parents' defenses against their pain and shame prevent these feelings from erupting into consciousness. If the parent were to let the child express those feelings, it would threaten his own defenses. The parent must stop the child's feelings of neediness and pain, so that he doesn't have to feel his own feelings of neediness and pain.

The Inner Voice As Automatic Thoughts

It is crucial for you to learn to pay attention to your internal dialogue, your own inner voices. The most destructive aspect of your inner voice has been referred to as your automatic thoughts.

Imagine the following situation: At a crowded football game a woman shrieks loudly, stands up, slaps the face of the man next to her and rushes out of the stadium. Several people are watching. Each reacts differently. One man is frightened; a teenage boy is angry; a middle-aged man is depressed; a therapist is curious; a clergyman is embarrassed. The same event triggered very different emotions in each of the observers.

The reason lies in the automatic thoughts of each observer. The frightened man was slapped repeatedly by his shrieking mother as a child. He heard his mother's voice yelling, "What do you use for brains?"

The angry teenage boy thought, "Women can get away with hitting men. Just like my sister can hit me without getting punished. It's just not fair."

The recently divorced middle-aged man thought, "Doesn't anyone get along anymore? It's really sad."

The therapist thought, "I wonder what he said to trigger that reaction?"

And the clergyman thought, "Wasn't that woman one of my parishioners? How embarrassing!"

In every case the observer's emotion was the result of a thought. The emotional response followed the thought that interpreted the event. Our mental life is teeming with thoughts, *many of them going on unconsciously and automatically.*

Internalized shame causes you to focus on a particular group of automatic thoughts, to the exclusion of all contrary thoughts. This preoccupation creates a kind of tunnel vision in which you think only one kind of thought and notice only one aspect of your environment. Aaron Beck uses the phrase "selective abstraction" to describe this tunnel vision. Selective abstraction means that we look at one set of cues in our environment to the exclusion of all others. Tunnel vision is the product of toxic shame.

Confronting Inner Voices

I hope it is clear that the negative voice fosters and intensifies toxic shame. It initiates and exaggerates shame spirals. The voice is powerful. Once the voice system is set up, it becomes the key dynamic of toxic shame's functional autonomy. Many techniques have been devised for confronting and changing the voices in our head.

Adaptation Of Firestone's Voice Work

Robert Firestone has done pioneering work in identifying the origins and destructiveness of the voice. He has developed some powerful ways to bring these hostile thoughts into the patient's awareness. He writes that the "process of formulating and verbalizing negative thoughts acts to lessen the destructive effect of the voice on the patient's behavior."

In voice therapy patients are taught to *externalize* their inner critical thoughts. By so doing they expose their self-attacks and ultimately develop ways to change their negative attitude into a more objective, nonjudgmental view. As the voice is externalized through verbalization, intense feelings are released which result in powerful emotional catharsis with accompanying insight.

Historically voice therapy developed out of Firestone's observations of both "normal" and neurotic individuals. He especially noted how groups of so-called normal therapists became angry and defensive when told certain things about themselves that they construed as critical or negative.

"Their defensiveness," writes Firestone, "was not usually related to the accuracy or inaccuracy of the feedback they were receiving, but appeared to coincide with their own negative self-evaluations." In other words, the stronger and reactive their defensive response, the more they were probably criticizing themselves the same way. Firestone came to the conclusion that "appraisals and evaluations from others, when they validate a person's distorted view of himself tend to arouse an obsessive thought process." Since we are already tortured by our own critical thoughts and self-attacks, we feel very threatened whenever others attack us the same way.

Methods For Externalizing The Shaming Voice

Firestone's methods are mainly used in the context of individual and group therapy. I have adapted these methods so that you can use them outside of therapy. I've attempted to show you how powerful your inner voices are and why you do not want to give them up. If you work on the following exercises and find yourself feeling overwhelmed, stop immediately. This means you need to do them with someone who is trained to help you.

Over-reaction Diary

The first method I would suggest flows directly from the early work Firestone did in testing the triggering of the obsessive critical voice process. It involves keeping a diary of your defensive over-reactions. It is best done when you are involved in some kind of feedback share group. But it can also be done simply in the context of your daily interpersonal life.

Each evening before retiring, think back over the events of the day. Where were you upset? Where did you over-react? What was the context? Who was there? What was said to you? How does what was said to you compare with what you say to yourself?

For example, on December 16th my wife and I were talking about remodeling rooms in our house. At one point in the conversation, I felt my voice tone accelerating and intensifying. Soon I was ranting about all the stresses that my current work entails. I heard myself saying, "Don't expect me to supervise this job. I can just barely keep up with my basic obligations." Later, I entered this outburst into my diary. I used the following form:

Date: Wednesday, December 16, 8:45 p.m.

Subject: My wife.

Content: Discussion of improvement of a room in our house.

Over-reac- After she said, "I'm going to need some help from you."
tion: I said in an increasingly agitated tone, "Don't expect me to supervise this job, etc."

Underlying You're a rotten husband. You don't know how to fix
Voices: anything. You're pathetic. Your house is falling apart. What a phony! Real men know how to fix things and build. Good fathers take care of their homes.

It's crucial to take time with the voices. I recommend you get in a relaxed state when it's quiet all around. Really let yourself listen to what you're saying to yourself. Write it down and then say it out loud. Be spontaneous about the expression of the voices. Once you start saying it out loud, you may be surprised at the automatic outpouring.

In Firestone's group work he encourages the person to express the sentiments aloud and emotionally. He will tell him, "Say it louder," or "Really let go." I encourage you to do the same. Blurt out spontaneously anything that comes to mind. Say it in the second person. Let yourself enter into the emotional voltage triggered by the voice.

Answering The Voice

Once you've expressed the voice, you can start answering the voice. You challenge both the content and the dictates of the voice. In my diary entry I answered that I am a good husband and I've provided a fine home. My manhood doesn't depend on my doing anything. I work hard and I can afford to pay someone to fix my house. I would hire someone even if I knew how. I've better things to do with my time. Many fine men are carpenters and builders. Many are not.

I repeat this dialogue the next day. I always answer both emotionally and matter of factly (logically). *Firestone recommends that one take action by consciously not complying with the voice, or by directly going against it.* In my example, I called a carpenter I knew and told him exactly what I wanted and left him alone. I played golf and exalted that I could afford to hire someone to fix my house.

Tracking Down The Inner Critic

A second way to expose the shaming voices comes from Gestalt therapy. I simply call it *Tracking Down The Inner Critic.*

An inner self-critical dialogue goes on in all shame-based people. This game has been called the "self-torture" game. It is almost always so habitual that it is *unconscious.* The following exercise will help you make it more conscious, and give you tools to become more self-integrating and self-accepting. I've taken this exercise from the book, *Awareness,* by John O. Stevens.

Sit comfortably and close your eyes . . . Now imagine that you are looking at yourself, sitting in front of you. Form some kind of visual image of yourself, sitting there in front of you, perhaps as if reflected in a mirror. How is this image sitting? What is this image of yourself wearing? What kind of facial expression do you see?

Now silently criticize this image of yourself as if you were talking to another person. (If you are doing this experiment alone, talk out loud.) Tell yourself what you should and shouldn't do. Begin each sentence with the words, "You should _____", "You shouldn't _____" or their equivalent. Make a long list of criticisms. Listen to your voice as you do this.

Now imagine that you change places with this image. Become this image of yourself and silently answer these criticisms. What do you say in response to these critical comments? And what does the tone of your voice express? How do you feel as you respond to these criticisms?

Now switch roles and become the critic again. As you continue this internal dialogue, be aware of what you say, and also how you say it, your words, your tone of voice, and so on. Pause occasionally to just listen to your own words and let yourself experience them.

Switch roles whenever you want to, but keep the dialogue going. Notice all the details of what is going on inside you as you do this. Notice how you feel, physically, in each role. Do you recognize anyone you know in the voice that criticizes you and says, "You shouldn't _____?" What else are you aware of in this interaction? Continue this silent dialogue for a few minutes longer. Do you notice any changes as you continue the dialogue?

Now just sit quietly and review this dialogue. Probably you experience some kind of split or conflict, some division between a powerful, critical, authoritative part of you that demands that you change, and another less powerful part of you that apologizes, evades and makes excuses. It is as though you are divided into a parent and a child. The parent or "topdog" always trying to get control to change you into something "better", and the child or "underdog" continually evading these attempts to change. As you listened to the voice that criticized and made demands on you, you may have recognized that it sounded like one of your parents. Or it might have sounded like someone else in your life who makes demands on you, i.e., your husband or wife, a boss, or some other authority figure who controls you.

This critical voice can be activated in any situation of vulnerability or exposure. Once activated, a shaming spiral is set in motion. And once in motion, this spiral has a power of its own. It is imperative to externalize this internal dialogue, since it is one of the major ways you keep yourself nonself-accepting and divided. This exercise helps make the critical dialogue conscious. This is a first step in externalizing the voice.

The second step is to take each of the critical messages and translate them into a concrete specific behavior. Instead of "You are selfish," say, "I didn't want to do the dishes." Instead of "You are stupid," say, "I do not understand algebra." Each critical statement is a generalization. As such, it is untrue. There are some times when everyone wants his own way. There are areas in life in which everyone is confused. By translating these generalizations (judgments, conditions or worth) into concrete specific behaviors, you can see a real picture of yourself and accept yourself in a more balanced and integrated way.

The third step is to take these generalizations (judgments, conditions of worth) and make positive statements that contradict them. For example, instead of saying, "I am selfish," say, "I am unselfish." It is important to verbalize this and hear yourself saying it. I recommend going to someone, a person in your support group, your best friend, your husband or wife and verbalizing the positive self-affirming statement to him/her. Be sure that the person you go to is a nonshaming person.

Stopping Obsessive Shaming Thoughts

This exercise is adapted from the work of Bain, Wolpe and Meichenbaum. It is most helpful in stopping a first thought or a recurring thought which triggers a shame spiral. This four-step exercise is my adaptation of the work of Joseph Wolpe.

This technique amounts to interrupting the shaming thought with a sharp command to stop and putting a new thought — a more self-affirming thought in its place. Shame-inducing thoughts tend to fall into three categories: self put-downs; catastrophic thoughts about one's inability to handle the future; and critical and shaming thoughts of remorse and regrets.

Shaming thoughts about future sickness and catastrophe can make one chronically anxious. The "if only" I hadn't done such and such are sure ways to trigger shame spirals. And self put-downs like, "I'm too shy to make friends or get what I need," or "I'm so stupid," are ways to trigger shame spirals. Obsessions about your failures and limitations trigger spirals, resulting in severe depression. The more you obsess about something, the more intense the shame spiral. Thought-stopping aims at stopping the spiral at its source.

Pause for a moment and write down five of your most shaming thoughts.

For example, the following five are thoughts I worked on while doing this exercise a few years ago.

1. Your pants are so tight, it's really disgusting. (Obsession on weight)
2. I'm a failure as a father. (Obsession on parental duties)
3. I think I'm really sick. (Obsession on physical illness)
4. What's the use. I'm just going to die. (Obsession on death)
5. You're really selfish. (Obsession on morality)

Try to find thoughts that come up over and over again and continue to shame you. Rank order these on the basis of how disturbing and shaming they are to you. Rank the next most shaming thought number 1 and next the most shaming number 2, etc. Look at your numbers 1, 2 and 3. Now choose one of these shaming thoughts to work on. Don't necessarily choose the worst one. The important thing is to have a success experience. So choose the one you have a positive feeling about overcoming. Later you can go back to the more shaming ones as you acquire skill at thought-stopping.

Thought-stopping requires a real commitment to be constantly alert. You can't wish a shame thought away, you have to drive it out. It involves concentrating on your shaming thought and then quite suddenly shutting off and emptying your mind. Here are the four steps for stopping an obsessive shaming thought.

STEP ONE: IMAGINE THE THOUGHT

Close your eyes and create a situation in which your obsessive thought is likely to occur. Let yourself go and drift into that situation. If you have trouble visualizing, feel the feeling that goes with this shaming thought. Or perhaps hear a voice that says this thought to you. Imagine as many details as possible relating to that scene: the clothes you have on, the colors, the smells, the feelings, the sounds of the other person(s) in the scene . . . Now start to follow the chain of thoughts you had then. Immerse yourself in the self-talk. Be vividly in this scene before beginning step two. If you start feeling the shame, that's a good sign because if you can voluntarily intensify the shameful feelings, you can voluntarily reduce it.

STEP TWO: THOUGHT INTERRUPTION

Thoughts can be interrupted by using any number of startle techniques. Egg timers and alarm clocks are often used. I like to use a tape recorder. Turn it on and record yourself saying out loud *STOP*. Record it at varied intervals, none less than two minutes. Sit or lie down and get as relaxed as you can. Situate yourself so that you are near the recorder. Close your eyes and float back into the shameful situation. Really get into the details of that scene and let it develop all its typical associations. Recall the pictures, self-talk and persons, etc., that go with the shame experience. Start your recorder after you are getting into the self-talk associated with the scene. When you hear the word *STOP* (it should be recorded with loud energy), set a goal of about 30 seconds after the shouted *STOP* during which your mind can remain completely blank. Then try it again. Return to your painful thoughts, turn your recorder back on and when you hear the alarm, shout out *STOP*, notice how long your mind is free of the painful thought. Try it again and see if you can be free for a full 30 seconds. Remember your thoughts will return. To get more practice, keep your recorder going as you go back into the obsessional thought. Vary the intervals and when you hear your voice say *STOP*, work on your mind being free for a full 30 seconds. Keep doing this over and over.

STEP THREE: UNAIDED THOUGHT INTERRUPTION

Now you need to get in a place where you can be uninhibited. You need to be able to shout the word *STOP* without worrying about it. Set an alarm clock to ring in three minutes. Let yourself return to your obsessive thought. Let yourself experience it with all the attendant feelings. When the alarm rings, shout out *STOP* and notice how long your mind stays clear of the painful thought . . . Now set your alarm and try it again; return to the unwanted thoughts . . . If you're having trouble shutting off the thoughts, try one or more of the following while you shout *STOP*. You can suddenly jump up, snap your fingers, slap a desk with a ruler, hold your hand up like a traffic cop or, my favorite choice, snap a rubber band that's around your wrist . . . Continue with the exercise by putting the alarm on a tape recorder at about three minute intervals.

Once you can turn off the obsessive thought for 30 seconds, it's time to start saying *STOP* in a normal voice. Replay your tape recorded alarm clock. Now return to your obsessive thought. When you hear the alarm, say *STOP* in a normal voice. You can still bang a ruler, snap your fingers or pop the rubber band. Do this until you can stop the obsessive thought for 30 seconds by saying *STOP* in a normal voice. Once you can achieve stopping the thought for 30 seconds in a normal voice, start the whole procedure again, this time saying it in a whisper. Practice until you can stop the thought with a whispered *STOP*.

When the whisper is sufficient, use the subvocal command to stop. Just imagine hearing the word *STOP* shouted inside your head. You might tighten your vocal chords and move your tongue as if you were saying *STOP* aloud. Do not play the recorder with the alarm clock this time. Now say *STOP* to yourself silently, just as the obsessive thought is entering your mind. You simply cut it off the second it begins before it starts a shame spiral.

If you need to bang the ruler or pop the rubber band at first, do it. The idea of saying *STOP* silently is so you can stop the obsessive shame thought anywhere without calling attention to yourself. Now practice saying *STOP* silently. Let your mind drift and the moment a painful thought appears, wipe it out.

STEP FOUR: THOUGHT SUBSTITUTIONS

Now you can stop the shame thought the very moment it enters your mind. No matter how good you are at stopping thoughts, the mind will not stay blank for more than 30 to 60 seconds. Nature abhors a vacuum, so within 30 to 60 seconds the old thought may come back if you don't replace it with a positive thought.

Here are some examples of things you can say to yourself: "This is distressing but not dangerous." "You can only live one day at a time." "You can only take it one step at a time." "Take a deep breath, pause, relax." "It will soon be over; nothing lasts forever. Let it flow over." "Say goodbye to your past; it's okay to forget." "Look for what you like about you." "It's okay to be imperfect." "It takes courage to be imperfect." "Accomplish one thing today and you'll be all right."

These are only suggestions. You should choose the ones you like and then make up some of your own. If you're in a 12-Step program, use some of the common slogans like, "Let go and let God", "One day at a time", "This too will pass", "Turn it over to your Higher Power".

These new positive thoughts are called covert assertions. Using covert assertions after thought interruption was first developed by Meichenbaum. He originally called it "Stress Inoculation Training".

Effective assertions remind you of your power to control your shame spirals and shame reactions. "You" statements are usually more effective than "I" statements. Putting your assertions in the second person imposes some distance between you and your reactions and implies a degree of outside control.

Another important key to good assertions is to focus on facts. A pain in my chest is usually gas, not an impending coronary sent by God to punish me for my past wickedness.

Above all, remember that our old shaming internal self-talk has been reinforced for years and years. You must practice "stopping" the shame thoughts and repeating the covert assertions. It is a skill and like all skills, it takes time and patience. You will have setbacks. Start with a thought that is not the most shaming or difficult, like a skier on a gentle slope. I also recommend using the rubber band on your wrist. When the disturbing thought comes and you subvocalize *STOP*, also snap the rubber band. Then say your covert assertion.

The Work Of Albert Ellis And Aaron Beck

What follows is my adaptation of the work of Albert Ellis and Aaron Beck. These men have made a great contribution to our understanding of how to change our shame-producing thoughts and internal dialogue. While I do not agree with Ellis that all feelings are directly related to thoughts or internal self-talk, I do believe that his techniques are a powerful way to do maintenance work on our basic shame-based self-concept and the distorted thinking that such a belief fosters.

Our shame-based identity is predicated on the belief that we are flawed and defective persons. Such a belief is the foundation for shame-based thinking, which is a kind of egocentric tunnel vision, composed of the following types of distortion.

SHAME-BASED DISTORTED THINKING

Catastrophizing

A headache signals an impending brain tumor. A memo to see the boss means you're going to get fired. Catastrophizing results from having no boundaries or sense of worth. There are no limits to the "what ifs" that can occur.

Mind-Reading

In mind-reading, you make assumptions (without evidence) about how people are reacting to you. "I can tell by their faces, they're getting ready to fire me." "She thinks I'm immature or she wouldn't ask me these questions." These assumptions are usually born of intuition, hunches, vague misgivings or one or two past experiences. Mind-reading depends on projection. You imagine that people feel as bad about you as you do about yourself. As a shame-based person, you are critical and judgmental of yourself. You assume others feel the same way about you.

Personalization

Shame-based people are egocentric. I compare it to having a chronic toothache. If your tooth hurts all the time, all you can think of is your tooth. You become tooth-centered. Likewise if your self is ruptured and it is painful to experience your self, you become self-centered.

Shame-based people relate everything to themselves. A recently married woman thinks that every time her husband talks about being tired, he is tired of her. A man whose wife complains about the accelerating price of food, hears this as an attack on his ability to be a breadwinner.

Personalization involves the habit of continually comparing yourself to other people. This is a consequence of the perfectionistic system that fosters shame. A perfectionistic system demands comparison. "He's a much better organizer that I am." "She knows herself a lot better than I do." "He feels things so deeply. I'm really shallow." The list of comparisons never end. The underlying assumption is that your worth is questionable.

Overgeneralization

This distortion results from toxic shame's grandiosity. One slipped stitch means, "I'll never learn how to sew." A turn-down for a date means "Nobody will ever want to go out with me." In this thinking distortion, you make a broad, generalized conclusion based on a single incident or piece of evidence.

Overgeneralizations lead to universal qualifiers like, "Nobody loves me . . . I'll never get a better job . . . I will always have to struggle . . . Why can't I ever get it right? . . . No one would love me if they really knew me . . . " Other cue words are *all, every* and *everybody.*

Another form of overgeneralization is what's called a Nominalization. In nominalization a process is made into a thing. "My marriage is sick", is a nominalization. Marriage is a dynamic process. Only some aspect of it is troubled, not the whole marriage. I heard a classic example recently. A guy said, "This country is going down the tubes." This country involves countless dynamics, processes and people. Some aspect of all these dynamics bothers this man. But the whole country is not an entity.

Overgeneralizations contribute to a greater and greater restricted lifestyle. They present a grandiose absolutizing, which implies that some immutable law governs your chances of happiness. This form of distorted thinking intensifies one's shame.

Either/Or Thinking

Another consequence of shame-based grandiosity is polarized thinking or either/or thinking. The chief mark of this thought distortion is an insistence on dichotomous choices: You perceive everything in extremes. There is no middle ground. People and things are either good or bad, wonderful or terrible. The most destructive aspect of this thought distortion is its impact on how you judge yourself. If you're not brilliant or error-free, then you must be a failure. There is no room for mistakes. A single-parent client of mine was determined to be a perfect parent to her two children. The moment she felt confused and tired of parental chores, she began bad-mouthing herself to me. She was disgusted with herself as a parent.

Being Right

As a shame-based person, you must continually prove that your viewpoint and actions are correct. You live in a completely defensive posture. Since you cannot make a mistake, you aren't interested in the truth of other opinions, only in defending your own. This thought distortion really keeps you in the shame squirrel cage, because you rarely hear any new information. You get no new data that would help you change your belief system about yourself.

"Should" Thinking

Karen Horney wrote about the "Tyranny of Shoulds". Should thinking is a direct result of perfectionism. In this thought distortion you operate from a list of inflexible rules about how you and other people should act. The rules are right and indisputable. One client told me that her husband should want to take her on Sunday drives. "Any man who loves his wife ought to take her for a drive out in the country and then to a nice eating place." The fact that her husband didn't want to do this meant that he was selfish and "only thought about himself". The most common cue words for this thought distortion are *should, ought* and *must.* A shame-based person with this thought distortion makes both himself and others miserable.

Control Thinking Fallacies

Control is a major cover-up for toxic shame. Control is a product of grandiosity and distorts thinking in two ways. You see yourself as helpless and externally controlled or as omnipotent and responsible for everyone around you. You don't believe that you have any real control over the outcome of your life. This keeps you stuck and in your shame cycle.

The opposite fallacy is the fallacy of omnipotent control. You feel responsible for everything and everybody. You carry the world on your shoulders and feel guilty when it doesn't work out.

Cognitive Deficiency Or Filtering

In this thinking distortion you pick out one element of a situation to the exclusion of everything else. The detail you pick out supports your belief about your personal defectiveness. A client of mine, who was a fine management consultant, was highly praised for a marketing report he created. His boss asked if he could get the next report out in less time. My client was depressed. When questioning him, I found that he was obsessing on the fact that he thought his boss was suggesting that he was lazy. He had completely missed the enthusiastic praise in his shame-based fear of defectiveness.

Filtering is a way to magnify and "awfulize" your thoughts. This triggers powerful shame spirals.

Blaming And Global Labeling

Blaming is a cover-up for shame and a way to pass it on to others. Blaming lends itself to global labeling. Your grocery store has rotten food. The prices are a rip-off. A reserved and quiet gal on a date is a dull wallflower. Your boss is a gutless dumbo.

Blaming and Global Labeling are ways to distract from your own pain and responsibility. They are thought disorders and keep you from honestly looking at yourself and feeling your own pain. It is your pain that will move you to change.

EXTERNALIZING YOUR THOUGHT DISTORTIONS

To begin dealing with your shame-based thought distortions, you can go back to a time when you were experiencing a painful episode of shame. The following three-step procedure will help you identify your thought distortions in that situation. It will also help you to restructure your thinking. The three steps are . . .

1. Describing the shame-producing situation or event by writing it out
2. Identifying your thought distortions
3. Restructuring and eliminating your shame-based thinking by rewriting the distortions

Step three seems to offer people the greatest problem. Our distortions are so ingrained that we have trouble knowing a more logical way to think. The following is a guide for logical corrections to the thinking distortions I have described here.

Catastrophizing

The most logical counter to catastrophizing is an honest assessment in terms of realistic odds or percent of probability. What are the chances? One in a thousand (1%), one in ten thousand (.01%), or one in a 100,000 (.001%)?

Mind-Reading

Mind-reading is a form of imagining and fantasizing. In the long run you're best off making no inferences about people. Treat all your interpretations about other people as hallucinations. Use that word when you give your interpretation. Say, "My fantasy or hallucination is . . ." The best policy is to check out the evidence for your conclusion.

Personalization

Force yourself to get evidence to prove what the boss's frown means. Check it out if possible. Abandon the habit of comparing. Make no conclusion unless you have reasonable evidence and proof.

Overgeneralization

Use a three column technique for overgeneralizations.

Evidence for my Conclusion	Evidence against my Conclusion	Alternative Conclusion

Write on a 3 x 5 card, "There Are No Absolutes" and put it on your desk. Challenge words like *all, every, never, always, nobody, everybody* by exaggerating them. Say: Do I really mean I never, never, never, etc.? Learn to use words like maybe, sometimes, often.

Check out nominalization by asking yourself if you could put it in a wheelbarrow. You couldn't put a marriage or our country in a wheelbarrow. The statements, "My marriage is sick," and "This country is going down the tubes," involve the nominalization distortion.

Polarized Thinking

Use your "There Are No Absolutes" card for this one. Either/or is a form of absolutizing. Toxic shame is more than human or less than human. This is the basis of its grandiose thinking. There are no black and white judgments. The world is grey. Think in terms of percentages. About 5% of the time I'm selfish, but the rest of the time I'm loving and generous.

Being Right

Own your own good healthy shame. If you're always right, you stop listening and learning. The key to overcoming being right is to become an active listener. Carl Rogers did pioneering work in developing this skill. As an active listener you listen for the content as well as the process. You learn to listen with your ears as well as your eyes. You learn to give feedback and to check things out.

Here is an example. A man began to tell me about how great his childhood was and that his father was the finest man he ever knew. He described how his father worked from morning until night. He allowed that because his father worked so hard, he never had time for him. He couldn't even come to his state championship game. As the man said this his breathing changed; his hands tensed and he looked away from me. I gently told him what I heard him say. I told him what I had seen when he spoke of the championship game and asked him how he felt about that. He said, "Oh, it was okay. I understood. But I vowed I would always be there for my own kids." When he said that, his voice sounded angry to me. So I checked that out. I could go on and on with this example; by listening and clarifying we learn to see things as another person sees them. The checking-out process helps us grasp the other's point of view. It is important to remember that others believe what they are saying as strongly as we believe our own convictions. I like to ask myself, "What can I learn from the other person's opinion?"

Should Thinking

Use the words *should, ought* and *must* as red flags. Flexible rules and expectations don't use these words because there are always exceptions and special circumstances. Rigidity is the mark of mental illness; flexibility is the mark of mental health. Without flexibility, there is no freedom.

Think of at least three exceptions to your rule and then imagine all the exceptions you can't even imagine.

Control Thinking Fallacies

Aside from acts of God, you are responsible for what happens in your world. I suggested earlier that neuroses and character disorders are disorders of responsibility. Learning to be responsible and to allow others that privilege is to live in reality. Ask yourself, "What choices have I made that resulted in this situation? What decisions can I now make to change it?" Also remember that respect for others means letting them live their own lives, suffer their own pains and solve their own problems.

Cognitive Deficiency Or Filtering

Stop using words like terrible, awful, disgusting, horrendous, etc. Write out the phrase — "No need to magnify. I can cope. I can stand it." My favorite phrase of all comes from Abraham Low. Say to yourself, "This is distressing, but not dangerous."

To stop filtering, you have to shift focus. Place your attention on coping strategies to deal with the problem rather than obsessing on the problem itself. Focus on a theme such as Danger or Loss. Then think of things that represent safety or think of things that you have which are valuable.

Blaming Or Global Labeling

Accept responsibility for your own behavior and choices. Focus on your own problems. Look at the beam in your own eye, rather than the speck in your brother's eye. When you start labeling, ask yourself, "What am I trying to avoid?" If you find you are not avoiding, be specific rather than global. My boss is often conservative. He is rarely a risk-taker. This is accurate. Calling him a gutless dumbo is about your need to vent anger at your own situation by having to answer to him.

Changing Inner Voices Through Positive Affirmations

This is literally a positive brain-washing technique. It attempts to replace old negative judgmental and critical shaming tapes with new realistic and positive affirmations about yourself. Since most of the old critical voices came from someone else's opinion of you, they represent a subjective opinion about you, rather than who you really are. New affirmations will help you change your internal self-talk so that you can be the person you want to be.

The technique of affirmations involves writing a positive statement about yourself 15 to 20 times (ideally, twice daily). Once the positive statement is written, you are to wait for the first spontaneous response that comes to you. Usually these responses will be negative. Wait about a minute. If no response comes, continue the affirmations, writing exactly the same statement as before.

The purpose of the response is to externalize all the negative shaming messages in the unconscious. The monotony of writing over and over again catches the shame control mechanism off-guard. It is important to remember that some of the most shamed parts of our self-image were told to us repeatedly. For example, "Why can't you be like your sister/brother, etc.," or "You are so sloppy, lazy, stupid, etc." The outline for affirmations is as follows:

Affirmation	Response
1. I, _____ am often loving and kind.	Wait for first spontaneous response each time.
2. I, _____, am often loving and kind.	Whatever comes.
3. I, _____, am often loving and kind.	Whatever comes.
4. Repeat above statement.	Whatever comes.

This is to be done for 21 days. Research has shown that this amount of time is needed to be optimally effective.

Making Affirmations Work For You

1. Work with the same affirmation everyday. The best times are just before sleeping, before starting the day and especially whenever you feel "bummed out".
2. Write each affirmation 10 to 20 times.
3. Say and write each affirmation to yourself in the first, second and third persons, as follows:
   "The more I, _____, love myself, the more others love me."
   "The more you, _____, love yourself, the more others love you."
   "The more she/he, _____, loves her/himself, the more others love her/him.

Always remember to put your own name in the affirmation. Writing in the second and third person is very important since your conditioning from others came to you in this manner.
4. Continue working with the affirmations daily until they become totally integrated in your consciousness. You will know this when your mind responds positively, and when you begin to experience mastery over your goals. You will be using your mind to serve you.
5. Record your affirmations on cassette tape and play them back when you can. I very often play them while driving the car on the freeway or when I go to bed.

6. It is effective to look into the mirror and say the affirmations to yourself out loud. Keep saying them until you are able to see yourself with a relaxed, happy expression. Keep saying them until you eliminate all facial tension and grimaces.

7. Use visualizations with your affirmations.

As the responses accumulate over a period of time, you may see patterns of negative voices. You may also experience a voice you had not been previously aware of. These negative voices can become sources for new contradicting positive affirmations.

Self-Esteem Affirmations

1. I, _____, like myself. I am a lovable person.

2. I, _____, am highly pleasing to myself.

3. I, _____, am highly pleasing to others and others are highly pleasing to me.

4. I, _____, am a self-determined person, and I allow others the same right.

5. I, _____, have the right to say "no" to people without losing their love.

6. The more I like myself, the more others like themselves.

7. I, _____, am attractive and lovable and the more I acknowledge that, the truer it becomes.

8. I, _____, deserve credit for my success and accomplishments whether they were difficult or not.

9. I, _____, am now a worthwhile woman/man even if I am _____.

10. I, _____, can satisfy myself in the presence of anyone.

11. I, _____, am loved and appreciated whether I am with someone or not.

12. I, _____, am precious and incomparable whether I like it or not.

11

Dealing With Toxic Shame In Relationships

"For there is but one veritable problem — the problem of human relations. We forget that there is no hope or joy except in human relations."

Antoine de Saint Exupery
Wind, Sand And Stars

A common joke among 12-Step recovering people is the oft-quoted statement, "We don't have relationships; we take hostages." This is one of those jokes that is aimed at lightening the pain experienced by shame-based folks in trying to establish an intimate relationship. Indeed, I would say that intimacy is the number one problem resulting from internalized shame. It certainly has been for me.

Intimacy requires the ability to be vulnerable. To be intimate is to risk exposing our inner selves to each other; to bare our deepest feelings, desires and thoughts. To be intimate is to be the very ones we are, and to love and accept each other unconditionally. This requires self-confidence and courage. Such courage creates a new space in our relationship, a true intimus. That space is not yours or mine; it is ours.

As a shame-based person all this was impossible for me. I had no relationship with myself. I was in hiding, not only from you but also from myself. I was a human "doing", because I could not go inside myself.

There was no one there. I had no self. My relationship with myself was rejecting and contemptuous. What I feared most of all was exposure. I had no self to give to anyone.

Adult Child Co-dependency Issues

I suggested earlier that co-dependency and toxic shame were the same reality. In looking at relationships the word co-dependency defines the problem very accurately. The phrase Adult Child also helps us see the problem.

Attachment And Bond Permanence

Because of the abandonment trauma, shame-based people become adult children who form co-dependent relationships. These relationships are dominated by the fear of abandonment. They are the result of the "bond permanence" Alice Miller speaks of. Such relationships are dominated by attachment.

As an Adult Child it's hard for me to let anything go. I have notes I took in my first year of college 30 years ago! I have boxes full of odds and ends I've been keeping for years. Change for me is extremely difficult. Having been abandoned gives me a feeling of scarcity. I'd better hold on to what I've got because there may not be anymore. It's hard for me to delay gratification for the same reason. There may not be anymore.

I have had a hard time being flexible in my relationships. I have a monumental time giving up control. It seems impossible to leave any relationship. I also have tried to set relationships up in such a way that I become so important to the other persons that they cannot leave me.

Control

Control is the great enemy of intimacy. By definition, intimacy excludes one person controlling the other. Control is the product of your disabled will. It is an attempt to will what cannot be willed. You cannot change another person. You cannot fix your parents, spouse, lover or children. You cannot control their life or their pain.

Enmeshment

Having no authentic self, you look for a relationship with the only self you feel you have, your false self. If you are a victim, the only relationship you know anything about is with a persecutor. The opposite is true if you are a persecutor. I was my mom's Surrogate Spouse and the Family Caretaker. As my mom's Surrogate, I always looked for women I could take care of. What this amounts to is a re-enactment of the fantasy bond I spoke of earlier. The fantasy bond is an enmeshed co-dependent entrapment. It's based on the bond permanence that was set up by the abandonment trauma. Once fantasy bonded, we only have one relationship, and we repeat it over and over again.

The way out of all of this is through the original pain and inner child work, the basic grief work. Our bond fixation resulted from our authentic self being fixated and frozen by the unresolved abandonment trauma. Each time we re-enact with a new fantasy bond relationship, we are trying to do the grief work. We choose the same kind of person in order to have another chance at resolution. Each new partner represents aspects of one or both of our parents. We try to make our partner into our parent(s) so that we can resolve the conflict and move on. Since we are no longer children, it never works.

The only way out is to do the legitimate suffering that the grief work demands. To do this we have to give up the false self and leave home. That is the only way we can gain our true self.

Overinvestment Of Power, Esteem And Expectation

Because any adult/child relationship is an immature child's relationship, it results in an overinvestment of power and esteem in the other person. Such an investment flows from the abandoned child's need to have a nurturing parent. Expecting one's partner to provide what one's parent failed to provide is a delusion. It is an unrealistic expectation and ends in disappointment and anger.

Projection Of Disowned Parts Of Selves Onto Relational Partners

One of the most damaging aspects of shame-based relationships is the projecting of our disowned parts onto our partner. In the movie, *Terms of Endearment*, the fascination and repulsion of disowned selves was portrayed artfully. Jack Nicholson portrayed a man who was totally identified with his wild, impulsive sexually indulging self. Shirley MacLaine portrayed a sexually repressed, perfectionistic, overly controlled, moralistic widow who lived next door. Each incarnated the extreme polarities of toxic shame. Jack Nicholson was dissipated and acted less than human. Shirley MacLaine was "holier than thou" and acted more than human. The couple had a lot to teach each other as they danced back and forth between attraction and repulsion. Finally each helped the other to integrate the self that had been disowned. He allowed her to embrace her sexual self, while she acquainted him with his conservative and nurturing self.

When I counsel people in destructive relationships, they usually are
relating through their disowned parts. Generous men often marry selfish
women; perfectionistic women marry sloppy men; nurturing women fall in
love with emotionally unavailable men. Instead of learning from each other
by incorporating their disowned selves, they live with these selves
expressed in their mates. Since each disowns the part expressed by the
mate, they are judgmental and angry about that part in their partner.

The integration of all the parts of self is primarily a process of self-
acceptance. Wholeness and completeness result from total self-acceptance.
Wholeness is the mark of mental health. Total self-acceptance means that
every part of ourself is okay. It's equivalent to unconditional love.

Attraction/Repulsion Collages

A variation of the exercise, "Making Peace With Your Villagers", was
suggested by Reverend Mike Falls. Mike is an Episcopal priest now serving
as Chaplain of Stephen F. Austin College in Nacogdoches, Texas. Mike has
been counseling for some 20 years. He is a highly gifted and intuitive
counselor. When a client comes in with relational problems, Mike often has
them do the following.

He tells them to go through a series of magazines and select all the
pictures of the people they feel attracted to. Next they are to make a collage
of these pictures on a large poster board.

Then they go through the magazines and select the pictures of people
they feel repulsed or turned off by. They also make a large poster board of
those pictures. The collage of pictures that attracts you is more than likely
the parts of you that you are overidentified with. The pictures that turn you
off may very likely be composed of parts of yourself that you disown. Once
you are aware of the parts that turn you off, you can dialogue with the
disowned parts in the manner described in Chapter 4. I've used this
procedure many times with outstanding results.

It's good to do the poster board exercise with same sex turn on's and off's
as well as opposite sex turn on's and off's. Often men are ashamed of their
feminity and women of their masculinity.

Carl Jung believed that a part of each person's shadow was his
contrasexual opposite. Every man and woman is the union of male and
female hormones. Men have minority female hormones and majority male
hormones. Women have minority male hormones and majority female
hormones. The feminine shadow side of the male Jung called his anima.
The male shadow side of the woman he called her animus. Integration of
the anima/animus shadow is crucial for full human integration.

I have pointed out how our rigid cultural sex roles are ways we develop a false self, i.e., overidentify with one part of ourselves. Men are shamed for being feminine by being called names like "sissy" or worse. Women are shamed for being masculine.

I've mentioned *Terms of Endearment* as a movie which dramatically portrays the male/female polarity. Another movie, *The African Queen*, which starred Humphrey Bogart and Katharine Hepburn, was a brilliant portrayal of the male/female polarity. Bogart as overidentified masculine energy and Hepburn as overidentified feminine energy dramatized the fascination/repulsion dynamic of disowned parts of self. Eventually there is an integration of the disowned selves by each person in the movie, and each character is transformed by the addition of the energies represented by the other. Both movies were Academy Award winners. It would be interesting to see how many Academy Award winners portray this universal struggle for integration and wholeness.

Dangerous Relational Situations

Certain relational situations seem to be more vulnerable to shame induction than others. Criticism and rejection are painful for anyone. They are excruciating for shame-based people. I will deal with each of them separately. For now, let me describe certain situations that regularly trigger shame spirals. These situations should be prepared for and kept on the tip of our consciousness. They are as follows:

Talking To Parents

Since parents are our source relationships, they present an ever present risk of triggering old shame spirals. If you've been severely shamed in the past, be wary of just casual talk with your parents. If you're working hard on shame reduction, and you've done your stage II work, you will be well prepared to avoid getting hooked. If you haven't done such work, you are in danger. Just talking on the telephone can trigger old auditory imprints.

Authority Figures

One of the common characteristics of children of alcoholics is fear of authority figures. This almost always relates to shaming abuse in a person's source relationships. It can also relate to shaming incidents in school. I know a psychology professor who begins to experience shame if he sees a policeman driving along the street. His mother used to threaten him, by telling him that the police were going to come and pick him up and take him to jail. Such a practice is not uncommon. Many shame-based people experience over-reactions of shame inducement just by the mere presence of a boss or authority figure.

New Relationships

Shame is often triggered in new relationships. The most common form it takes is in critical self-talk which usually starts immediately after the other person has gone away. The shaming voices will suggest things like "Boy, you bungled that one!" or "Nice job, Mr. Clutch," or "You with that mumbled conversation." New relationships are risky because they expose us to someone we've never been exposed to before.

When You Or They Are Angry

Most shame-based people have anger deficits. We do not know how to express anger and we are extremely vulnerable to being manipulated by anger. I'm thinking of a guy that I really dislike. One day he expressed anger to me in a totally off-the-wall transaction. I was actually praising him. Several other people had told me that he was jealous of me. When I praised him, he reacted with anger. He heard something totally different than what I said to him. I ruminated over this incident for weeks. I wanted to call him and make everything okay. I used lots of self-assertive positive self-talk to stop myself. His anger was about him and his personal history. It had nothing to do with me.

Most of us were shamed with anger and rage. When someone expresses anger, our first reaction is fear. The various techniques in the section on criticism can help a lot in handling anger.

When You Are Hurt Or You Hurt Someone

Because we've been hurt so badly, we fear hurting others. Often we don't handle it well when we are hurt. If you had parents who manipulated you with hurts, you are especially vulnerable to hurts. Shame-based parents manipulate their children with hurts whenever the child's behaving in a way they dislike. "Your kids will never know how you've hurt your father," or "I don't know if I can ever forgive you. You've hurt me so badly." A lot of hurts are pure manipulation. They are used to get one's own way. Healthy relationships are accountable. If I've hurt you, I want to own my part in it. I also know that some of it is about you and your history.

Successes

In *Man Against Himself*, Karl Menninger describes a number of people who had complete breakdowns after they achieved success. Some even killed themselves. Shame-based people do not believe they have the right to be so happy. Deep down their toxic shame tells them that they have no right to money or fun when other people are poor and suffering. The success is not limited to material prosperity. You can feel toxic shame for being rewarded with any kind of honor. Often this is a family system issue. If the other members of the family are still in their old frozen rigid roles, and one member breaks out and creates a unique life of her own, that member may feel shame for being so different and successful. Remember, in dysfunctional families no one is supposed to leave her role in the family.

Receiving Affection And Stroking

Shame-based persons have great trouble with compliments and praise. Deep down the toxic shame cries out, "You don't have the right to be loved and receive all this attention." If you've worked hard at the material I've presented in Chapter 5, you will know that you are lovable. Your own unconditional loving relationship with yourself will be the basis of your accepting all love and praise as truly your just due.

Criticism

Years ago I wrote half a book about how to live with a critical person. Somehow I never got around to finishing the book. I felt that criticism was a major blight on human relationships and that people needed help in defending themselves against it. Certainly shame-based people are repelled and pained by criticism. They are also attracted to it as a way to interpersonally transfer shame to others.

I've never believed there was any value in so-called "constructive criticism". In our share groups we give each other *feedback*. Feedback is high quality sensory based observation *without interpretation*. In a group setting, feedback can be enormously helpful. But criticism, as I define it, is always a subjective interpretation based on one person's experience and grounded in that person's personal history. As such, it is not very useful.

I encourage shame-based people to avoid being critical and I offer the following techniques as ways to handle a critic.

The main principle in handling criticism is *NEVER defend yourself.* If you defend yourself, you're taking on the toxic shame. To help you remember these techniques I've named each of the ways to handle direct criticism with a word starting with the letter *C.* My techniques are: Clouding, Clarifying, Confronting, Columboing, Confessing, Confirming, Comforting and Confusing.

CLOUDING

Clouding is an adaptation of a technique taken from assertive training. Manuel Smith calls it fogging. In this technique you acknowledge the truth, the possibility of the truth or the probability of the truth. You do not defend. You simply let the critic's statement go through you like a cloud. For example, you are talking to your mother on the telephone. She says, "Your children are undisciplined. They are going to get in trouble at school." You answer, "You're right. They may get in trouble at school." You acknowledge the possibility of the truth of your mother's statement. Then she might say; "Well, when are you going to give them more discipline?" You say, "I'll give them more discipline when they need it." This is vague enough and it acknowledges the truth of the statement.

CLARIFYING

Clarifying is a way to pin your critic to the wall and expose the shame transferring intention of the criticism. Let's imagine your spouse says, "You're not going to wear those brown pants are you?" You answer: "What is it about these brown pants you don't like?" No matter what the critic says, you ask for clarification. If the critic says, "They look cheap." You say, "What is it that you don't like about cheap pants?" or "Why do cheap pants bother you?" These questions force your critic into an adult part of her personality. The adult is not contaminated by repressed feelings. The adult is oriented toward logic and objectivity.

The usual outcome of this technique is a dissipation of the critic's energy. One question after another will smoke out the real issue that lies behind the criticism. The real issue is either purely subjective or an attempt by the critic to cover up his own shame and pass it on to you. This technique does not always work. None of them always work. However, the more techniques you have, the more protective choices you have in asserting yourself.

CONFRONTING

Confronting means what it says. You confront your critic. It is a form of assertiveness. In confronting, I recommend that you follow these guidelines:

1. Stay under your own skin. Say what you perceive (see and hear) what you interpret, what you feel, and what you want.
2. Use "I" messages. Be responsible for what you perceive, interpret, feel and want.
3. Use sensory-based behavioral detail, rather than evaluative words.
4. Look the person right in the eyes. This has to be practiced. I teach people who are severely shame-based to stare at a spot between the person's eyes.

I had an example of confronting recently. I had just bought a new BMW convertible. It is the most expensive car I've ever owned. I have some cultural shame around growing up poor. Whenever I get around someone who is rich, my shame comes out. I start feeling inferior, like I don't belong. This same shame comes out when I have something (like a new BMW) that costs a lot of money. It is especially bad if I'm around someone who has very little money. Although I've worked hard on this, it still happens from time to time.

When I showed my car to one of my relatives, he gave me a left-handed, critical comment. He said, "Wow, that's a beauty. I bet a whole family could live for a year on what you paid for that car." When I heard the statement my mind went blank. I started to feel shame. A voice said to me, "You could have got something for half the price and given some money to the poor and needy." I've worked hard on my voices. I countered with, "I love myself for celebrating my life with a fine new car." I looked at my relative and said, "When you make comments like that, I interpret that you feel bad about my good fortune. Somehow my good fortune triggered your shame. I'm sorry you have that shame and I'm going to send you a copy of my new book on healing shame." At that point my relative began a long defensive diatribe about my sensitivity. He allowed that he meant no harm and that I misinterpreted him. He said he was very happy for me; that I deserved it. I agreed and drove away!   Confrontation may trigger rage in your critic. In that case, I simply say, "I'll be happy to talk to you when you stop raging," and I leave. Withdrawal is an assertive behavior in the face of bully or offender type criticism.

COLUMBOING

Columboing is taken from the antics of the TV detective Columbo. Detectives come in all sizes, shapes and styles. Columbo is sloppy and unkempt. He is constantly asking questions. He seems in awe of the people he interrogates. He seemingly doesn't know enough to come in out of the rain. Yet there's a profound brilliance in his apparent ineptness. He never misses the most insignificant detail. He checks everything out. He is a master of concrete specific detail.

When you Columbo your critic, you play dumb and ask a lot of questions. You say, "Now let me see if I'm getting this straight . . . You think I should stop wearing my hair this way . . . What is it about my hairstyle that you don't like?" When they answer your question, you go through the same routine. The goal is to get to the bottom of it, to expose their subjectivity. The criticism is usually about their toxic shame, and not about your hairstyle. By columboing you avoid defending yourself and get the other person out of his critical parent cover-up.

CONFESSING

This response is useful if you have clearly and unequivocally done what you're being criticized for. If you spilled the milk, you say, "Yes, I did spill the milk." Simply make an acknowledging statement. *DO NOT* add things like, "How stupid of me!" The tenth step in 12-Step programs states, "When we were wrong, we promptly admitted it." This is a maintenance step. Its aim is to keep us focused on our healthy shame. We can and will make mistakes. We need not apologize for them. They are part of the human condition.

CONFIRMING

This is a technique you can use when talking to a parent. It can be used when talking to any critical person. I like to use it on the telephone. As you are talking and the other person becomes critical, put your hand over the telephone mouthpiece and say aloud, "No matter what you say and do to me, I'm still a worthy person." Repeat this statement over and over again.

You can also anchor this positive statement. As you say it aloud, visualize yourself as standing tall, looking confident and looking the other person in the eye. As you feel the strength and power of this, touch your left thumb and left finger together. (It doesn't matter what hand you use.) Hold the touch 'til you feel the power of confirming yourself. Later on, sitting in your boss's office, or in some context where an authority figure is criticizing you, you can fire your anchor by touching your left thumb and finger together. You can hear your own confirming voice as you look at the authority figure.

COMFORTING

I use this method when I'm clear that I've inadvertently and unintentionally violated another person's boundary. The goal of comforting is to allow the other person to express his feelings, not to blame or defend yourself.

Comforting is exactly the same behavior as active listening. Let's say my car was blocking the driveway. I am away from the house. I've gone jogging. When I return, my wife is upset and angry. She says, "I have a dental appointment, and I'm late. You should have asked if I needed to use my car." I say, "Gosh, I hear that you're upset and angry. I'll move the car right now," or "I hear your frustration," or "I know how upsetting that is."

Comforting is a form of accountability. It allows us to acknowledge another's upset concerning our unintentional trespass and to make reasonable amends. What it avoids is our triggering a shame spiral by putting ourselves down. Unintentional hurts are a part of the human condition.

When All Else Fails — Confusing

This is a technique I advise using in nonintimate relationships. It is a technique to use when you've tried other methods. Confusing is a way to get someone off your back. Use it when you feel vulnerable and you can't seem to confront or clarify.

In confusing, you use either a big word, or a made-up word, out of context. For example, a fellow employee scolds you for taking too much time on your lunch hour. You do not want a confrontation or hassle. You've been through this situation before with this person and it ended in a nonresolved harangue. So you look at him and say, "Boy the traffic was otiose today." The use of an unfamiliar word, or a word out of context is often a real stopper. You can see the perplexing look on the other person's face. His mind is now involved in a search for the meaning of what you just said. You just smile and walk away.

This technique involves the fun child part of you. You can feel gleeful as you see the other person's perplexity. It puts you in control. Remember criticism is a cover-up for shame and a way to control another person. Confusing is a technique that allows you to maintain control. It can afford you a moment of pleasure rather than defensiveness.

Nothing works all of the time. If one of these techniques does not work, try another. They form an arsenal of support to protect you from the interpersonal transfer of shame.

Rejection

There is no greater potential for painful shame than rejection. This is a truism for all relationships. But for shame-based people, rejection is akin to death. We have rejected ourselves, and for someone on the outside to reject us, it proves what we fear the most, that we are flawed and defective as persons. Rejection for us means we are indeed unwanted and unlovable.

There are degrees of rejection, ranging from the store clerk not smiling to being rejected and left by a cherished lover. The pain of such a rejection is physical as well as emotional. It feels like a knife in our chest. I've only exprienced it once; I certainly would not want to repeat it. I've been with scores of clients as they go through the pain of this kind of separation.

All the techniques I've outlined can be useful while going through the grief of a broken heart. The more one has done the original pain work and left one's fantasy bonded family enmeshments, the better one will be able to handle rejection. If one is still fantasy bonded and enmeshed, the rejection is equivalent to death. For a fantasy bonded person, the rejection impacts the hurt and lonely child who has never resolved the original grief.

So, I heartily recommend that you do original pain and inner child work as a way to lessen the pain of future potential losses. The more you have differentiated and separated, the better you can handle separation and aloneness.

I recommend Judith Viorst's book, *Necessary Losses*. It presents what I'd call a philosophy of loss. It will help you accept the fact of losses as a necessary part of the human condition.

I once thought of writing a similar book. I wanted to call it "I Grieve, Therefore I Am". I wanted to show that to live well is to grieve well. Everything you have ever done has ended. Life is a prolonged farewell. Grief is the process that finishes things. The end of grief work is to be born again. So to live well is to grieve well.

When going through the grief of personal rejection, you need legitimization, social support and time. You need a loving and significant other to be with you. You need your feelings mirrored and affirmed. It's better if you have more than one significant other. This is the advantage of having a 12-Step group or any kind of support group.

Grief goes through all the stages I've described: shock, denial, bargaining, depression, anger, remorse, sadness, hurt, loneliness, etc. You need time to go through your grief stages. The worst thing you can do is rush into a new quick-fix relationship. I've seen this happen disastrously. The new relationship covers up the grief core, and another layer of unfinished grief accrues. Grieving a rejection takes time. Stay close to nourishing and supportive relationships. You are a worthy and precious person, in spite of the other person's leaving you.

Finally, remember that your "internalized shame" resulted from your childhood abandonments. Your worst fear (rejection) *has already happened* and *you survived it.* You were a needy, vulnerable and immature child and you survived. Wow! You can and will survive again.

Making A "Shame Siren"

Lesser rejections are part of the "terrible dailiness" of life. I use an adaptation of a technique I first heard Terry Kellogg describe, to deal with the everyday rejections of life. It involves developing a "shame siren." A shame siren is a kind of anchor. When someone slights you, overlooks you, gives you an evaluation or out-and-out rejects you, do the following:

1. Imagine that you have a siren you can turn on by pulling your ear. (Either ear is okay). When you pull your ear, you hear a siren which shrieks out, "Shame, Shame, Shame, Shame, Shame, Shame." When you hear it loud and clear . . .
2. Say to yourself — "Oh it's only a feeling . . . I'm really a worthy person . . . " ' Say this several times to yourself. In this way you

externalize the internalized shame. You transform it from a state of being back into a feeling. Feelings rise and fall. They are over and done with.

3. Call at least one person in your most significant support group (or see her if that's possible). Ask that person to verify your goodness and lovableness. Say, "Tell me I'm a lovable and beautiful person." This restores the interpersonal bridge.

If you get in the habit of using the "shame siren" it will become second nature to you. I've found that I have less and less overreaction to being slighted and to being evaluated by others when I use my shame siren.

Love Is Work

There are many other things I've done to work on shame in my interpersonal relationships. I've spent hundreds of hours learning and practicing effective communication techniques. I've done several assertive training and awareness seminars. All of these have enhanced my relationship skills.

The Couples Journey

I reiterate my belief that love is work. It involves commitment. This means I have to make a decision to hang in there. A decade ago I almost left my marriage. That would have been a tragic mistake. Remember that shame-based people have an all-or-nothing core of grandiosity. If it's not going my way, I'll leave. It's all or nothing!

My own marriage is a living proof of the conclusions arrived at by Susan Campbell in her book, *The Couples Journey.* Susan based that book on a long study she had done of a large number of couples who had been together in excess of 20 years. She found that each of these couples had gone through similar stages and struggles in the journey to intimacy.

ROMANTIC STAGE

Each couple had been in love. This was the Romantic Stage. That stage was characterized by a fusion of boundaries. It felt oceanic and powerful. The couple felt they could conquer all! When they married, a new stage soon began.

POWER STRUGGLE

In this stage the boundaries bounced back. There was no longer a fusion of differences. Each person's family of origin rules came into play. The

Hatfield and McCoys had to battle it out. This was a stage of really coming to know each other's differences. Rules about money, sex, sickness, socializing, celebrating, household maintenance, and with the arrival of children, parenting had to be negotiated. This took 10 years for most of the couples. It was followed by a stable period of settling down. All was quiet and routine for a while. But soon aging, the empty nest, and the individuation process ushered in a third stage.

OWNING PROJECTIONS AND ACCEPTING PERSONAL RESPONSIBILITY

This stage was characterized by a soul-searching journey of personal responsibility and a quest for ultimate meaning. Each partner owned his/her anima/animus projections. The men became individuated by embracing their female side. The women owned their masculine side. They embraced their generative needs for self-actualization. As each partner became more and more complete, a new and fruitful stage began.

PLATEAU INTIMACY

Because the partners were complete within themselves, they could come to their partner out of desire rather than neediness. There was no longer any patching up of each other's deficits. The new bond was based on choice and decision, rather than fantasy bonding out of neediness.

Each could love more generously. Each gave because he/she really wanted to. A new plateau of intimacy emerged. Some of the qualities of the in-love stage returned. Each was fascinated with the other's uniqueness and differences. Each became the other's cherished friend. Each was bonded out of deep respect and appreciation of the other.

The journey towards intimacy is marked by the following: healthy conflict; learning to negotiate and fight fair; patience, hardwork, and the courage to risk being an individual. Above all, it is marked by a willingness to embrace a disciplined love.

The bottom line of all this is that achieving love and intimacy in a relationship is a dynamic process. Such a process ebbs and flows. It is marked by conflict and individuation. In the end it is all worthwhile. I believe with St. Exupery that, "There is no joy except in human relations."

CHAPTER

12

Spiritual Awakening

"Thou hast made us for Thyself, O Lord, and our hearts are restless til they repose in Thee."

St. Augustine

The work of transforming toxic shame into healthy shame leads directly to spirituality. Healthy shame tells us that we are limited; we need help; we are not God. There is something or someone greater than us. Healthy shame is the source of spirituality.

When we know our limitations, we know that there is something greater than ourselves. In the 12-Step programs this greater something is called "The Higher Power" or God as you understand God. I personally choose to call this power God. I further believe that such a power cannot be less than personal. The apex of human life is personhood shared in the embrace of intimate love. If God is a Higher Power, God cannot be less than our human fulfillment. I believe that spirituality involves a personal union with a personal God. My way to achieve this union is through a relationship with Jesus Christ.

For a shame-based person "spiritual awakening" is impossible until the "externalization" work is done. Without such work, our ego self remains ruptured and alienated.

Full Human Consciousness

All the exercises I've described to you in the previous chapters have to do with reconstructing your ego self and integrating your alienated energies.

This is essential work on our journey toward wholeness. But you need to know that the ego self is not your true self. Figure 12.1 is a common way of representing the fullness of human consciousness. The small circle in the center is the ego self. It represents your core psychosocial boundary. It is narrowed consciousness and deals with establishing a sociocultural identity. The ego's main concern is survival. The ego's primary purpose is the fulfillment of our dependency and survival needs. When our ego is strong, we know we can get our basic needs met. We know we are able to get enough food, clothing, warmth, love and protection. A strong ego is essential for survival.

Figure 12.1. Full Range of Human Consciousness

True Self-
Awareness

Personal
Unconscious

Sub   EGO   Person-
alities

Shadow

Paraconscious
Mind

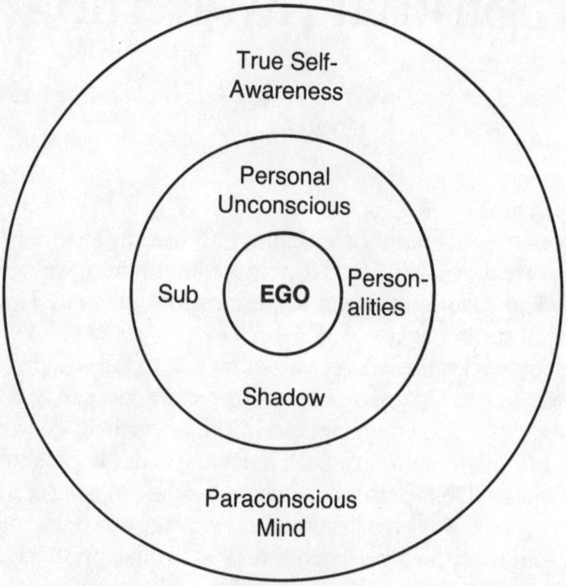

The second circle has to do with storing both current and past experience. It also represents the storehouse of our forbidden feelings, needs and drives. This circle is called the personal unconscious or subconscious. All the parts of us, which have been toxically shamed and split off, reside in the subconscious. The subconscious is the abode of our subpersonalities. Carl Jung called this part of consciousness our shadow. Once we have integrated our shadow, we are ready to expand. Expansion leads to the full range of consciousness. In Figure 12.1 the outer circle represents this full range of consciousness, Stone and Winkelman call this the level of awareness. Transpersonal psychologists often refer to this circle as the paraconscious or higher conscious mind. The paraconscious is the realm of our true beingness and selfhood. Once achieved, this level of consciousness is transforming. On this higher level of consciousness we see and experience everything differently. This is the level of discovery. Here we find a new self — not a better self. In Figure 6.1 (page 135), I called this discovery the work of Stage III.

Spiritual Awakening

This expanded consciousness is a way to describe "spiritual awakening", which is about the growth and expansion of awareness. Spirituality is about wholeness and completeness.

It is dangerous and counterproductive to work on this expansion until the lower self (ego) is unified. Spiritual masters often speak of the process of ego integration as the journey into the desert. In the Christian Scripture, Jesus goes into the desert for 40 days and 40 nights *before* beginning his spiritual work. The mystics speak of "the dark night of the soul". The dark night of the soul is the stage of preparation before entering the "unitive way". The unitive way is the way of bliss — the state of true intimacy with God.

The spiritual masters also tell us that if the ego work is not finished, we will be drawn back to it. Much of the ego work is about the bound and frozen energy caused by developmental arrest. Unless that energy is unfrozen and unbound, it will draw us back to it. You have seen that one of the major ways that your frozen and shame-bound energy is recycled is through reenactment. This can even happen with spirituality if the ego work is left undone.

Spiritual Reenactment

I've shown you how piety and righteousness can be a cover-up for toxic shame. The off-shoots of pious righteousness are perfectionism, judgment and blame. For me, one of the surest ways to know that a given style of spirituality is not true spirituality is to apply the following critieria to it. How blaming and judgmental is it?

Years ago I wondered about the judgmental rambling of both Jim Bakker and Jimmy Swaggart. As I listened to them, their words were divisive. It was always "us" and "them"; they condemned and accused others. They saw the speck but never the log. They hid from their shame. Their unresolved shame was ultimately "acted out" sexually. They were covering up their own unresolved ego issues and unresolved shame by blaming and judging others. They acted like spiritual leaders but their ego issues were unresolved.

No matter how much prayer and good work we do, if the ego needs are unmet, they will continuously draw us back to the level where the unmet need exists until that need is met.

In my own case, even though I was 10 years sober, teaching adult theology and probing the realms of ancient spiritual wisdom, I was still compulsive. *I was compulsive about my spirituality.* My *Inner Child* was still bruised and unhealed. I was still on an "insatiable quest" to fill the empty hole in my psyche. Such a quest is quite different from the healthy longing for God that St. Augustine wrote about. The issue in compulsivity is the issue of unmet developmental ego needs. Although saints may look compulsive, compulsivity is not what their yearning for God is about. Their yearning for God flows from a higher human need. It is a being need. Such a need arises when our dependency needs have been adequately met. Figure 12.2 gives you my adaptation of what Abraham Maslow called The Hierarchy of Human Needs.

Figure 12.2. The Hierarchy of Human Needs

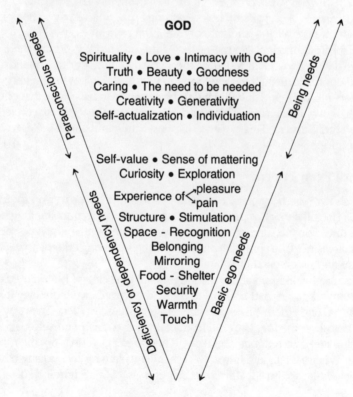

The bottom half of the pyramid represents your human dependency needs. Maslow called these deficiency needs. These needs depend on others for their fulfillment. When left unmet, the energy which should accrue from the meeting of these needs is frozen. This energy continually expresses itself in patterns of projection or repetition compulsion.

According to Maslow, these basic human needs are hierarchical. You will not be concerned about structure and stimulation if you have no food, warmth or shelter. The same is true of the being needs. You will not seek truth, beauty or God when your ego has unfinished business.

Spirituality is a basic human need. It is the reason we develop our ego. The higher reality always explains the lower. The ego serves as a platform from which to expand. A shame-based ego fears letting go of control. It guards lest it is ever caught off-guard. A strong ego structure allows you to let go and expand. *We must let go in order to grow.* As you will see in a moment, meditation, a vehicle for consciousness expansion, demands a strong ego. To meditate well you must be willing to give up ego control. A strong integrated ego is like a first stage booster rocket, allowing you to go into the outer space of higher consciousness.

Meditation

One way to achieve higher consciousness is through meditation. True meditation is the ultimate overcoming of toxic shame. Meditation aims at an immediate union with God. Physical love gave you an awareness of union. True love brought you into the chambers of the source of all union. Prayer allows you to dialogue with the source of union. And meditation allows you to be united to the source of union in a relationship of bliss.

Techniques

There are many ways to meditate. Each involves a technique. It is important to understand that the techniques of meditation are not the goal of meditation. There is no goal for meditation in the usual sense of the word.

Meditation is a search for immediate intimacy with God. The various techniques aim at creating the conditions for such intimacy. The main condition for this intimate union is called "the silence". Whatever the meditation technique, it aims at creating the "silence". The techniques range from simple breath awareness to the activity exercises of the whirling dervishes. In between there are mandalas, mantras, music, manual arts, mental imaging and massage exercises. The choice of a technique depends on your personal preferences. No one technique has greater value than any other. Each technique aims at distracting your mind and absorbing all your conscious attention.

After much practice you can create a state of mindlessness. This state is called the silence. Once the silence is created, an unused mental faculty is activated. It is a form of intuition. With this faculty one can know God directly. Spiritual masters present a rather uniform witness on this point. They speak of this intuitive knowing variously as "unitive consciousness", or God consciousness, or higher consciousness. It is direct union with God. In this union one also "knows" oneself as one really is. This "knowing" is unmediated. With such inner vision one has new *in-sights* and in-lightenments.

Three Ways To Higher Consciousness

In what follows I will outline three approaches to higher consciousness (higher power meditations). For best results, I recommend that you record the meditation instructions on your tape recorder.

Reframing Your Life Through The Eyes Of Your Magical Child

INTRODUCTION — THE MYTH OF THE MAGICAL CHILD

Figure 3.1 (page 72) shows the various layers of cover-ups for toxic shame. In the center circle there is a diamond. This diamond represents what Wayne Kritsberg calls "The Magical Child". The magical child is a psychic energy which withstood the onslaught of toxic shame. The magical child emerges when the wounded inner child is embraced and nourished.

As the reparenting process takes place, you recognize that there was a part of your authentic self which endured. This is the part of you that bought this book and leads you to seek recovery from the shame that binds you. The Magical Child is that part of you that can laugh even amid the pain; that can have fun and enjoy rich moments in life in spite of your toxic shame. The Magical Child is the part of you the scripture calls you to when it says, "Unless you become as little children". The Magical Child is the core of your essence. The Magical Child is what I understand the Zen Masters to mean by the "beginner's mind". The Magical Child is what makes you, you. When the poet Gerard Manley Hopkins writes, "What I do is me, for that I came," he's talking about this core psychic energy.

As a theologian, I see the Magical Child as the image of God in us. It's the part of you that is Godlike. In creating you, God looked at all the possible ways His reality could be manifested. You became the incarnation of one of those ways.

This way of thinking is mythical. Myths are the ways we structure meaning about realities that are transcedent. We use myths and symbols when speaking about God. All God talk is mythical and symbolic. The question of

God cannot be avoided. It is demanded by our healthy shame. As Agustine said, "Woe to him who speaks of God, yet mute are even the most eloquent." We cannot avoid speaking about God.

Paul Tillich used to scold his students for saying God talk is only symbolic. Symbols participate in the reality they try to describe. Symbols are more holistic then logic. Over half of the Judeo/Christian scripture is written in symbols, (e.g., visions, dreams, parables, psalms, etc.). Symbols are the stuff of myth.

In my myth, each of us is a unique and unrepeatable creation of God and each of us incarnates some aspect of the Divine Reality. Each of us came into the world in order to manifest that unique part of God's reality. We do that by being ourselves. *The more we are truly ourselves, the more we are truly Godlike.* To truly be ourselves, we need to accept our eternal mission and destiny. This consists in manifesting in a fully human way our Godlikeness. I follow Jesus Christ because he is for me the perfect expression of this.

Our destiny is known by the Magical Child. Once we've done our shame reduction work, we have our Magical Child available, and we can continue our journey to selfhood and true beingness. Our abandonment trauma pushed us off track. We momentarily lost our way. Our Magical Child pushed us to do our recovery work. As we resolve our grief, we resume our journey. We reintegrate our ego self and establish our ego boundaries. This forms our human identity. However, even when our ego identity is fully restored, even when it is positive and life affirming, it is socially and culturally limited. It is time bound; it is limited by language and constricted awareness. Our true self is eternal and enduring. It persists throughout all changes. It survives as our Magical Child.

Using that mythology, I invite you to expand your consciousness with your Magical Child. Since this part of you has been alive but hidden, it is now time for expansion and unfolding. The following meditation is one way to continue this unfolding.

MAGICAL CHILD MEDITATION

Find a quiet space where you will not be interrupted. Take the phone off the hook or turn off the ring signal. Find a comfortable chair. Sit in an upright position. Do not cross your arms and legs. Choose a time when you're not too tired.

Meditation is most effective when your mind is producing alpha and theta brain waves. Alpha and theta brain waves create an altered state of consciousness which resides in-between waking and sleeping. This is the proper context for meditation.

Record the following:

   Start by focusing on your breathing . . . Breath is life. It symbolizes the
most fundamental rhythm of life, holding on and letting go. As you breathe
in . . . and out . . . imagine an ocean with the waves rising (as you breathe
in) cresting and spilling over (as you breathe out). Hear the power of the
ocean as the waves spill over and wash onto the shore . . . (Do this for two
minutes) . . . Now let your mind become full of breathing . . . Be aware of
your chest as you breathe in . . . and as you breathe out . . . Just be mind-
full of breathing . . . (one minute) . . . Now be aware of the air as it comes
in and as it goes out . . . Be aware of the difference in the air as it comes in
and as it goes out . . . Is it cooler or warmer as it comes in? . . . As it goes
out? . . . (one minute) . . . Now breathe into your forehead and feel any
tension that may be there and breathe it out . . . Repeat . . . Now breathe in
around your eyes; look for any tension and breathe it out . . . Repeat. Now
breathe in around your mouth and jaws; look for any tension and breathe
it out . . . Repeat. Continue this process with your neck, shoulders, arms,
hands and fingers, chest, stomach, buttocks, knees, calves, feet and
toes . . . Now let your whole body relax . . . Relax every muscle and every
cell . . . Imagine that you are hollow on the inside, like a human bamboo
stalk . . . Breathe in a warm golden sunlight through the top of your head
and breathe it out down through your whole body and out through your
toes . . . Repeat this several times . . . Now imagine you are standing at the
base of three stairs leading to a door . . . Place all your worries in an
imaginary ball of sunlight . . . Make the ball with your hands . . . Put all
your worries in the ball of sunlight and bury them . . . You can have them
back later on . . . Walk up the three stairs and open the door . . . You will
see three more stairs leading to a door . . . Make another ball of sunlight
and place all your presuppositions and rigid beliefs in the ball and bury
it . . . You may have them back when you're finished . . . Walk up the next
three stairs and open the door . . . You will see three more stairs leading to
a door . . . Now imagine another ball of sunlight by cupping your hands
together. This time place your ego in it. Include all the Roles you
play . . . Put them in the ball one by one . . . Now open the door and walk
out on a porch . . . Imagine that you are looking into the abyss of outer
space . . . Look straight ahead and see a stairway of light beginning to
form . . . When it is completely formed, look to the top of the
stairs . . . Your Magical Child will appear there . . . the child will begin
walking down the stairs toward you . . . Notice everything you can about
this Magical Child. What does the child have on? . . . Look at the child's face
as the child comes near . . . Notice the child's eyes . . . hair. When the child
steps onto the porch embrace the child . . . Feel the connection with this
powerful part of yourself . . . Talk things over . . . Imagine the two of you

could review your life . . . The moment you were conceived . . . what was your mother's emotional condition? . . . What about your father? . . . See their union and your conception from God's point of view. Ask your Magical Child about your purpose . . . Why are you here? Who are you? What is your specialness and uniqueness? . . . What unique part of God do you manifest? . . . What is the difference about you that makes a difference? . . . Accept whatever your Magical Child tells you . . . The answer may come in words . . . You may receive a symbol or a collage of symbols . . . You may have a strong feeling . . . Just accept what you receive . . . even if you cannot make sense out of it. If you do get a clear answer to your sense of purpose, review your life from that perspective . . . See the significant persons who affected your life. You may see someone who seemed to be a negative influence in the past as an integral part of your plan or divine purpose. You may also see someone who seemed to be a positive influence in the past as less important for your true destiny. Go through all the events of your life step by step . . . View them all as part of a larger plan and purpose . . . See them from your Magical Child's point of view . . . Let the film of your life run up until the present moment . . . Reflect on what you are experiencing now . . . Feel the presence of your Inner Child . . . Get a sense of the unity and coherence of your life . . . See it all from a more expanded point of view . . . See it all . . . your whole life . . . differently than ever before . . . (one minute) . . . Embrace your Magical Child . . . Tell your child when you will meet with her again (sooner rather than later) . . . Hear your child assure you that she is there to guide you . . . Your child is your ally . . . She has been there holding on to you through all the bad times . . . Now is the time for ripening and expanding . . . See your child walk up the magic stairway of light . . . Take two minutes to reflect on what has transpired . . . Let yourself dream a dream of integration . . . Let all your life come together in one unified purpose . . . Feel your willingness to commit to your purpose . . . Now for just two minutes of clock time, which is all the time in the world to the unconscious . . . dream your dream . . . (allow two minutes on the recorder) . . . Now begin to feel the place where you are located in the room . . . Feel your clothes on your body . . . the air on your face . . . the sounds in the room . . . Let feelings of your worth and value flow over you . . . Tell yourself that there has never been anyone like you . . . (10 seconds) . . . nor will there ever be anyone like you again . . . (10 seconds) . . . Make a decision to go forth and share yourself with others . . . (10 seconds) . . . Go back through the door and down the stairs . . . Pick up the ball of sunlight with your ego in it . . . Reintegrate your ego . . . Feel yourself coming back to your normal walking consciousness . . . Walk through the next door and down the stairs . . . Decide whether you want your old beliefs and presuppositions . . . If you do, take them out of the ball of sunlight . . . If not, walk through the third door, down the stairs and pause . . . Decide if you want your worries back . . . Remember that many worries are forms of fear and have a quality of wisdom about them . . . It is wise to fear certain things . . . You decide if you want some or all of your worries . . . Take the ones you want out of the ball of sunlight . . . Leave the rest buried . . . Walk to some beautiful place you know about and gaze into the sky . . . See the white clouds form the number three . . . Feel your feet and hands; feel the life coming back into all of your body . . . Feel every cell and muscle awake . . . See the clouds blow away the number three and new clouds form the number two . . . Feel yourself returning to your normal waking consciousness . . . See the clouds blow away the number two and new clouds form the number one . . . When you see the number one, open your eyes and be fully awake . . .

Always sit for a few minutes after you've meditated. Let yourself integrate the experience. Parts of the experience may come back later in the day. Meditation is an inner exprience. It feels strange, even weird at first. The inner life has its own language. Inner experience is expressed in images, symbols and feelings.

As a shame-based person I had rarely been in my inner castle, as it were. I was busy guarding and defending myself lest I be found out. I was so busy guarding the outside that I never went inside. I lived in the front yard.

Meditation takes time and it takes practice. My grandiosity and impulsiveness wanted it all at once. I wanted the floodgates to open and for God to appear . . . My Magical Child has often punctured my grandiosity. I use my Magical Child as an inner guide. I remember once asking him what I needed to do to resolve a spiritual dilemma I was having. His answer was, "Start by cleaning off your desk!" I was terribly disappointed with this answer. I wanted him to tell me to go to a Trappist monastery or fast for seven days. Clean off your desk? Come on! The way of the spirit is very simple. It is simple but difficult. The way of the ego intellect is complex and complicated. Analyzing and intellectualizing are complex but easy.

The answer to your purpose in life is most often very simple. For me, my purpose is to be the person I was meant to be. That means that I'm supposed to be me. It's the only thing I do not have to work at. To be me is to love myself in the ways I've described. This includes loving others since I couldn't really love myself without wanting to expand and grow, and that can only happen through love.

Looking At Yourself Through The Eyes Of Your Higher Power

This meditation is a short one. It can be done in a 10 to 15 minute time span. It allows you to look at yourself from the point of view of your higher consciousness or Higher Power.

Use your own experience of God as you understand God. *Record the following instructions on your tape recorder.*

Close your eyes and focus on your breathing . . . (10 seconds) . . . Be aware of your breath as it comes in . . . and as it goes out. Focus on the difference in the feeling of the air as it comes in and as it goes out . . . Is it cool as it comes in? . . . It it warm as it goes out? . . . Feel the difference as completely as you can . . . (30 seconds) . . . Now take several very deep breaths . . . as you breathe in and out begin to see the number five . . .(20 seconds) . . . Then see the number four . . . (20 seconds) . . . Then see the number three . . . (20 seconds) . . . Then see the number two . . . (20 seconds) . . . Then the number one. See the number one turn into a door and see it open . . . (10 seconds) . . . See a long winding corridor leading to a field of light . . . Walk down the corridor, noticing that there are doors on either side . . . Each door has a symbol on it . . . Walk toward the field of light . . . (10 seconds) . . . Walk through the light field into an ancient church or temple . . . (10 seconds) . . . Look around this holy place . . . (20 seconds) . . . Sit down in a comfortable place and allow some symbolic image of your God or Higher Power to enter the church or temple . . . Allow the image to come toward you and to sit across from you . . . Be aware that this is the presence of truth, beauty, goodness and love . . . Imagine that you could float out of your body into this presence . . . When you can see yourself sitting across from you, make a kinesthetic anchor with your thumb and a finger on your right hand. Hold the anchor while doing what follows:

Imagine that you are your Higher Power. You are the Creator of life, love and all the humans on earth. You are looking at you this very moment. You see yourself through the eyes of Love itself. You are in the very heart and mind of Love itself. You can see yourself completely and perfectly. You begin to recognize qualities and aspects of yourself that you've never seen before . . . (20 seconds) . . . You see and hear what your Higher Power cherishes about you . . . (20 seconds) . . . You feel yourself totally and unconditionally accepted . . . (30 seconds) . . . Holding all that your Higher Power loves and cherishes about you, especially those aspects of yourself you were unaware of with your own eyes, slowly come back to your own body. Be totally you. Let go of your thumb and finger anchor. Feel all the love and value that is you. Thank your Higher Power and walk out of the place where you are. As you come to the entrance, see a scene of natural beauty. Walk out into it. Feel yourself part of the universe. Feel yourself as a necessary part of nature. You are supposed to be here . . . (30 seconds) . . . Look up in the sky and see the clouds form the number one — Tell yourself you will remember this cherished feeling. See the cloud become a two — then three — feel your hands and feet. Be aware of your body. See the clouds form the number four, know you are coming back to your normal waking consciousness. See the number five and slowly open your eyes . . .

Mindlessness — Creating The Silence

This meditation aims at enhancing your "beingness". When you are in touch with your beingness, you are one with everything that is. There is no longer any separation. Without separation there is no object or event outside of you to achieve.

One meditation master, Suzuki Rashi said, "As long as you are practicing meditation for the sake of something, that is not true practice." In meditation we simply let ourselves be. The more we stop thinking and doing, the more we just are. Since God, as I understand God, is Being itself, to let ourselves be is to enter into union with God.

In this meditation you can begin to experience pure moments of just being here. These moments feel open and spacious because they are devoid of personal needs, meanings and interpretations. This larger space is one way to describe the *silence*. Meditation can teach us how to contact this larger space or (silence). Since this space lies beyond the constant search for personal meaning, it can affect a radical transformation in the way we live. In shame-based lingo, this means you will give up your hypervigilance and guardedness. Meditation can lead you to this larger sense of aliveness. Such a sense of aliveness is not about anything we do; it's about who we are. As Jacquelyn Small says, "There is nothing that has to be done; there is only someone to be."

Creating the state of silence or mindlessness involves discipline. It is best compared to water dripping on a rock. Over the years the rock gets eaten away. The following is one of many ways the state of mindlessness can be approached.

Begin this meditation using the same instructions for the Magical Child meditation. Creating a state of mindlessness involves following your awareness wherever it goes. Start with your breathing and let your thoughts come and go. Do not try to control them or direct them in more pleasant directions. Whenever you become aware of your thoughts, gently bring your awareness back to focusing on your breathing.

Start by becoming aware of the sensation of air passing through your nostrils. Feel its touch. Notice in what part of the nostrils you feel the touch of the air when you inhale, and in what part of the nostrils you feel the touch of air when you exhale . . . Become aware of the warmth or coldness of the air . . . Breathe into your forehead and become aware of any sensations in your forehead . . .

Continue to be aware of any sensation around your eyes, around your mouth, . . . in your neck and shoulders . . . Just be aware of the sensation . . . Continue through your whole body. Omit no part of you . . . You may find some parts of you completely devoid of sensation . . . Keep focused on those parts. If no sensation emerges, move on . . .

Once you get to your toes, start over again . . . Do this for about 10 minutes . . . Then become aware of your body as a whole. Feel the whole of your body as one mass of various types of sensations . . . Now return to the parts — focusing on your eyes, mouth, neck, etc. . . . Then once again rest in the awareness of your body as a whole.

Notice now the deep stillness that has come over you . . . Notice the deep stillness of your body . . . Go back to a part and come back to the stillness . . .

Try not to move any part of your body . . . Each time you feel an urge, don't give in to it, just be aware of it as sharply as you can. This may be extremely painful for you at first. You may become tense. Just be aware of the tenseness . . . Stay with it and the tension will disappear . . . (one minute).

Now imagine you are entering a holy place . . . Walk toward a circular altar with a dirt floor . . . There is a book buried in the dirt and you know where it is . . . Dig it up and start looking through it until you find a page that draws you to it . . . You may see a symbol on this page . . . You may have a strong feeling about something you see . . . or you may read something that engages you . . . Take whatever comes to you and return the book to the place you found it . . . Walk out of the holy place and see yourself as you come out . . . See the symbol or feeling or message you got from the book as if it were on a screen . . . If what you experienced was a feeling, imagine that feeling taking some form. See yourself interacting with your symbol, feeling or message . . . (1 minute) . . . Then let the whole horizon become darker and darker until there is nothing but darkness . . . Gaze into the darkness . . . (1 minute) . . . Begin to see a candle flame in the center of the darkness . . . See the light from the flame growing brighter and brighter until the whole landscape is illuminated . . . Gaze into a field of pure white light; let yourself be absorbed by the light . . . Let yourself flow into the light . . . Be aware of nothing. There is nothing, only a great abyss and emptiness . . . Flow into the "nothingness" . . . (3 minutes) . . .

Slowly begin to see the number one on the horizon; then the number two. Very slowly see the number three, number four, five, six; when you see the number seven, open your eyes. Sit in reverie for a few minutes.

To be "mindless" is to be free of any mental content. In the silence, you stop all the inner voices. You turn off your mental chatter. The mind is emptied and focused on nothing (no-thing). Such a state is a state of pure being. Being is the ground of all the beings that are. There are human beings, animal beings, tree beings. Each is a specific form of being. Each is a thing. When the mind reaches a state of nothingness, it goes beyond all things to the ground of all things. When you get beyond anything you arrive at a place beyond any form of being. You arrive at pure being. So to get to the nothingness, you actually get to the ground of everything. You become united to being itself. In such a state you are connected to everything.

Unity Consciousness — Bliss

It is at this point that you've arrived at unitive consciousness. In this state there is no division or separation. All the dichotomies are synthesized. There is a coincidence of opposites. The veils of appearance break down. You see the interconnection of all consciousness. This state is also known as bliss. It is a state of pure joy and peace. In this state everything is transformed. All your egoic understandings are transcended. You do not become a better self; you become a different self. You see your whole life as perfect; as something that had to be. You get a view of the whole puzzle not just the pieces of the puzzle.

Ego Integrity

You arrive at what Erik Erikson calls ego integrity. Ego integrity means that you totally and unconditionally accept yourself. Erikson writes: "It is the acceptance of one's one and only life cycle as something that had to be . . . the possessor of integrity is ready to defend the dignity of his own lifestyle against all threats" (*Childhood and Society*).

With ego integrity you can truly say, "If I had my life to live over, I'd do it all the same!" *Ego integrity is total self-acceptance, the complete overcoming of toxic shame.* Once such a state is experienced, it has no opposite. You thirst for it. It is a "land more kind than home", according to Thomas Wolfe.

Synthesis Of Opposites

In a state of bliss you no longer see things in opposites. There is no "us" and "them". You experience unity. The ego boundaries you worked so hard to establish have become the very structure which allowed you to transcend all boundaries. The naive mysticism of your Magical Child has expanded into the reflexive mysticism of the adult. You feel a oneness with all creation. You are aware that separation is an illusion.

Higher Power

The mystics and physicists tell us that in the state of bliss, we have a *Higher Power* available to us. Being connected to all consciousness gives us resources of insight and knowledge that are more powerful than any we've ever imagined. The only condition required for such knowledge is the letting go of all ego control. A slogan in 12-Step groups says, "Let go and let God". Another one reads, "Turn it over". Both slogans urge you to let go of ego control.

Mind Over Matter

The physicists also tell us that both mind and matter are forms of energy (Quantum Theory). Matter is a less radiant form of energy; it vibrates at a lower frequency. Mind or consciousness is a higher frequency energy; it can ensconce matter and powerfully affect it. This may involve phenomena like psychokinesis.

Delores Kieger has taught thousands of people how to alleviate pain through the laying on of hands. This phenomena is achieved through concentration and the development of kinesthetic sensory acuity. Anyone can learn to do this. Mind can create events outside itself through the use of imagination. This includes the creation of wealth. It also includes the power of mind to heal the body.

Prayer

Prayer can powerfully influence events in the natural order. Prayer depends on a higher level of spirituality. Prayer depends on God as we understand God. In prayer we let go and let God. We give up control and allow a childlike trust and faith to emerge.

The Intentionality Of Consciousness

All consciousness is intentional. This means it is purposeful. "Nothing walks with aimless feet," says the poet. I've suggested that "people make sense" no matter how bizarre their behavior may appear to us. When we are in higher consciousness, we are united to all consciousness. We share in the purposefulness of all consciousness. Many physicists and transpersonal psychologists believe that there is a "plan" for our lives. As we look back over our lives, it is often clear that there was such a plan. I knew things at 12 years of age that have acutally happened in my life. Over the years it has become clear to me that if I get out of the way and quit trying to control things, they always work out. Barry Stevens calls this "flowing with the river". Our ego, with its limited vision can't see the proverbial forest for the trees. To "Let go and let God" is to turn it over to higher consciousness.

Nonattachment

Spiritual masters and saints have always practiced letting go. They call it nonattachment. They tell us that our suffering stems from our attachments. What we are emotionally invested in is what causes our pain. Since all human events have an ending, emotional pain is inevitable as long as we are emotionally invested.

In the movie, *Zorba The Greek*, Zorba exhibited this nonattachment when he met with calamity. He had totally committed himself to the project of building a lumber conduit down a mountain side. No one could have worked harder or been more committed. After months and months of hard work, the project was ready to be tested. As the lumber flowed down the mountain, the momentum created too great a force and the conduit collapsed. Zorba was stunned. He took it all in. Then he began to laugh! He laughed and laughed! Then he began to dance! He danced and danced! The laughing and dancing were a kind of cosmic chuckle and cosmic dance. From the perspective of "unitive consciousness", no single event has importance. What is important is the whole.

The whole is what wisdom is all about. "The mountain to the climber is clearer from the plane," says the poet. We can only understand the parts when we see the whole. As Sri Aurobindo says, "You must know the highest before you can truly understand the lowest." Unitive vision and nonattachment are the fruits of bliss.

There are other fruits that flow from spiritual bliss. Some of these are serenity, solitude and service. Each is manifested differently in accord with each person's unique lifestyle.

Serenity

Serenity is characterized by what Robert Frost called "riding easy in harness". With serenity, your life will become less problematic and more spontaneous. You will act without analyzing everything and without ruminating. You will quit trying to figure it out. You will stop over-reacting; your hypervigilance will leave you. You will enjoy each and every moment as it comes along. You'll quit believing in scarcity and give up your impulsiveness and instant gratification. You'll accept the richness of life moment by moment. You'll see what you see, hear what you hear, know what you want and need, and know that you can get your needs and wants met. Serenity changes life into a childlike vision where "meadow, stream and every common sight" take on a newness. Those who are serene, love the earth and all things. Life is its own splendid justification.

Solitude

Each of us is alone. This is the hard and fast boundary of our material condition. Aloneness is a fact of life. How we embrace our aloneness determines whether it will be toxic or nourishing. Toxic aloneness is fostered by toxic shame. It is a consequence of being self-ruptured. Nourishing aloneness is a fruit of blissful spirituality. It flows from the union with God, giving us immediate knowledge of our self. From such knowledge flows self-love, self-acceptance and self-valuing.

Because you love and value yourself, you want to spend time with you alone. This is called solitude. When you know the joys of solitude, you want more of it; you also want it for the ones you love. Instead of your old shame-based possessiveness, you will become a protector of your own and your beloved's solitude.

Goethe said this well when he wrote:

> "Once the realization is accepted that even between the closest human beings infinite distances continue to exist, a wonderful living side by side can grow up, if they succeed in loving the distance between them which makes it possible for each to see the other WHOLE against the sky. A good marriage is that in which each appoint the other guardian of his solitude."

Solitude is possible because you have done your ego work, especially the "original pain" work. With the completion of that work, you accepted your separateness. The fear of separation is why you stayed "fantasy bonded" in the first place. The fantasy bond is an illusion; the illusion that you will always be protected by your parents.

Once you've accepted your separation and aloneness, you've come to believe that your ego is strong enough to take care of you. Your ego is strong enough for you to survive alone. This is also the precondition for meditation. As you come to experience the blissful union with God through meditation, you come to know your true self. You also come to know that there is a place where you are never alone. With such awareness, solitude is most desirable.

Service

Spiritual bliss synthesizes life's polarities. The more solitude you come to know and enjoy, the more you will want to serve others in ways that enhance their spirituality. As Ken Wilber says,

> "To intuit and know your true self is a commitment to actualize that self in all beings, according to the primordial vow. However innumerable beings are, I vow to liberate them."

> Ken Wilber
> *No Boundaries*

Service may also mean a commitment to worshiping in a way that fits your own beliefs. You may want to go back to your old church and religious denomination. If you return, you will have a new outlook and an expanded awareness. You can then see worship and ritual as ways to incarnate the "pooled memories" of your religious tradition. If your religious preference is a sacramental church, you can participate in the commemoration of the mighty acts of God as you understand God. As you participate in the symbolic reenactments of your ancestors' collective memory of their God, you can experience yourself as part of the past and part of a living tradition. You can experience your actions in the now as bringing the past into the present and the present into the future.

Service means caring for others and giving back what you have received. The 12th Step urges its participants to carry their spiritual awakening to others who suffer from toxic shame. All of us who have come out of hiding need to bring the light to others. Carrying the message is done by modeling, not by moralizing. It is done by those who "walk the walk as they talk the talk". This means that there are no gurus. There are only those who have walked a little further down the path. Anytime you make someone into a guru, you have relinquished your own power. Service and love for others flows directly from service and love for ourselves. I love the motto of the Dominican Priests, "To hand on to others what you yourself have contemplated". We truly cannot give what we haven't got. We cannot teach our children self-valuing if we are shame-based. We cannot take our clients where we have not been as therapists.

Service is a true mark and fruit of spiritual bliss. In bliss we know what Paul Claudel meant when he wrote:

> "There is no one of my brothers . . . I can do without . . . In the heart of the meanest miser, the most squalid prostitute, the most miserable drunkard, there is an immortal soul with holy aspirations, which deprived of daylight, worships in the night. I hear them speaking when I speak and weeping when I go down on my knees. There is no one of

them I can do without. Just as there are many stars in the heavens and their power of calculation is beyond my reckoning so also there are many living beings . . . I need them all in my praise of God. There are many living souls but there's not one of them that I'm not in communion in the sacred apex where we utter together the *Our Father.*"

Empowerment

Bliss engenders empowerment. We move from our childish belief that we will always be victims to a childlike spontaneity and optimism. We embrace our imagination and creativity. We refuse to be victims any longer. We become the artistic creators of our own lives. We take risks. We go after the things we really want.

As you come to the end of this book, my most sincere hope is that you have gone a long way in healing the shame that binds you. In so doing you've opened yourself to the awesome, but limited possibilities, of your human nature. Such possibilities are modeled by the magnificent outpouring of human creation. Our great musicians were limited by the laws of the musical scale, but within those limits the variety of their compositions are almost unbelievable.

Our great painters were limited by their canvas, but walking through a museum of fine art can be an awesome and overwhelming experience. Within our human limits, there are still miracles to come. *You* are one of the miracles!

E P I L O G U E

Fear of exposure lies at the heart of shame. As we allow our shame to be exposed to others we are exposed to ourself. As the writer of the book *Shame* says:

> "Exposure to oneself lies at the heart of shame: we discover, in experiences of shame the most sensitive, intimate, and vulnerable parts of ourself."

In this sense, the healing of the shame that binds you is a revelatory experience. Because your shame exists at the very core of your being, when you embrace your shame, you begin to discover who you really are. Shame both hides and reveals our truest self.

Healing toxic shame is also revolutionary. As you truly feel your toxic shame, you are moved to change it. This can only happen by being willing to come out of hiding. We have to move from our misery and embrace our pain. We have to feel as bad as we really feel. Such a feeling moves us to change ourselves. It is revolutionary.

Toxic shame, with its more than human/less than human grandiosity, is a problem involving the denial of human finitude. Being human requires courage. It requires courage because being human is being imperfect. Alfred Adler first used the phrase, "The courage to be imperfect". You need the courage to be imperfect. As I've tried to show, our families, religions, schools and culture are based on perfectionistic systems. And perfectionism is the major cause of toxic shame. Perfectionism sets us up for being measured, which in turn sets us up for perpetual disappointment. Perfectionism is boundariless. There are no limits. You can never do enough. It takes courage to do battle with these perfectionistic systems. But it's worth it!

The courage to be imperfect engenders a lifestyle characterized by spontaneity and humor. Once you've accepted that mistakes are natural products of limited human awareness, you stop walking on eggs. You take more risks and feel freer to explore and be creative.

Most importantly, you will laugh more. *A sense of humor may be the ultimate criterion for measuring a person's recovery from internalized shame.* Being able to laugh at events, other persons, and ourselves requires true humanness. To have a sense of humor you have to straddle the more than human, less than human polarity. This demands that you be a paradox juggler.

A sense of humor is based upon the juxtaposition of the incongruous. To have a sense of humor is to take life less somberly and more seriously. As Walter O'Connell has so well written, "Humor results from re-solution of human paradoxes." Every human paradox has two extremes. It is by reuniting these extremes that we gain energy and hope. These are the fruits of our humor. It also gives us perspective and balance. It lets us laugh at both our overinflated egos and our flaws. Give yourself permission to enjoy every minute of every day of your life. Ride easy in harness, as Robert Frost would have it. Go for enlightenment. You'll know you're there when you lighten up!

A P P E N D I X

Note To Psychotherapists

There is a growing awareness concerning the lack of studies on shame in modern psychology. Joseph Campos, a developmental psychologist at the University of Illinois, writes, "We know too little about shame. It has been the ignored emotion in psychology." This neglect has seriously affected the success of psychotherapy in treating shame-based people. Dr. Donald Nathanson, a psychiatrist at Hahnemann University in Philadelphia, states that "Shame is the tacit issue in psychotherapy, but its importance has been under-recognized by many therapists." Dr. Nathanson recently led a course on, "Shame In Psychotherapy," at the annual meeting of the American Psychiatric Association.

Helen Block Lewis, a psychologist at Yale University, has been one of the first to study the issue of toxic shame in psychotherapy. In a study of transcripts from 180 psychotherapy sessions, Dr. Lewis found that, "When the therapist failed to recognize the patient's feelings of shame, the patient's problems were prolonged or worsened. When the therapist recognized the shame and helped the patient deal with it, the treatment was shorter."

Dr. Lewis' work verifies my own experience as a patient and as a therapist. At a point in my life of deep confusion and despair, I spent a three-month therapy complying with my psychiatrist and dutifully taking the tranquilizers and sleeping pills he prescribed. Six months after the termination of this treatment, I was carried into Austin State Hospital.

I have some serious doubts about the effectiveness of the traditional mental health models of treatment in regard to the various syndromes of toxic shame. Maybe a more precise understanding of toxic shame can open up some new and innovative approaches.

The following chart is a raw bones contribution to the emerging dialogue. It compares and contrasts toxic shame and toxic guilt. The problem is more

239

complicated than what I present. But it clearly suggests a different treatment design for shame and guilt.

My chart offers some general guidelines for the treatment of toxic shame. The restoration of the "interpersonal bridge" is the sine quo non in treating shame-based people. This may be the key.

Martin Buber said long ago that what heals in any model of therapy is the "I and Thou" relationship. Once the interpersonal bridge is established, the client will accept the therapist's nonjudging acceptance. I recommend that toxically shamed people be directed into groups as soon as possible. The group is crucial, no matter what the specific syndrome of shame happens to be. The group seems to provide a sense of mattering and of being important in a way that a one-to-one alliance cannot provide.

Cermak has pointed out the advantages of group psychotherapy. His belief is that it provides "a setting in which the issues of co-dependency emerge spontaneously." People will behave in the group much as they do in real life. They will be distrustful, controlling, people-pleasing, critical, etc. As they come to understand that those behaviors reflect unconscious patterns of defense against toxic shame, the group can become a laboratory for alternative behaviors. (Diagnosing and Treating Co-dependence.)

The 12-Step programs are the therapist's greatest ally. I hope my chapter on the power of the 12 Steps to reduce toxic shame sheds some light on the subject. I believe it would be useful to develop 12-Step programs for all the syndromes of toxic shame.

There are already jokes circulating about such an idea. For example, 'They tried to start a paranoids anonymous meeting but no one would tell where it was being held!" In all seriousness, 12-Step groups would be difficult for character disordered "shamies". But aren't all approaches difficult in treating the character disorders? I guarantee that there are plenty of alcoholics who are character disordered and they are making it in AA.

I believe that people with shame-based identities must work on changing both the collages of visual shame memories and the auditory imprints that store the internal voices which triggered shame spirals. I'm excited about the powerful methods used in NLP for achieving these ends.

Finally, I would offer a word to those clinicians who wince at the word "spiritual". The 12-Step programs have had incomparable success in healing addictions. The 12th Step makes it crystal clear that one has not healed his addiction until he has had a "spiritual awakening". The millions of recovering addicts using that step are raw data enough to compel any scientist worth his salt to investigate this spirituality. Toxic shame is spiritual bankruptcy in the sense I've defined. Healing this shame requires spiritual awakening in the sense I've defined.

Appendix I

	Toxic Shame	Toxic Guilt
Rapport with Therapist	This is absolutely essential. The "interpersonal bridge" *must* be restored.	Rapport is useful but not crucial.
Confrontation of Denial	Cover-ups must be confronted. Rapport must be adequate to demand "surrender" of control.	This is not relevant.
Feeling Work	Feeling work is essential. To feel any feeling is shame-reducing. Ultimately "original pain" grief work needs to be done.	Guilt often is a racket for anger. The racket must be confronted and anger work must be done.
Confrontation of False Beliefs	When "interpersonal bridge" is restored — gently confront false self-image.	"Grandiosity" must be confronted from the beginning. Grandiosity is about the false sense of super-responsibility and denied uniqueness.
12-Step Group	This is the most effective treatment for all forms of addiction (and possibly for all syndromes of shame).	This is not relevant.
Imagery and Affirmations	These are crucial for remapping the visual and auditory collages of shame.	Affirmations are useful in changing false beliefs.
Spirituality	This is crucial for trust. The goal for healing spiritual bankruptcy is "spiritual awakening".	A stern and punitive God as well as a rigid moralism often have to be confronted and challenged.
Group Therapy	Group is crucial for continued progress. Group allows exposure of co-dependent traits, which emerge naturally in group interaction.	This may be useful, but is not critical.

The felt sense of toxic shame and toxic guilt may be quite similar. A person can experience toxic shame and guilt simultaneously. The toxic shame and guilt may result from the same behavior.

BIBLIOGRAPHY

*The author gratefully wishes to acknowledge the following books. I
enthusiastically recommend them to the reader.*

Alberti, Robert, and Emmons, Michael. **Your Perfect Right**. San Luis Obispo,
    California: Impact Publishers.

Bach, George, and Goldberg, Herbert. **Creative Aggression**. New York:
    Doubleday & Co.

Bandler, Leslie. **They Lived Happily Ever After**. Meta Publications, 1978
    (now published under the title **Solutions**. Future Pace)

Beck, A.T. **Cognitive Therapy and Emotional Disorders**. New York: New
    American Library, 1979.

Carnes, Pat. **Out of the Shadows: Understanding Sexual Addiction**. Irvine,
    California: CompCare Publications.

Cermak, Timmen. **Diagnosing and Treating Co-dependence**. Minneapolis,
    Minnesota: Johnson Institute.

Dwinell, Lorie, and Middelton-Moz, Jane. **After the Tears**. Pompano Beach,
    Florida: Health Communications, 1986.

Ellis, Albert, **A New Guide to Rational Living**. North Hollywood, California:
    Wilshire Books, 1975.

Erikson, Erik H. **Childhood and Society**. New York: W. W. Norton.

Faber, Leslie. **The Ways of the Will** and **Lying, Despair, Jealously, Envy, Sex,
    Suicide, Drugs and the Good Life**. New York: Harper Colophon,
    Harper & Row.

Firestone, Robert. **The Fantasy Bond**. New York: Human Sciences Press.

Forward, Susan. **Betrayal of Innocence**. New York: Penguin Books.

Fossum, M. and Mason, M. **Facing Shame**. New York: W. W. Norton.

Hendricks, Gay. **Learning to Love Yourself**. Englewood Cliffs, New Jersey:
    Prentice Hall.

Johnson, Robert. **Inner Work**. New York: Harper & Row.

Kaufman, Gershen. **Shame: The Power of Caring**. Cambridge, Massachusetts: Schenkman Books.

Kopp, Sheldon. **Mirror, Mask and Shadow**. New York: Bantam Books.

Kritsberg, Wayne. **Adult Children of Alcoholics Syndrome: From Discovery to Recovery** (1986) and **Gifts for Personal Growth and Recovery** (1988). Pompano Beach, Florida: Health Communications.

Lankton, Stephen, and Lankton, Carol. **The Answer Within: A Clinical Framework of Ericksonian Hypnosis**. New York: Brunner/Mazel.

Lynd, Helen Merrell. **On Shame and the Search for Identity**. Eugene, Oregon: Harvest House Publications.

Norwood, Robin. **Women Who Love Too Much**. New York: St. Martin's Press, 1985.

Maslow, Abraham. **The Farther Reaches of Human Nature**. Esalen.

Masterson, James. **The Narcissistic and Borderline Disorders**. New York: Brunner/Mazel.

Meichenbaum, D. **Cognitive Behavior Modification**. New York: Plenum Press.

McKay, Matthew, Davis, Martha, and Fanning, Patrick. "Thoughts and Feelings." **The Art of Cognitive Stress**. New Harbinger Publications.

McKay, Matthew, and Fanning, Patrick. **Self Esteem**. New Harbinger Publications.

Middelton-Moz, Jane, and Dwinnel, Lorie. **After the Tears**. Pompano Beach, Florida: Health Communications, 1986.

Middelton-Moz, Jane. **Children of Trauma: Rediscovering The Discarded Self**. Deerfield Beach, Florida: Health Communications, 1989.

Miller, Alice. **Pictures of Childhood**. Toronto: Collins Publishers.

Peele, Stanton, and Brodsky, Archie. **Love and Addiction**. New York: Signet: New American Library.

Satir, Virginia. **Conjoint Family Therapy: Your Many Faces**. Palo Alto, California: Science & Behavior.

Simon, S.B., Howe, L.W., and Kirschenbaum, H. **Values Clarification: A Handbook of Practical Strategies for Teachers and Students**. A & W Visual Library.

Small, Jacquelyn. **Transformers**. Marina del Rey, California: Devors Publishers.

Smith, Manuel. **When I Say No, I Feel Guilty**. New York: Bantam Books.

Stevens, John O. **Awareness**. Real People Press.

Stone, Hal, and Winkelman, Sidra. **Embracing Our Selves**. Marina del Rey, California: Devors Publishers.

Subby, Robert. **Lost in the Shuffle: The Co-dependent Reality**. Pompano Beach, Florida: Health Communications, 1987.

Viorst, Judith. **Necessary Losses**. New York: Simon & Schuster.

Wegscheider-Cruse, Sharon. **Choicemaking** (1985) and **Learning to Love Yourself** (1987). Pompano Beach, Florida: Health Communications.

White, Robert, and Gilliland. **Elements of Psychopathology: The Mechanisms of Defense**. San Diego, California: Grune & Stratton.

Whitfield, Charles, L. **Healing the Child Within**. Pompano Beach, Florida: Health Communications.

Wilber, Kenneth. **No Boundary**. Boston: Shambhala Publications.

Woititz, Janet G. **Adult Children of Alcoholics**. Pompano Beach, Florida: Health Communications.

Wolpe, J. **The Practice of Behavior Therapy**. New York: Pergamon Press.